FOR DUMMIES™

BESTSELLING
BOOK SERIES

mySAP™ ERP For Dummies®

W9-AHX-668

Functional Areas of mySAP ERP

Analytics	End-User Service Delivery	Strategic Enterprise Management	Financial Analytics	Operations Analytics	Workforce Analytics
Financials		Financial Supply Chain Management	Financial Accounting	Management Accounting	Corporate Governance
Human Capital Management		Talent Management	Workforce Process Management		Workforce Deployment
Procurement and Logistics Execution		Procurement	Supplier Collaboration	Inventory & Warehouse Management	Outbound and Inbound Logistics / Transportation
Product Development and Manufacturing		Production Planning	Manufacturing Execution	Enterprise Asset Management	Product Development / Life-Cycle Data Management
Sales and Service		Sales Order Management	Aftermarket Sales and Service	Professional Service Delivery	Foreign Trade / Incentive & Commission Management
Corporate Services		Real Estate Management	Project Portfolio Management	Travel Management	Environment, Health & Safety / Quality Management
SAP NetWeaver™		People Integration	Information Integration	Process Integration	Application Platform

For Dummies: Bestselling Book Series for Beginners

mySAP™ ERP For Dummies®

Cheat Sheet

Industry Solutions

Industry solutions are offered by SAP to provide a tailored solution system that gives a company an overview of industry-specific business processes. Industry solution maps were created in a cooperation with industry-specific user groups, partners, and SAP development teams in an effort to define the requirements of individual sectors of industry. mySAP ERP comes with more than 25 industry solutions:

Aerospace and defense

Automotive

Banking

Chemicals

Consumer products

Defense and security

Engineering, construction, and operations

Financial service providers

Healthcare

High-tech

Higher education and research

Hospitality services

Industrial machinery and components

Insurance

Life sciences

Logistics service providers

Media

Mill products

Mining

Oil and gas

Pharmaceuticals

Postal services

Professional services

Public sector

Railway services

Retail

Telecommunications

Utilities

SAP Resources

Here are some great resources you can explore for more SAP information, insight, and tips:

- ✔ **Your SAP account representative:** If you are new to the SAP family or do not currently have an SAP account representative, visit www.sap.com/contactsap/directory to locate the closest office.

- ✔ **The SAP Web site:** For up-to-the-minute information on SAP, check out www.sap.com. The mySAP ERP section can be found in the Solutions area or by visiting www.sap.com/erp; the SAP NetWeaver section (with information on ESA) is at www.sap.com/netweaver.

- ✔ **The SAP Developer Network:** For information that is slightly more technology-focused, try http://sdn.sap.com (registration necessary).

- ✔ **The SAP Community:** The SAP community Web site can be found at www.sap.com/community (registration necessary). Here you can browse and watch replays of recent SAP and SAP customer presentations on all aspects of mySAP ERP and ESA, as well as discuss issues in various forums.

- ✔ **SAP Events:** There are many SAP events, from the elaborate SAPPHIRE conference and SAP TechEd to local events such as The Best of SAP World Tour. All can be found under www.sap.com/events.

- ✔ **SAP Partners:** Go to www.sap.com/partners to find out about the myriad of partners that can extend or help you with mySAP ERP.

- ✔ **SAP User Groups:** Go to www.sapgenie.com/usergroups (not an SAP-owned site) for a list of user groups.

For Dummies: Bestselling Book Series for Beginners

mySAP™ ERP

FOR

DUMMIES®

mySAP™ ERP FOR DUMMIES®

by Andreas Vogel and Ian Kimbell

Wiley Publishing, Inc.

mySAP™ ERP For Dummies®

Published by
Wiley Publishing, Inc.
111 River Street
Hoboken, NJ 07030-5774
www.wiley.com

For general information on our other products and services, please contact our Customer Care Department within the U.S. at 800-762-2974, outside the U.S. at 317-572-3993, or fax 317-572-4002.

For technical support, please visit www.wiley.com/techsupport.

Wiley also publishes its books in a variety of electronic formats. Some content that appears in print may not be available in electronic books.

Library of Congress Control Number: 2005927621

ISBN-13: 978-0-7645-9995-8

ISBN-10: 0-7645-9995-X

Manufactured in the United States of America

10 9 8 7 6 5 4 3 2 1

1B/RU/QZ/QV/IN

WILEY

About the Authors

Andreas Vogel joined SAP in the Corporate Consulting Team/Office of the CEO in 2003, where he worked on various projects related to SAP strategy. In the beginning of 2005, Andreas joined the Solution Management Team for mySAP™ ERP, where he lead the effort to service-enable mySAP™ ERP. Andreas now serves as vice president of Field Support for mySAP ERP, where he is responsible for the introduction of mySAP ERP 2005 into the market.

Before joining SAP, Andreas held various research, technology, and business positions around the world, among them principal research scientist at the DSTC (Brisbane, Australia), chief scientist at Borland (San Mateo, CA), and CTO and cofounder of Mspect Inc. (Sunnyvale, CA).

Andreas holds MSc and PhD degrees in computer science from Humboldt University, Berlin, Germany. Andreas previously published three books on CORBA and Enterprise Java Beans with Wiley.

Ian Kimbell joined SAP in the marketing organization in February 1998, where he held several positions in industry and solution marketing, which culminated in developing the SAP Solution Maps and marketing mySAP.com® Ian then spent a two-year assignment in the SAP Chairman's office as a board assistant before moving on to development as VP for mySAP ERP Strategy and Business Development for mySAP ERP 2004. He has now returned to marketing and is vice president of Solution Marketing for mySAP ERP.

Before joining SAP, Ian held various international IT and marketing positions during his 11-year tenure with DuPont.

Ian has become well known at the SAPPHIRE conferences in recent years, where he has regularly appeared in the keynote presentations, demonstrating the mySAP Business Suite.

Ian holds two business degrees, including a British Bachelor of Arts with honors in European Business and a German Diplom Betriebswirt.

Authors' Acknowledgments

We would like to thank SAP's executive management team, Shai Agassi, Jim Hagemann Snabe, Peter Kirschbauer, Peter Graf, Archim Heimann, Stefan Schaffer, and Thomas Baur, for their support and sponsorship of this book.

Many thanks to the following individuals who tirelessly reached into their depths of knowledge in their specific areas of expertise and contributed to this book: Amit Chatterjee, Catherine Courreges, Bob Cummings, Ralf Dehos, Frank Eck, Steffi Eger, Stefan Elfner, Claudius Fischer, Markus Fischer, Joachim Foerderer, Amy Funderburk, David Grasso, Matthias Haendly, Christian Hastedt-Marckwardt, Markus Kuppe, Karolin Laicher, Jürgen Lindner, Salvatore Lombardo, David Ludlow, Thomas Mattern, Doris Moellgaard, Gordon Mühl, Angeline Ng, Tatjana Nikolic, Tsafrir Oranski, Boris Otto, Gunther Piller, Klaus Pohl, Michael Rademacher, Ingo Rothley, Janet Salmon, Christof Schmoll, Horst Schnörer, Tim Steinmayr, Jeff Stiles, Jeremiah Stone, Ralf Strassner, Kaj van de Loo, Karin Weis, Jens Weitzel, Harry West, and Jeff Word.

A special mention goes to contributing authors Andreas Frank (for his work on analytics) and Hanif Ismail (for his contribution on composite applications).

We would like to extend our special appreciation to Tesha Harvey, for all her support during the writing of this book: We couldn't have done it without you, Tesha.

We appreciate the hard work and focused effort that was put in by the Wiley project team. Thanks to Katie Feltman for keeping us in line with the tight deadlines and ensuring this book was published.

Finally, this book would not exist without the tireless support and patience of Nancy Stevenson. Thank you, Nancy.

Publisher's Acknowledgments

We're proud of this book; please send us your comments through our online registration form located at www.dummies.com/register/.

Some of the people who helped bring this book to market include the following:

Acquisitions, Editorial, and Media Development

Project Editor: Linda Morris

Acquisitions Editor: Katie Feltman

Copy Editor: Linda Morris

Editorial Manager: Jodi Jensen

Media Development Supervisor: Richard Graves

Editorial Assistant: Amanda Foxworth

Cartoons: Rich Tennant (www.the5thwave.com)

Composition Services

Project Coordinator: Maridee Ennis

Layout and Graphics: Joyce Haughey, Stephanie D. Jumper, Barbara Moore, Shelley Norris, Barry Offringa, Heather Ryan, Ron Terry, Julie Trippetti

Proofreaders: Laura Albert, John Edwards, Leeann Harney, Joe Niesen, Carl Pierce

Indexer: TECHBOOKS Production Services

Publishing and Editorial for Technology Dummies

    Richard Swadley, Vice President and Executive Group Publisher

    Andy Cummings, Vice President and Publisher

    Mary Bednarek, Executive Acquisitions Director

    Mary C. Corder, Editorial Director

Publishing for Consumer Dummies

    Diane Graves Steele, Vice President and Publisher

    Joyce Pepple, Acquisitions Director

Composition Services

    Gerry Fahey, Vice President of Production Services

    Debbie Stailey, Director of Composition Services

Contents at a Glance

Table of Contents

Foreword

Jim Hagemann Snabe
General Manager, Industry Solutions, SAP AG

*E*nterprise resource planning (ERP) is nothing new. In fact, ERP software has been around for more than 30 years. Although long regarded as old and boring software, ERP is hotter than ever before.

ERP is traditionally associated with process efficiency in the back offices of companies. Although ERP helps companies increase process integration and efficiency, many companies also associate ERP with long and costly IT projects combined with major change management efforts.

With mySAP™ ERP, a new generation of ERP solutions is now available: an ERP solution that will not only increase efficiency with best practices, but, at the same time, enable process innovation and business flexibility on an unprecedented level.

Through a new architecture, mySAP ERP goes beyond process efficiency and opens up new opportunities for companies to innovate and to better compete in their markets.

mySAP ERP provides you with

- **Analytics:** Giving the insight to enable the appropriate people to make the right decisions when they are needed

- **Business process flexibility through enterprise services:** Providing access to the rich functionality of mySAP ERP through services, which are defined in business terms and delivered through open-standard technology

- **Composites:** Applications that span various functional areas to solve problem issues with dramatically reduced investment, delivered by SAP and its rich partner community

✔ **Model-driven tools:** The service enablement of mySAP ERP in concert with SAP NetWeaver's® model-driven development tools dramatically reduce the investment needed to foster your own innovation

✔ **Industry best practices for more than 25 different industries:** For faster deployment and return of investment

This book provides you with a more detailed introduction to these topics. Enjoy reading *mySAP ERP For Dummies*. As soon as you are ready, SAP will be waiting to help you take the incremental step to a next-generation ERP solution.

Introduction

*E*nterprise resource planning (ERP) and the world of enterprise computing in general are undergoing a quiet revolution. With the introduction of enterprise services, businesses now have more of an opportunity to differentiate themselves, adapt to change quickly, and provide a common language for IT and business people to communicate — and do it while reducing the overall costs associated with their IT systems.

mySAP ERP, beginning with mySAP ERP 2004, heralded the start of this new service-enabled functionality. Building on top of the traditional features of SAP® R/3®, this new generation of ERP software helps businesses do things they could never do before — at lower cost.

In this book, we help you understand this brave new world, and how it can benefit your enterprise today and in years to come.

Why Buy This Book?

To be part of the ERP revolution, you have to understand more than mySAP ERP's features. You have to explore the world of Enterprise Services Architecture, or ESA, and discover how services work and how mySAP ERP embraces them. You need a basic understanding of the underlying technology, SAP NetWeaver, to see how flexibly you can work with out-of-the-box and custom business processes. And you need all of this in plain English that you can understand. That's where this book comes in.

For Dummies books all share a common goal: to avoid complexity like the plague and make topics easy to understand. Throughout this book, we explain concepts, both technical and nontechnical, simply with examples that make mySAP ERP accessible even to the non-IT people among us. When we throw out a technical term, we define it in a way you can understand, and we provide great tools like the Cheat Sheet (that yellow card at the front of the book that you can tear out and use as a handy reference), a glossary of terms, and easy-to-digest Part of Tens chapters that give you ten quick hits of information apiece.

We even include information about things like building an ERP Roadmap with tidbits like TCO and ROI to help you justify the move to mySAP ERP to your powers-that-be. This alone could be well worth the price of the book!

Foolish Assumptions

This book assumes that you are somebody who works in the corporate world (large or small) and has some basic understanding of business methods and business technology. But we don't assume that you know a thing about SAP or mySAP ERP. Although some of you may be from the world of IT, others aren't, so we try to explain technology in simple terms.

From the very first chapter, we introduce you to basic concepts that you need to understand the world of mySAP ERP and services. But if you already have a handle on the basics, you can easily jump to a later chapter and dive right in. (We also provide cross references to send you back to the relevant chapter for a refresher course.)

How This Book Is Organized

mySAP ERP For Dummies is organized so that you can quickly find, read, and understand the information that you want. It's also organized so that if you have some experience with ERP, you can skip some chapters and just jump to the parts that interest you.

Don't feel that you have to read this book from cover to cover. We provide handy cross references so if you skip over something important in rushing to a later chapter you know where to go to bone up on it.

The chapters in this book are divided into parts that help you find the information that you're looking for quickly and easily.

Part 1: mySAP ERP in a Services-Enabled World

We start right off in Chapter 1 with a lot of the basic concepts you need to understand mySAP ERP, such as ERP itself, Service-Oriented Architecture, Enterprise Services Architecture, and more. Chapters 2 through 5 give you the lowdown on four key ways that mySAP ERP benefits your business: by providing the framework for differentiating your business, upping the productivity and efficiency of your people, providing business insight through stellar analytics, and giving your IT people the tools to be flexible and put technology to work to support your business strategy.

Part II: Getting Under the Hood: The Underlying Technology

mySAP ERP has a ton of functionality, but it all rests on top of a technology platform called SAP NetWeaver. To understand the full potential of mySAP ERP, you need a bit of a grounding in SAP NetWeaver. The chapters in this part introduce you to SAP NetWeaver, tell you how you use it to design and run applications, and show you how SAP NetWeaver works with services. Finally, you explore the world of composite applications, where you can orchestrate functionality from several applications to make technology support your business processes.

Part III: Implementing Change

If you read the book from cover to cover, by the time you get to this point in the book, you will probably have gained a great deal of knowledge about the benefits of mySAP ERP. Armed with this knowledge, you'll probably be eager to find out how to get the thing up and running. Chapter 10 explores some up-front prep in the form of calculating your total cost of ownership, as well as preparing your organization for change. Chapter 11 lays out a roadmap for implementing mySAP ERP, including several useful programs and tools to make it relatively painless. Finally, Chapter 12 is where we pull out our crystal ball (with a little help from the folks at SAP) to tell you where SAP and mySAP ERP are headed in the future. This helps you understand how your investment today locks you into further advances tomorrow.

Part IV: The Part of Tens

This part contains three chapters in the ever-popular top-ten list format. This is where you discover ten great ways to make your employees more productive using mySAP ERP, ten approaches to help you differentiate yourself and innovate in a services-enabled environment, and ten resources that can help you get going with mySAP ERP.

Icons Used in This Book

We're a visual society, inundated with images from big-screen movies and computer games, so this book uses little picture icons to visually point out information that's handy to know.

 The Tip icon indicates information that may help save you time or aggravation. These icons tend to point out to you interesting little factoids that could prove very useful as you conquer the world of ERP.

 Oops! The world can be a dangerous place, and the world of ERP has its own little pitfalls. Warnings alert you to areas where you could make a misstep that could cost you money or result in frustration.

 Remember icons are gentle reminders about important ideas or facts that you should keep in mind while finding out all about mySAP ERP. We also use these icons to note where in the book a subject is introduced or covered in more detail.

 Geek alert! This little icon points out a definition of a word or a description of a process that wanders over into the realm of the high-tech. These tidbits are informative but not crucial: Feel free to skip these paragraphs if you like.

 This icon is a special kind of tip that points out ways in which mySAP ERP or its underlying technology can save you money or speed your return on investment.

 We use this little icon to alert you whenever we mention a big advance that's introduced by mySAP ERP.

Part I

mySAP ERP in a Services-Enabled World

In this part . . .

In this part, you pick up a lot of the basic concepts that you need to be familiar with in order to understand mySAP ERP, such as ERP itself, service-oriented architecture, Enterprise Services Architecture, and more. Then we explain four important ways that mySAP ERP benefits your business: by providing the framework for differentiating your business, upping the productivity and efficiency of your people, providing business insight through great analytics, and giving your IT people flexible tools to put technology to work in support of your business strategy.

Chapter 1

ERP: Yesterday, Today, and Tomorrow

*T*he leading enterprise resource planning software in the world is mySAP ERP. So, what's the real lowdown on ERP? Software can be like a person: Unless you know where a person came from, where he grew up, what his family was like, and what he studied at school, you don't know him. In some ways, understanding how a software product has evolved requires a similar bit of history.

To understand ERP and where it's headed, you have to take a brief peek at its life to date. Where was ERP born, how has it grown, and what does it still have to learn to fulfill its promise?

In this chapter, we take a look at the life of ERP up until now, including SAP's ERP offerings. Then we make some predictions about its future based on something called *Service-Oriented Architecture* (SOA) and, specifically, SAP's Enterprise Services Architecture (ESA).

Just What Is ERP?

Enterprise resource planning (ERP) has many definitions. In a nutshell, it is a set of software applications that are intended to integrate and streamline business processes.

Traditionally, the processes ERP concentrated on were

- Financials, including all the traditional business processes that deal with money (such as accounts receivable, accounts payable, and general ledger)
- Human resources (also called human capital management), which involves all the people-related business processes such as payroll, time and labor tracking, and benefits administration
- Logistics, involving all the rigmarole you have to go through to get stuff, such as sales, procurement, transport, and manufacturing

ERP is part of a broader landscape called *enterprise computing*, which is essentially a map of IT assets and business processes held together by a set of principles that support your business strategy. Although other sets of applications, such as Customer Resource Management (CRM) or Product Lifecycle Management (PLM), have evolved over time as part of the broader enterprise world, ERP was the first and is still the core set of applications for most organizations.

Take a look at how ERP has grown and you begin to understand how it has reached a point today where it (along with some nifty new technologies) can begin to deliver efficiency and productivity more effectively for your business.

A Brief History of ERP

Enterprise resource planning as a category of software was born about 30 years ago in the early 1970s. Essentially, SAP presided at the birth. SAP was started by five former IBM employees who thought that the future of computing for businesses was at the enterprise level. They opened an office near Heidelberg, Germany.

Starting with basic applications for survival

Think back to the early 1970s, if you were alive then. The software landscape was dominated by mainframe computers — basically, fast calculating machines that ate punch cards all day long. Very simple character-based word processing programs were starting to emerge and spreadsheets could only be dreamt of. (Lotus 1-2-3, the first real PC spreadsheet program, wasn't even on the horizon for another 10 years.) The potential for finding ways to automate simple business functions was wide open.

In 1973, SAP created part of what was to become ERP, a basic financial and logistic system called the R/1 system. R/1 wasn't even enterprise resource planning software, but it was the precursor of ERP. In 1981, SAP introduced its second generation of application software, SAP R/2®, which was installed on mainframe computers and implemented on an enterprise-wide basis. SAP R/2 was the first enterprise resource planning system. SAP R/2 automated financial, accounting, human resources, sales, procurement, and manufacturing functions that have always been so vital for the survival of any large company.

Adding to the mix with expanded applications

In 1992, SAP got on board with the benefits of the emerging client/server architecture and brought out the next generation of SAP software, SAP R/3. SAP R/2 had provided most of the core functionality, and SAP R/3 initially didn't add a ton of features; instead, it made the technological leap from mainframe to client/server architecture, which had a huge impact on the market.

Shortly after SAP R/3 came out, this suite of applications and others like it became known by the term *ERP software.*

ERP software during this time kept track of all financial and accounting information and helped with planning, forecasting, and reporting. For most IT professionals, SAP R/3 *was* ERP because it set the standard for the entire set of ERP solutions that came out in the 1990s from a variety of vendors. SAP R/3 was therefore the most popular ERP solution at most large companies around the world. (Today, SAP serves more than 12 million users and over 28,000 customers in 120 countries, just to put its dominance of the market in perspective.)

With the widespread adoption of ERP systems in the 1990s, organizations demanded more functionality for specific areas. Although ERP still covered the "basics," SAP started to develop new applications. For example, ERP systems would still cover order management, but new stand-alone applications such as Customer Resource Management (CRM) started to emerge. Logistics and production planning became Supply Chain Management (SCM). A whole generation of acronyms was born!

What Early ERP Did Right

The SAP R/3 generation of ERP software offered some key benefits that supported increased integration and efficiency, and companies jumped on the ERP bandwagon. Their experiences largely depended on how well they understood their own businesses, and how well they implemented SAP R/3 or any other ERP product.

But in general, ERP in the era of SAP R/3 offered many benefits.

Made businesses more productive

In SAP R/3, enterprise applications essentially grew to automate core business processes in all directions. As businesses developed needs for common business processes, new ERP modules appeared. For example, Product Lifecycle Management (PLM) and Supplier Relationship Management (SRM) both appeared on the scene around the year 2000.

The good news was that companies could now use standard software to run most of their processes. They didn't have to develop their own applications (referred to as *home-grown* or *proprietary*) in various business areas, and that made life simpler.

 One approach that SAP took to ERP was to work with customer partners to build best practices into its applications. *Best practices* were guidelines or templates for how certain processes, such as payroll, could best be run. This meant that companies did not have to create their own standards or programs for these processes; the standards were already there, right out of the box, based on the success of other SAP customers. For this reason, SAP's ERP product was more connected to the way businesses work than competing products.

New ERP systems also offered a better user interface. No longer were people forced to enter cryptic codes to call functions. The graphical, easy-to-understand screens offered new ways to support the way people worked.

Additionally, the rise of industry-specific functionality made ERP even more useful to more people. Many companies, including SAP, introduced specific, integrated industry functionality to make the adoption of ERP more palatable. For example, the adoption of FDA requirements for the pharmaceutical industry was built right into the system.

Offered a scalable solution with a three-tier client/server architecture

Part of the success of ERP was due to the widespread adoption of Unix as a platform for enterprise networks and the use of client/server architecture for applications. Client/server architecture moved away from the monolithic mainframe to a more flexible and scalable architecture. With client/server technology, the processing of an application could be split between the server and workstations, and data management was separate from the servers. In a client/server setup, the server usually handles the centralized functionality, whereas the client workstation is maximized for users. SAP R/3 was one of the first products to adopt this architecture.

Client/server architecture offered a three-tier model (see Figure 1-1) that made the system more scalable and made some changes easier. That's because these tiers were essentially layers: the user interface layer, the business logic layer, and the database layer. With this structure, you can make changes or scale one layer without having to retool the whole system.

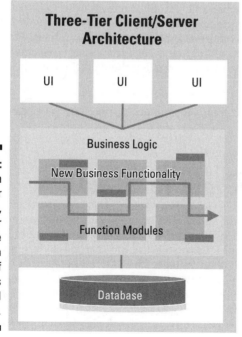

Three-Tier Client/Server Architecture

UI   UI   UI

Business Logic

New Business Functionality

Function Modules

Database

Figure 1-1:
In client/server architecture, the user interface (UI) sits on top of business logic and data.

Centralized data all over the place

Data has always been one of the major assets of any company. Customer data, product data, vendor data — you name a business process, and it's probably got data associated with it.

One of the big wins of SAP R/3 was that all the data for a particular application was integrated. For example, in the financial area, all the various databases for accounts payable, accounts receivable, and every other accounts-type thing came together, both physically and logically. With this integration of data, companies saw huge leaps in efficiency because information was easier to enter, maintain, and access.

Provided a bit of integration

SAP R/3 was a tightly integrated system with centralized data. As other applications were developed, such as SCM or CRM, they filled up functionality gaps in useful ways, but this functionality came at a price. Because each used its own centralized repository, eventually, these applications became silos of functionality and data, somewhat isolated from each other. Although it took some doing, with a lot of code and something called *point-to-point integration,* you could connect silos in different applications so that information could flow back and forth. However, creating these little stovepipes between the silos of data was not easy, and synchronizing the data through these conduits was sometimes difficult.

So ERP solved many big problems for the enterprise, but there was still a ways to go.

Where ERP Had Room to Grow

The good news was that ERP automated business processes and made many processes more efficient. However, as time moved on and more organizations developed efficient processes, companies had to start considering where they could gain a competitive advantage. The SAP R/3 generation of ERP was excellent for integrating and managing standard processes (like keeping your books, administrating your workforce, and controlling your costs), but now companies demanded more flexibility to adapt faster to market conditions. ERP, as it existed even a few years ago, was not designed to address these business pain points.

Focused on transactions

One big issue with ERP was that it was not always modeled after how people in a company work, and the way the technology worked was not always in sync with the way people performed business processes. It piled up software features and functionality in the form of transactions, which were useful, but not always a reflection of how people get work done.

One big disconnect was that, although transactions might take place in a single department using a single application, most business processes actually cross the functionality of application silos. Think about a customer order. The order may be placed with sales, go to manufacturing, wander over into shipping, and end up being invoiced in accounting. What was needed was a business process–based approach that would have all the functionality you'd need to get from a customer placing the order to your accounting department processing the payment. (This approach would eventually arrive in the form of scenarios, which you'll read more about soon.)

A customer inquiring about that order may be passed from department to department. What was needed was a more role-based approach. Think about it: We all have a job in a company, but we play many roles. A worker in one department may require access to data and people in other departments to do her job. A person in sales might have access to CRM functionality, but not to SCM functionality that could tell him whether materials to fill the order were being procured correctly.

But people can't get much done without information, and that was another challenge. How could you get analytics — the reports, graphs, and various other data that help businesspeople keep on top of trends — in the hands of people who needed them in the context of their day-to-day work? This, too, required a role-based approach that SAP had yet to develop.

ERP had lots of great features, but, in some cases, the people who needed them couldn't get at them.

Kept IT busy

The SAP R/3 generation of ERP software definitely improved business efficiency. But because it was not easy to make changes to the system, companies had to scramble a bit when they had to make quick changes or retool their processes to stay ahead of their competition.

In this landscape, IT and businesspeople often were at loggerheads over how to do things because technology wasn't designed to easily support business change.

Chapter 2 takes a closer look at how mySAP ERP, SAP's latest ERP offering, addresses ways to differentiate and innovate.

Technology presented challenges

As many separate applications evolved, and, in many cases, as technologies from many different companies were taped together with complicated code, change became harder and harder, especially when companies took the "best of breed" approach, selecting different IT vendors whose products best fit a particular company silo.

But even when selecting a single vendor, the *tightly coupled* features of previous versions made it hard to change a single piece without changing everything. Think of it this way: You move into a new office and want to rearrange the furniture to suit you. How much harder would it be to move your chair to the other side of the room if it was tied to your desk, the computer, and the coat rack? That's kind of what tight coupling had done to make changes in the world of ERP cumbersome.

In addition, when you connect two systems using point-to-point integration, you run into problems. Data in one system might be incompatible with data in another. One application might hold different fields of data for a customer than another. One set of data might use a five-digit ZIP code and the other a nine-digit ZIP code. One may have a system-assigned customer ID number, whereas the other uses the Social Security number for a customer ID.

To add to the inflexibility, whenever one application was changed, the other applications it was connected to had to be changed as well. Sadly, today's ERP landscape often looks something like Figure 1-2.

Challenged by the changing demands of customers and business

Think about how you come to demand bigger, better, and faster things in your own lifetime. Do you sit at your computer today and wonder why it takes 15 seconds for the thing to boot up? Don't you remember when it took two minutes? Or if you're a real computer veteran, do you remember when you ran the operating system from a floppy disk? Businesses have likewise gone from being thrilled with simple calculation software to being hungry for advanced customized computing capabilities.

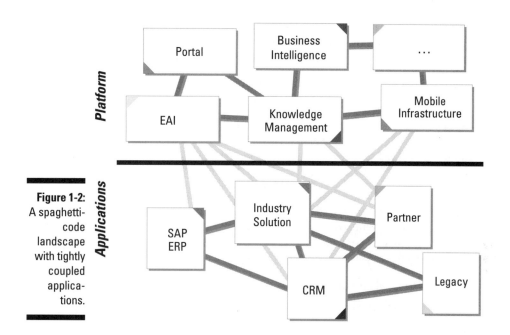

Figure 1-2:
A spaghetti-code landscape with tightly coupled applications.

Remember, the enterprise application had started life as a container for automating basic business functions. In the 1970s, that seemed like a great leap. But as ERP evolved and made businesses more efficient, a new set of demands sprang up. Today, companies not only want to automate the standardized core business functions; they also want to automate processes that are unique to their operations. Nobody in his right mind wants to pay for writing all the custom code to do this, so another solution is needed.

Additionally, customers have become more savvy. The Internet has allowed customers to take a peek inside your company's technology via your Web site or online store. This means you have to find new ways to interact with customers and make your processes look good from the outside in.

Needed to address specific industry requirements

Although industries have certain things in common, such as the need to hire employees and process payments, in other areas, they are amazingly diverse. That's why a one-size-fits-all enterprise product just can't work, anymore than a one-size-fits-all clothing store would fly in your local mall.

What's needed is an infrastructure that gives you the flexibility to create industry-specific ERP solutions, without having to build each one from scratch. That involves gathering best practices in every major industry, and building solutions based on them (something SAP just happens to excel at).

The New ERP: mySAP ERP at Your Service

Although SAP R/3 revolutionized the way in which IT supported business, it had reached a turning point where it now had the technology and the opportunity to make technology serve business strategy. This involved providing a more flexible infrastructure, one that could adapt more quickly to change, and one that could really support people and the way they work.

Here are the features that the new mySAP ERP would have to provide:

- Cross-functional scenarios, such Order2Cash, Procure2Pay, or Hire2Retire, that help IT work in a framework that matches business processes you work with every day. See Chapters 2–5 for more about scenarios.

- Analytics that provide information when and where your employees need them. See Chapter 4 for more about analytics.

- Dashboards with an easy-to-understand and -use interface that places everything a person needs to get his job done in one place. See Chapter 3 for details about control centers and work centers, and Chapter 9 for more on dashboards.

- Embedded roles that make it easy to provide the information and functions each person needs based on his role in your company. See Chapter 3 for more about how roles make you more productive.

- Industry solutions that extend and customize generic ERP to make sense in every industry setting.

- Real-time integration through SAP NetWeaver, and specifically SAP NetWeaver Exchange Infrastructure (SAP NetWeaver XI). Part II tells you all about what SAP NetWeaver makes possible for mySAP ERP.

Service-Enabled: The Foundation of Flexible ERP Today

The future of ERP was contained in one word (no, not *plastics*): services. The whole idea behind services is that flexible little packets of functionality help to solve the challenges that ERP needed to address going forward.

Breaking functionality up for flexibility

The way to create flexibility is to break up the functionality into small pieces that can be assembled or reassembled quickly to do something new, or do something in a different way. Ideally, these pieces can be presented easily to users, in a way that meshes with how they work.

Luckily, a technology framework called *Service-Oriented Architecture* (SOA) appeared on the scene to do just that. SOA is a technical framework for building software applications that use available pieces in the form of Web services. Service-Oriented Architecture is essentially a guidebook for taking advantage of a Web services–enabled world.

Web service technology is the enabling technology for SOA. Web service technology has been adopted by all major players in the software industry, such as SAP, IBM, Microsoft, Sun Microsystems, and so on.

Building processes from services

The concept of *services* is one of compartmentalizing and sharing business functions, rather than creating long strings of code. Web services began as a way to allow applications to talk to each other over the Internet, where one application provides some data or functionality to share with another. That data or functionality is exposed as a service. Enterprise services takes this a step further by adding a set of principles and a roadmap to make sense of the possibilities that services and SAP NetWeaver make possible.

Services provide a new way for applications to work with one another. A service might be something used by a lot of people in most companies, for example, a credit check on a customer or vendor. Alternatively, a service could be more specific to a particular company or industry.

Web services primer

Web services extend the end-user-focused, browser-based Web technology to enterprise applications. The major technologies behind the Web are the communication protocol HTTP, which manages the exchange of data over the Internet, and the mark-up language HTML, which enables browsers to read Web documents. HTML has been generalized to XML, which allows the separation of data and its presentation.

Web services also use HTTP as their communication protocol. The data that is exchanged is formatted in XML. A specific language has been defined for Web services: the Web Service Description Language, or WSDL. WSDL is defined in XML. A Web service contains a group of one or more related operations or methods. Each of these methods has input and output parameters (how information goes in and comes out). WSDL allows you to specify the operations of a Web service, including the data types used in specifying its input and output parameters.

You can build a business process just by assembling these services. For example, for an order entry process, you could group together services for taking orders, checking credit ratings of customers, and creating orders in an order entry system.

A service-enabled environment is, quite simply, the future of enterprise computing. Services and composites will grow the functionality of applications and play a more important role as time goes by. These services will crisscross the functionality of several applications that you use today. You'll use some services again and again for various business processes.

Besides being flexible, tools built around a service world offer a graphical, easy-to-use approach to building business process functionality. Think of the way you can access a world of data online with a browser interface. Now think what it means to a business to access its entire universe of data, services, and functionality with one browser-like interface, instead of opening and closing individual applications all day long.

Getting to Enterprise Services Architecture

In the offices of SAP, SOA was enhanced and morphed into *Enterprise Services Architecture* (ESA). Although related, Service-Oriented Architecture and SAP's ESA are not identical twins. Simply put, ESA is SAP's blueprint for a business-oriented approach to SOA.

In general terms, SOA is a technical framework for building software applications that use services available via the World Wide Web. Applications in SOA are built as Web services, which are encapsulations of well-defined business functionality. These services are *consumed* (which is a techie word for "used") by clients in different applications or business processes.

ESA is SAP's interpretation of an SOA that expands the concept of Web services. This expanded vision of SOA enables an enterprise-wide, service-enabled business architecture.

ESA extends SOA by service-enabling the most common business scenarios, such as Procure2Pay, Order2Cash, and Hire2Retire. Whereas SOA can be seen as more of a technical concept, ESA is the blueprint that enables services to provide flexibility, openness, and speed: elements critical to your business success.

SAP calls services in the context of ESA *enterprise services*. Technically, enterprise services are based on Web service technology. Enterprise services take Web services further, however: They provide access to business content and functionality presented in business terms.

All this flexibility and openness provides a different ERP picture (see Figure 1-3) from the tightly coupled scenario shown in Figure 1-2.

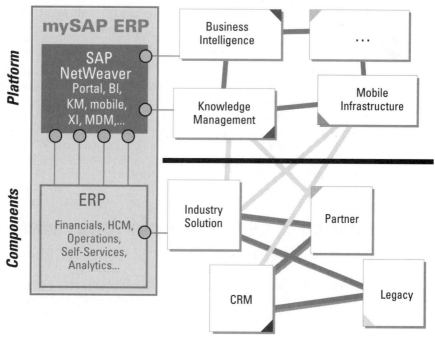

Figure 1-3: The applications landscape changes in a service-enabled world.

Exploring the Benefits of Enterprise Services

How do enterprise services make your business more flexible and quick to make changes? A combination of features make this all possible.

Starting with standardization

Assembling sets of enterprise services is essentially a way to turn functions into commodities. What does that mean? Think about the automobile industry. At one point, each model a company made had its own set of parts, and each manufacturer made its own parts. At some point, parts became standardized. That's why you can go out and buy a part for your car from any corner auto parts store without having to go back to the manufacturer. This commoditization gave automobile manufacturers huge economies of scale. In a similar way, enterprise services using standardized technology make it simple to log on to the Internet, grab a service, and pop it into your process, no matter who designed the service.

Luckily, the Web is a natural environment for standardization. One great thing the Web does, for example, is to use a standard way of formatting and transmitting information to and from a browser using HTML and HTTP. The broad acceptance of standards online has virtually replaced proprietary technology on the Internet.

But standardization extends beyond HTML and HTTP. When one application wants to have a chat with other applications to access some data or function, it uses a standard format called Web Service Description Language (WSDL) to describe itself to the other application. This description allows the two applications to understand just how to connect to each other. After the applications make a connection, WSDL describes commands to control the flow of information back and forth. Data is transmitted as messages in XML, another useful standard for describing any data format.

Making applications platform- and vendor-independent

Web services allow applications to talk to one another in a platform-independent way, regardless of which company actually produced them. This means you can be running Linux, Unix, Windows, or whatever, and no one vendor is in control of your applications.

Inside your company's four walls, you might have a Web service for your intranet (your own little Internet) that lets you check the status of a customer order. If that Web service is available to all your applications, your employees could easily call up the information without even knowing what application or database was involved, or what platform the applications are running on. You could also give other companies access to this Web service, so they could look up the status of their orders in your system directly without having to worry about whether they have a certain application on their own network to read those orders.

Web service connections are much cheaper to create, maintain, and access than earlier technologies. Web services are also reusable, meaning that one Web service can be used by any number of applications.

Hiding technology details through abstraction

The functions that applications provide may be useful (for example, allowing you to run a calculation in your system), but your employees don't necessarily have to see that functionality. Just as a driver doesn't need to understand how a spark plug works in order to get somewhere, a business user doesn't always need to see the code that drives a calculation. Because services are business processes, not technology functions, they are meaningful to your users. This process of *abstraction* hides the technology from the user and presents only the relevant information in a friendly interface. In fact, you have many more options about how the results of a Web service are displayed to users than you did with older technologies.

Enterprise Services Provide Building Blocks

Enterprise services are normally individual steps or parts of a bigger process; for example, deleting an order or placing an order might be steps in the overarching ordering process. In fact, you can combine a string of services to form a business process. These *composites* are constructed using enterprise services as the building blocks. Composites essentially gather together all the functionality of existing applications to work in a more flexible way.

Chapter 9 is all about how composite applications come together.

Enterprise services are designed, which is a key differentiator between them and ordinary Web services. Part of that design is that enterprise services can provide business content and functionality at a granular enough level that they can be easily consumed by composites. Enterprise services are also designed to be used with handy modeling tools, which you find out more about in Chapter 7.

Using enterprise services in this way, you can build entire business processes that map to the way you do business. Finally, ERP came into its own in the form of mySAP ERP, which offers built-in scenarios that invoke a series of services to build a business process. mySAP ERP, introduced in 2004, started a whole new way of approaching ERP applications at SAP.

The Procure2Pay scenario of mySAP ERP, for example (see Figure 1-4), may involve services such as Purchase Request Processing, Purchase Order Processing, Supplier Invoice Processing, and so on.

Before: People-driven process, transaction-based

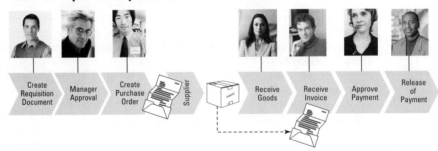

After: Event-driven process, automated

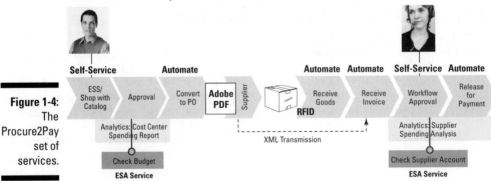

Figure 1-4:
The
Procure2Pay
set of
services.

Services integrate applications and people

Enterprise services architecture brings a revolution to the way people do business and the way mySAP ERP can serve companies. Being able to call functionality from any ERP application with a Web service in a consistent user interface (see Figure 1-5) means your technology gets more flexible; your business processes start to control your operations, rather than technology; and you can innovate and stay competitive rather than wasting time on rewriting code and maintaining nondifferentiating tasks.

Applying this concept to ERP means that you can find new ways to achieve greater efficiency in areas that you never dreamed of before. You can more easily outsource standard processes to free your resources for strategic and differentiating endeavors. All this is made possible with Web services.

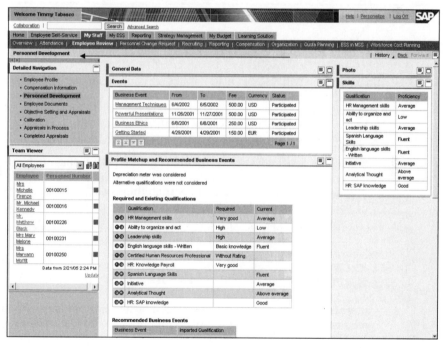

Figure 1-5: Far friendlier user interfaces make business processes much easier to use.

How SAP is shifting gears

How, specifically, is SAP taking advantage of Web services? Chapter 12 maps the company's future vision out in detail, but in a nutshell, SAP is

✔ Making every application ready to provide and consume Web services

✔ Basing integration on Web services and providing all the necessary support tools

✔ Changing the way applications are created to take advantage of Web services

✔ Prepackaging the connections between applications, between tools, and between applications and tools so that as much integration as possible is available out of the box

✔ Using a hub and supporting services to manage cross-application processes and many-to-many connections based on Web services

✔ Reducing the cost of owning applications and changing them to adapt to new processes

---

Where does ESA take you?

So just where will ESA have an impact on your business? ESA has these implications:

✔ As applications are presented to the user as a Web service, the cost of creating, maintaining, and connecting applications drops.

✔ Companies can work with people outside their walls much more easily, connecting two unique systems in days, not months, or interacting with customers online. This enables such things as business process outsourcing that can keep your company more efficient and competitive.

✔ Business and IT people can communicate better because the focus is now on business processes, not on applications.

✔ You can extend automation in your processes because you can work across applications and even across company boundaries more easily.

Using ESA, SAP can provide prepackaged business processes with built-in connections for applications and tools right out of the box, such as mySAP ERP.

ERP has been reborn as service-enabled ERP, and it's the way of the future. But will you have to replace your current ERP system to take advantage of all this? Luckily, the answer is no. ESA fits on top of and integrates with your current ERP system. All the benefits of ERP are still there, but with ESA, you have a platform for innovation and differentiation.

Where Does ERP Fit In?

mySAP ERP provides the applications functionality for performing business processes. But it's hard to isolate ERP in reality, so we won't try to. Throughout this book, we talk about mySAP ERP, but we also refer to the underlying principles of ESA and, in some cases, the technology platform that enables much of mySAP ERP's functionality, SAP NetWeaver (see Figure 1-6). (You can find out more about SAP NetWeaver and its relationship to ERP in Part II.)

Think of building a house: ESA is the architect with the vision that supports the building process, mySAP ERP is the contractor out there doing the work, and SAP NetWeaver is the power tool that makes certain functions possible.

In the next four chapters, you see how these three elements come together to empower a revolutionary change in ERP and the way you do business.

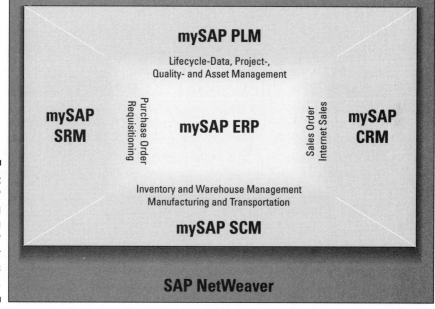

Figure 1-6: ERP connecting through SAP NetWeaver to business services.

Chapter 2

Differentiating Yourself with ERP

*I*magine that you are the CEO of a company. You come to work every day with great ideas about how to make your business more agile, and to adjust your business processes to changing business conditions. What are the stumbling blocks to all this progress? One big one could be that your IT department can't make changes quickly enough, and any changes they do make come with a huge sticker price.

Putting Enterprise Services Architecture–enabled ERP applications in place in your business allows your IT systems to enable, rather than get in the way of, change by providing a flexible, cost-effective foundation for innovation.

ERP and ESA are a dynamic duo that creates an environment that helps you handle your business processes more easily and flexibly, while lowering the investment necessary for innovation. You can save money because the interface to technology is simplified, and the underlying technology is open (meaning it plays well with other technologies) and far easier for developers to change with no special training required. With an ESA-enabled ERP, you can implement your business innovations and adapt to changing markets quickly and with a lower up-front investment.

In this chapter, you think about a new approach to your enterprise computing practices that can make a big difference in how competitive you are.

Start by Being Business Model–Driven

How do you approach your business processes so that they take less time, freeing resources to anticipate the next big thing? You need to change your thinking from technology-driven to business model–driven.

'Fess up: In the past, have you allowed technology to drive your business, forcing your processes to accommodate technical limitations? Probably so — most companies have. But that approach has a flaw: Traditional applications software is designed to automate individual activities and maybe sub-processes, but not overarching business processes. The business processes that control these activities are typically defined outside of software and are executed by users.

Being business model–driven means that you start by thinking about the priorities your organization must set to survive in the long term — how to make your business more efficient or better serve your customers, for example. Then you have to make the technology do what's needed to support those priorities.

Sounds logical enough, but how do you do it? Enterprise Services Architecture is part of a roadmap for becoming business model–driven: It outlines how technology can support business processes, and how services can provide the flexibility for your business to innovate.

Being business model–driven: A case in point

A service-oriented architecture enables your enterprise to adapt to continuous change in an economical way because you modify those processes at the top level by calling different services, not by retooling the underlying technology.

Consider this example of a business that had to reinvent itself. A major European computer manufacturer found it harder and harder to compete in the market based on price. So, the company decided that instead of designing a computer, buying parts and materials, building the computers, and then trying to find customers to buy them, it would reverse the process. The company began to shop for the best parts prices and then design its computers around those parts. It offered these computers in an auction; if there was enough demand for a particular model, the company built it.

Imagine trying to make a switch to that kind of business model–driven model in your company. What tangle of data and technology would you have to rearrange to support the change? How could you feed information about available parts to your design group quickly when the design group is usually the starting point for your product data? Is your IT group and your ERP system flexible enough to quickly support these kinds of changes?

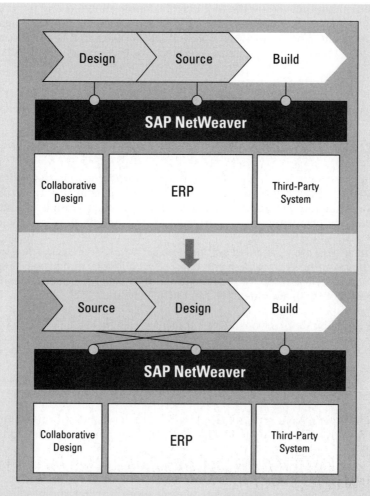

A company using ERP based on ESA (enabled by SAP NetWeaver) can make these kinds of changes. That's because IT is driven by the business model at the top of the heap. The services called up at the top level can be easily moved around; you have no need to retool the underlying business objects, components, or engines.

Services are preconfigured steps of business processes that come out of the box in mySAP ERP. They work in a services-enabled architecture such as ESA. See Chapter 1 for an introduction to services and ESA.

Other chapters go into the technological underpinnings and features of ERP. But a successful implementation of ERP rests on an understanding of ESA and the business model–driven approach that we offer in this chapter. Start by understanding your business, and make the technology support it.

Differentiating versus Standard Processes

Think about it: In any business, you do some *differentiating* activities that help you get ahead, gain a competitive advantage, and stand out from the crowd. For example, maybe you design a great new product or think of a new incentive to bring customers to your Web site by the thousands, money in hand.

Then there are your *standard* business activities, such as keeping and reconciling your books, creating and controlling budgets, and processing orders. Everybody has to do these types of things to keep the doors open for business, but these activities don't help you leap ahead.

Huge pain points for businesses today are to figure out

- ✔ How to reduce the cost of standard activities (what keeps your head above water)
- ✔ Where to invest in what moves your company forward

How do you balance these two types of business activities to become innovative and gain a competitive edge? That's what the next two sections are all about.

Hop over to Chapter 3 for more detail about how to reduce the cost of your standard business processes by getting more efficient and productive.

Bringing in Innovation

Innovation is a pretty simple word to define: It simply means to introduce something new that brings some kind of benefit. But innovating in business today is not so simple. In part, that's because there is fierce competition and the playing field changes every day (if not twice every day).

Defining business innovation

Innovation in business terms means identifying that magic bullet that can make your business stand out from the crowd. You have to define new processes, change your current processes to adapt to changing needs, bring new products or services to the market, and be prepared to meet changing market conditions.

No ERP product can help you identify how to differentiate your company. You know your industry, markets, and customers best, and you have to figure out how to gain a competitive advantage. But after you identify how to innovate and differentiate your business from the business next door, ESA and mySAP ERP can enable you to support that innovation at a dramatically reduced investment.

The changing cycle of innovation

Say that you get the difference between standard and differentiating processes. You have figured out how to reduce the cost of standard activities and put more resources into finding the next great innovative idea. Are you done? Unfortunately, not: The things that differentiate your business change over time. What was once innovation eventually shifts into maintenance mode.

Here's an example: A bookstore decides to sell books online. What an innovation in 1996! People flock to the bookstore's Web site to buy books, that is, until every other bookstore chain starts a Web site and customers come to expect that they can buy books online. So all bookstores switch into maintenance mode to support this now nondifferentiating aspect of their businesses. Maybe one of the pack then decides to offer used books, or electronics, or music. This also works for a while, 'til everybody else jumps on the bandwagon.

Think about your industry and you'll probably come up with similar scenarios.

Meeting the Two Challenges of Innovation

Because of the changing cycle of innovation, being ready to innovate in business involves

✔ Having the flexibility to change your business processes quickly

✔ Enabling IT and businesspeople to communicate with a common language about your business's strategies and goals, and getting them to have this dialogue on an ongoing basis

Gaining the flexibility to change

ERP has given you solid business applications for years, but making changes to your business processes was cumbersome. Your IT staff had to rework functionality and interfaces by writing lines and lines of code. This was anything but flexible.

How do you get the processes you need with the flexibility for change? ESA-enabled ERP, in the form of mySAP ERP, provides you with best of both worlds. On the one hand, all the functionality you need is available as services, the basic building blocks you can use to model your business processes. On the other hand, you can compose new processes from these services, tweaking or extending or reorganizing your existing processes at the drop of a hat.

Building processes with services

Services are the individual steps you use to build a business process, and they can be combined in a variety of ways. You can think of the process of working with services as similar to assembling one of those model toys where the parts can go together in many different ways. You place the blocks in one sequence, and you get a truck. Assemble them differently, and you get a spaceship. Still another organization of the basic parts produces a fire engine. In your business, if you decide you want your process to change, you just reorganize the services as you would rearrange the pieces in a model toy kit. It's fast, it's easy, and it makes you very flexible.

The assembly process is simplified through SAP model-driven tools. Using these tools, you don't have to program anymore; instead, you create a graphical model that allows you to control how services fit together (see Figure 2-1). The ability to create and rearrange processes as you need them reduces the investment you have to make when making changes to your technology.

Check out Chapter 7, where you discover all about SAP's model-driven development approach using SAP NetWeaver.

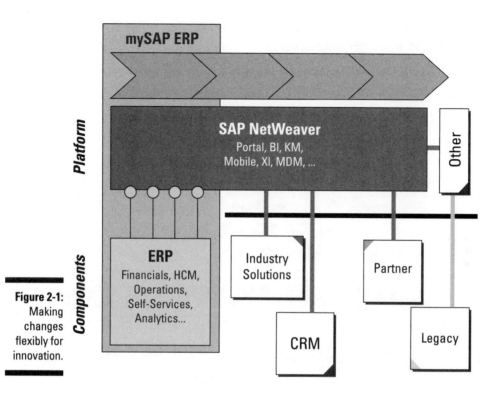

Figure 2-1: Making changes flexibly for innovation.

Administrative Intelligence: Services in action

Administrative Intelligence (AI), an SAP partner, has used enterprise services to extend the purchasing functionality built into mySAP ERP. AI focused on the bidding process (also called *tendering*) for the public sector. This is an area with some pretty unique regulatory requirements.

The steps in ERP's Procure2Pay scenario are shown in Figure 2-2. AI has a very basic integration with Procure2Pay, at the beginning and the end of the RFQ process steps. This integration was implemented by a simple file transfer from SAP to AI's system. Six to nine months later, AI transferred a file in the reverse direction. This simple integration was all they could afford.

This is all well and good from a technology slant, but from a business perspective, things aren't that simple. During the RFQ process, various business interactions naturally pop up. For example, before moving the bidding process ahead, you have to check the available budget in the ERP system. Next, the budget needs to be allocated in the ERP system. After you select the vendor, that company needs to be checked against the vendor list in ERP; if the vendor isn't listed there, somebody has to create the vendor record in the ERP system. All of this stuff was done by telephone and e-mail in the past because the investment to automate these processes was simply too high.

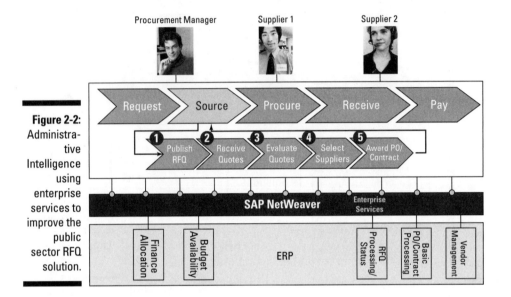

Figure 2-2:
Administrative Intelligence using enterprise services to improve the public sector RFQ solution.

Using ESA, SAP enabled AI to implement these interactions by drastically lowering the entry-level investment. AI developers didn't have to understand the teensy techie details of the ERP system and its ABAP programming language, or work on cross–programming-language and cross-platform integration. AI developers just needed to call the appropriate enterprise service using standard Web services technology.

This newly automated interaction between the AI solution and ERP provided great usability to AI's end users and improved the efficiency of their work and the quality of what they produce.

Day & Zimmerman: Another example of services flexibility

A good example of a company that had to reinvent its business is Day & Zimmerman. With annual revenues of about $1.3 billion, the company employs 20,000 people in approximately 150 sites worldwide. Its business is geared toward managed services in areas ranging from staffing and maintenance to engineering, construction, security, and logistics. The company must do an outstanding job of sharing information with its partners and updating and distributing content rapidly.

Like every company, Day & Zimmerman has both standard and differentiating processes to manage. It faces big challenges in getting the greatest employee productivity and managing a large number of people in different locations; for example, the company must provide all these far-flung people with instant access to large files to get their jobs done. On the other hand, differentiation for Day & Zimmerman comes in how well they deal with the areas of collaboration and content distribution for customers.

"We realized that we were relying on a variety of methods for communicating with our customers, as well as our own staff, with no enterprise view of the world," says Anthony Bosco, CIO for Day & Zimmerman. The company was using e-mail as well as static and dynamic Web sites. The bad news was that the company was generally being driven by current technology rather than its business needs.

At one point, Day & Zimmerman was processing time and expense records and tracking approvals for one of its largest customers, a major entertainment and television network. To support a strict schedule for weekly billings, Day & Zimmerman entered into an ambitious service-level agreement (SLA) with the client. This new way of doing business could be a big differentiator for the company, but it required the company to retool its expense reporting processes. The company also had to consolidate its collaboration and communications methods into a single, uniform approach.

Day & Zimmerman brought in SAP to help it create a solution. That solution involved the knowledge management and collaborative capabilities of SAP NetWeaver, and an enterprise portal that provides a single, enterprise-wide window into a whole range of services. The company applied a service-oriented approach to its business processes, extending its reach with customer-driven content and making tools such as time and expense reporting available to its customers.

"Our goal is to simplify the tools employees use in their jobs," says Bosco. "This way, instead of getting bogged down in trying to figure out how to use the core system, they can use their time to focus on delivering to our customers and on creative problem solving." ERP and SAP NetWeaver brought together a variety of integration technologies and provided preconfigured business content, which saved Day & Zimmerman from expending effort on custom integration.

Within a month, the company had significantly reduced the time it took to handle weekly billing; in fact, the company beat its already ambitious SLA commitment for weekly billing, giving it a serious edge over its competition.

Outsourcing the management of Day & Zimmerman's application to SAP Hosting also freed its IT people to focus on innovative activities that produce higher value. See Chapter 3 for more about the benefits of outsourcing.

Remember that innovation change cycle challenge? What happens when the value of today becomes the routine deliverable of tomorrow? Day & Zimmerman is already planning for new ways to add value. The company plans to extend its portal so customers can requisition, qualify, and approve talent for their projects online. The company is moving toward becoming a virtual organization, available to customers 24 hours a day, 7 days a week through its enterprise portal. SAP NetWeaver, ERP, and an ESA environment has made it flexible enough to expedite that kind of change.

The solution SAP delivered to Day & Zimmerman provides a great return on investment, so much so that the company anticipates full payback for its investment within just three years.

Creating a common language for IT personnel and businesspeople

If, in the brave new world of enterprise computing, business drives technology, IT has to deliver business solutions, not technology solutions. Making IT more adaptable is one piece of the innovation puzzle. But to help IT understand the business challenges so that it can respond to them quickly, you have to get IT personnel and businesspeople speaking the same language.

One of the goals of ESA is to provide that common language as well as interfaces to technology that businesspeople understand. In a services-enabled world, transactions are transformed into enterprise services. These services have to be defined with a granularity that's meaningful to businesspeople. So what, exactly, is granularity? There are two sides to the granularity coin:

- ✔ *Granularity* simply refers to defining services so that they relate to the individual steps of a business process. If you define these steps in just the right granular way, they can be more easily and flexibly rearranged and modified. Think of granularity as a fashion statement: If you put on a jumpsuit with pants and a shirt all in one piece, you can't change the top when you want to dress things up. If you wear a separate top and pants, you've got more granularity, and more fashion flexibility.

- ✔ Granularity also relates to the definition of services, and more specifically, to the definition of service parameters. In this context, the right granularity means that you make parameters visible only to users who are necessary from a business perspective. That means all the techie stuff that deals with systems, such as security, transaction controls, database layout, and so on, never hits the radar of the enterprise service interface.

You know you've defined an enterprise service at the right granularity when it exposes ERP functionality in pure business terms. The enterprise service then becomes the interface between business and IT.

When IT starts talking in business language, it becomes better able to respond to business process changes. With business processes built on best practices and composed of services, IT has a set of tools that allows it to make changes more easily, no matter what your underlying technology (see Figure 2-3).

This ease of change hits your bottom line in the form of significant cost savings, and impacts your business strategy in the ability to respond to your customers and market yourself aggressively.

Figure 2-3:
No matter what technology exists below, making changes in a business model—driven model is easy.

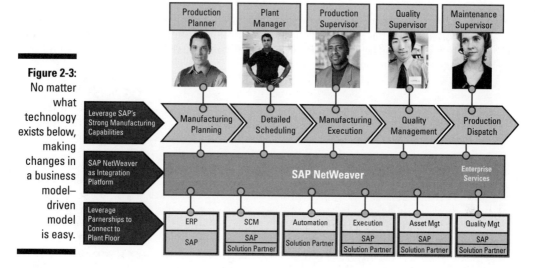

Best practices are generic or industry-specific predefined processes that come preconfigured in mySAP ERP; they are quick and easy to implement and can help drive down the cost of automating business processes.

Similarly, businesspeople get a much better understanding of what IT can do for them and can suddenly say what they need in regular business-speak because IT capabilities can be described in business terms through enterprise services.

Change the company or change the system?

This is a question many decision-makers face: Should the company change its business processes to fit in with an ERP system, or should ERP systems be changed to fit the company's existing processes?

Now that you understand standard and differentiating business processes, the answer to this question is easy: It depends. If you are looking for the straight answer, here it is: If the process in question differentiates your company, you change the system. If it doesn't, change your process.

Enterprise services come down to this: In deciding which business processes to take advantage of, your company is no longer limited by the capabilities of technology; instead, business processes begin to drive the evolution of information technology.

Chapter 3

Raising the Bar on Productivity

....

....

*O*ne of the big challenges to business today is to reduce the cost of standard business processes (those processes like running the payroll or processing invoices that are unglamorous but keep your doors open). Cutting these costs means reducing the total cost of ownership (or TCO, which is covered in more detail in Chapter 10) of your IT systems, including lowering costs associated with user productivity.

In an ESA-enabled environment, ERP can provide great tools to lower your TCO and increase productivity through improved usability with better access to applications and data, and the capability for self-service. These two tools can help your employees get their work done much more efficiently.

Out-of-the-box generic and industry-specific best practice scenarios can help streamline your processes and give you the ability to flexibly modify any process. You can also use shared services centers to centralize or outsource pieces of your processes, which can save you big dollars.

Upping Your Usability

You can give your employees all the software in the world, but if they can't use it easily, they won't be very productive. Usability is all about how people get at the tools and information they need to get their work done and how they interact with the computer interface they stare at over their coffee cups every morning.

Providing a control center for your work

You know that having an organized workbench in your garage makes that do-it-yourself project much easier to handle: The hammer, drill, and nails are all there in one place, easy to get your hands on. In a similar way, the interface you look at all day long on your computer screen shouldn't just look good; it should also give you the tools and data you need to become more productive.

Having access to data and functionality smoothly integrated in a single interface can improve efficiency and make for much happier workers. In an ESA environment with SAP NetWeaver, you can build something called a *control center*. A control center provides an intuitive central point of access to information and functionality for an individual. Using a control center, such as the one shown in Figure 3-1, employees can organize, monitor, and plan all their work and information. Along the left side of this center are activity-based items such as contacts and links to projects, budgets, collaboration features, and so forth; on the right are work triggers reflecting work activities, reminders, and analytics.

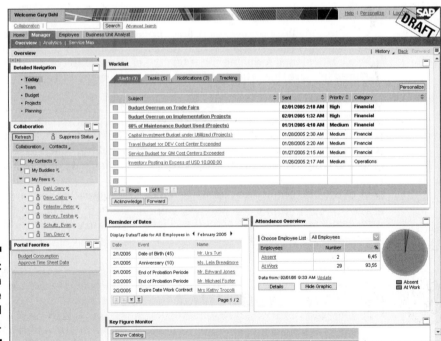

Figure 3-1:
An
employee
control
center.

The work trigger list is a really useful thing: In the past, it was your task to find all the relevant pieces you needed to get to work. Now your ERP systems obtain all the stuff you need to get your job done for you and put them into this universal work list.

Two new and important paradigms are behind this work list:

- Pull versus push
- Role-based

A *pull-versus-push* paradigm means that the ERP system is proactively pushing information to you so that you don't have to go out there and find what you need, possibly missing an important tidbit in the process.

A *role-based* paradigm means that your IT administrator defines sets of policies that belong to you based on your role in your company. Roles in an IT sense are sets of policies that enable you to gain access to information or functionality that you use to get your job done. After you have a role defined for you, you get all the access to the data and functionality that you need to do your particular job.

Read more about roles in the later section of this chapter, "How Roles Make Life Easier."

Taking advantage of work centers

You can easily create work centers in mySAP ERP. Whereas control centers are a kind of instrument panel that gives each employee an overview of all her work and activities, work centers are portals that are more specific to getting work done in certain areas. For example, Figure 3-2 shows a work center with an HR/manager focus. With work centers, employees can get organized and be proactive rather than reactive because relevant information is pushed to their desktops. With all this information at their fingertips, workers become much more productive.

All your work centers are accessible from your control center.

You can also build *guided procedures* into your control or work center user interface, like the one shown in Figure 3-3. These are wizard-like screens that step people through more nonroutine business processes. Some of these are built into ERP, but you can also build your own based on a best practice in your own organization. Guided procedures ensure that users take advantage of your system, instead of reverting to the old manual way of doing things. The ability to build guided activities is built into SAP NetWeaver.

Figure 3-2:
Specific
information
about
headcount,
sick time,
and
attendance
populate
this HR-
focused
work center.

Figure 3-3:
A step-by-
step
process in
your
interface
helps users
to avoid
mistakes.

Easy collaboration

Control and work centers also give you access to several tools for collaboration. Some of those tools come from SAP NetWeaver. Others are built into various applications such as mySAP ERP.

Collaborative tools allow you to

✔ Organize contacts and buddy lists for instant messaging.

✔ Check people's availability for meetings.

✔ Share applications.

✔ Create appointments.

✔ Use folders to share documents.

✔ Create collaboration rooms, which are essentially project-based work rooms that end users can create themselves. All collaboration rooms appear in your control center.

✔ Send a view of a report to others using the SAP Business Information Warehouse information broadcasting feature. Recipients can look at the snapshot of data and, with the right permissions, even drill down to find and view background documents.

Integrating with Applications You Use Every Day

Think how useful it would be if your enterprise data could be connected with the applications that folks use for their everyday work. What if you could place an application like Excel in the context of your accounting business processes, for example?

The whole idea here is that when you record data in one system, you shouldn't have to repeat that data entry in another. After it is entered into what is called a *primary* system, the data should flow through to other systems easily. This reduces the inefficiencies and inconsistencies that often happen with repeated data entry. It also delivers enterprise processes in the context of the standard *information worker environment* — a fancy term for those familiar screens, menus, and toolbars you use everyday.

Besides being more efficient, this method is easier because nobody has to be retrained: Just about everybody is comfortable with ubiquitous products such as Word, Adobe, PowerPoint, and Outlook.

Going into the office

Tapping into Microsoft Office (one of the most popular office productivity suites) as a front end to SAP data and processes is a logical move. So you'll be happy to hear that SAP and Microsoft announced a joint product to do just that at the SAPPHIRE conference in the spring of 2005. Named Mendocino, this product essentially leaps over the gap between the desktop and the enterprise in a single bound. It connects the best-practice processes that SAP has worked so hard on with the easy-to-use and familiar interface of Microsoft Office applications.

What is Mendocino?

Essentially, Mendocino Version 1.0 is a set of employee and manager self-service applications that connect Office and ERP. To help you understand how it works, here are some ways you might use Mendocino in your business:

- ✔ **Time management** enables you to use the Outlook calendar to streamline employee time reporting.

- ✔ **Budget monitoring** allows you to receive SAP budget reports in your Outlook inbox and work with them offline. You can be proactively alerted to time-critical budget information.

- ✔ **Leave management** lets you receive leave requests via your Outlook calendar.

- ✔ **Organization management** means getting up-to-date info about employees via mySAP ERP Human Capital Management (mySAP ERP HCM) using Microsoft Office InfoPath forms. (InfoPath is a set of tools you can use to create dynamic forms used to gather and share data across your business processes.)

- ✔ **Personnel change requests** send reports from mySAP ERP HCM through Excel or Outlook to keep you up to date about promotions, bonuses, new positions, and more.

What does Mendocino do?

So how does this all work? Say you use your Outlook calendar for doing your time scheduling, setting up meetings, and reminding yourself of appointments. So you enter information for a meeting next Tuesday on the new procurement project. If you also have to track the hours you spend on projects or accounts in a time-reporting program, why should you have to enter the information about the meeting when you already entered it in Outlook? Being able to integrate your Outlook schedule with an enterprise-wide time-reporting program makes much more sense. With Microsoft Office and Mendocino integrated with ERP, this is easy.

Here's another example. You open your calendar to look for a date when your are available to fly to San Francisco for a meeting. You can then create an event for that date, which takes you to your browser, where you can select a flight from a travel-planning window. When you book the flight, all the flight information is automatically recorded back in your Outlook calendar.

All the Office programs can be similarly integrated with your enterprise applications and data. You can customize the Microsoft Research pane so that it is specific to your ERP-related data, for example. All Office applications have easy connectivity with e-mail to exchange documents. You can deliver business analytics through Excel and smart documents in Word.

What will I see on my screen?

Mendocino delivers certain tangible elements to users. They get extended application menus that allow them to make the connection between Office apps and SAP data and functionality. They also get an SAP-specific smart panel as a tool to manage this connection. Business analytics are delivered via Microsoft Excel, whereas smart documents appear in Word.

But beyond these application-specific features are underlying technical benefits. For you IT types (everybody else can skip this section), here are some examples:

- ✔ Outlook can synchronize between Microsoft Exchange and mySAP ERP processes.

- ✔ There is unique interoperability between Office apps and mySAP ERP functionality.

- ✔ A metadata architecture delivers a way to connect Office apps with mySAP ERP data. (*Metadata* is simply data about data — for example, information about a file's size, author, last edit, and so on.)

- ✔ Security authentication and authorization capabilities put tiny technical guards at your corporate doors to control data access.

- ✔ Ease of configurability means that you can set Mendocino up the way you want.

The bottom line is that Mendocino makes collaborating, communicating, making decisions, and getting your work done easier. It also means that your business can leverage its existing investments in both SAP and Microsoft Office applications with little, if any, retraining required.

Taking paper forms online

Despite the dream of the paperless office, paper forms continue to play a big role in business. Just think about trying to do anything with your insurance company or, heaven forbid, the government: If you want something, you've got to fill in a form first.

SAP has integrated Adobe Interactive PDF forms into mySAP ERP using SAP NetWeaver. An application such as mySAP ERP HCM can use these electronic forms to create a new employee request and handle reporting. PDF forms can have exactly the same look as paper forms. And, of course, you can still print them, fulfilling your role in the paper-filled office lifecycle.

With Adobe Interactive PDF forms, you can stay in complete compliance with all the requirements established for paper forms. Electronic forms are easy to back up for recordkeeping, and you can e-mail them or use them from mobile devices. It is even possible to "sign" them digitally. So, for example, insurance adjusters could electronically file and sign claims while out of the office using Adobe forms.

Online interactive forms offer specific advantages over paper forms, specifically when they are combined with enterprise services.

Prepopulation

Paper forms are blank when you receive them, but you can prepopulate online forms with information. Think of this example: When you check into a hotel, the person at the reception desk typically asks you to fill in a form with your name, address, and so on. But if you're a member of the hotel's frequent guest program and have already entered all that information into its system, why should you have to stand around, all jet-lagged, and write it out again? With an online interactive form, that check-in form could be prepopulated with all the relevant information.

Input verification

With a paper form, the information you enter is checked when a person at the end of the paperwork food chain finally looks at the form. Some mistakes may be easy for them to spot, but if you mistyped something more subtle like a material number, you may just get rubber duckies instead of rubber mallets.

With an interactive online form, the system could call an enterprise service to verify the data you enter. If you make any mistakes (the item name doesn't match the item number, for example), the form itself flags them immediately.

Workflow

Forms don't just sit still: They make their way around your desk, through the hallways of your office, and even over to other offices in distant locales through snail mail or faxing. These busy little forms may even get stuck to other documents with paper clips or staples as part of your workflow process.

An online form can be attached to any document or workflow system and sent on its way in an instant, with no paper clip or stamp licking required.

There are some interesting applications for sharing electronic forms with others. For example, for your partners and customers who don't have direct access to your portal, forms are an easy way for them to interact with your systems. Forms are also an excellent way to satisfy the form-happy public sector's paperwork requirements.

Copying and archiving

Running to the copier is a thing of the past with online forms. (Although we won't kid you: If you need a hard copy, you still have to run to the printer.) You can print copies with a click or two. Similarly, you can store, archive, and retrieve paper forms without a trip to the filing cabinet. You don't have to wonder whether the temp filed Production Quotes under Q instead of P. Online forms are stored in centralized archiving systems and can be easily searched for by various criteria such as a keyword or date last saved.

How Roles Make Life Easier

To paraphrase Shakespeare, an office worker will play many roles in his or her work lifetime. For example:

- ✔ You are an employee, so you get a paycheck, take vacation time, and need updates on your benefits.
- ✔ You might be a manager who is responsible for your people's professional development and their performance reviews, bonuses, and raises.
- ✔ You probably have a specific functional role, such as being the senior purchasing agent.

The concept of role-based access uses the concept of your roles to make setting up and making changes to your place in the scheme of things much, much easier.

Defining roles for users

With roles, you define policies for users based on their organizational data, such as where they exist in the company hierarchy, what cost centers they are associated with, and so on. Policies might govern such things as what data gets pushed to the worker, what alerts get sent, and what data they have access to. Instead of defining access rights for each and every individual in your company one by one, for example, with roles, you can define sets of policies that apply to anybody in that role in the company.

When the next reorg comes along (and you know it will), an administrator only needs to update the organizational data and the roles everybody now plays, and you're done.

The combination of roles and workflows is extremely powerful. Compliance with company, government, and industry regulations and reporting becomes easier because all the appropriate forms, policies, and activities related to those regulations are built into the roles. If you're a purchasing agent, for example, policies are built into your role that keep all forms for overseas purchases in line with international customs regulations. If you are the plant manager charged with monitoring the yield of the production line, your role includes a policy to notify you of a jump in cost of materials instantly, rather than having you find out about those costs in a report you used to get in your inbox at the end of the month.

How roles show up in control centers

By associating you as an individual with the different roles you play, the ERP system can push all the appropriate tasks to your control center and provide you with information and analytics you need to do your specific job.

Here are some of the things that someone in a plant manager role would see in a control center, for example:

- ✔ Manufacturing intelligence dashboard with alerts
- ✔ Key performance indicators
- ✔ Manufacturing content
- ✔ Work lists
- ✔ Decision support to handle exceptions or changes in demand or supply

Self-Service for Productivity

Another big boon for productivity is the idea of self-service. When you rush to the airport to catch a flight, there's a handy kiosk there that lets you check yourself in with the push of a few buttons (and a swipe of your credit card). Usually this self-service capability gets you checked in faster and frees an airline employee behind the counter to deal with less routine issues.

If you add the capability for self-service to your business, allowing employees to get what they need themselves instead of going through somebody else, you also add to your organization's efficiency. For example, you might enable employees to check on how much vacation time they have coming. This spares some overworked soul in HR the hunt for the information.

Take a look at a business process in a typical organization that could benefit from self-service. Say this process involves an employee locating and signing up for a training course, and then having HR incorporate the resulting certification in her personnel file. Figure 3-4 is an HR business process that includes some of these steps, with certain steps enabled for self-service.

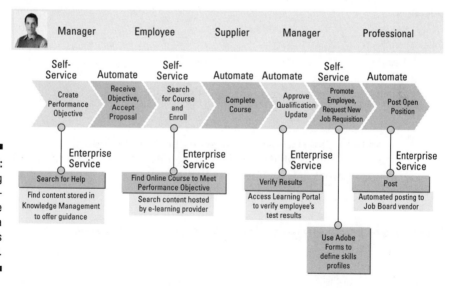

Figure 3-4: Identifying the self-service pieces of a business process.

In Figure 3-4, you can see some logical pieces of the process that could be designated as self-services:

✔ The employee could search an online course catalog to find the most appropriate training options (see Figure 3-5) without having to involve an HR person.

✔ The HR worker could access your company's learning portal to verify the employee's results in the course and update her records.

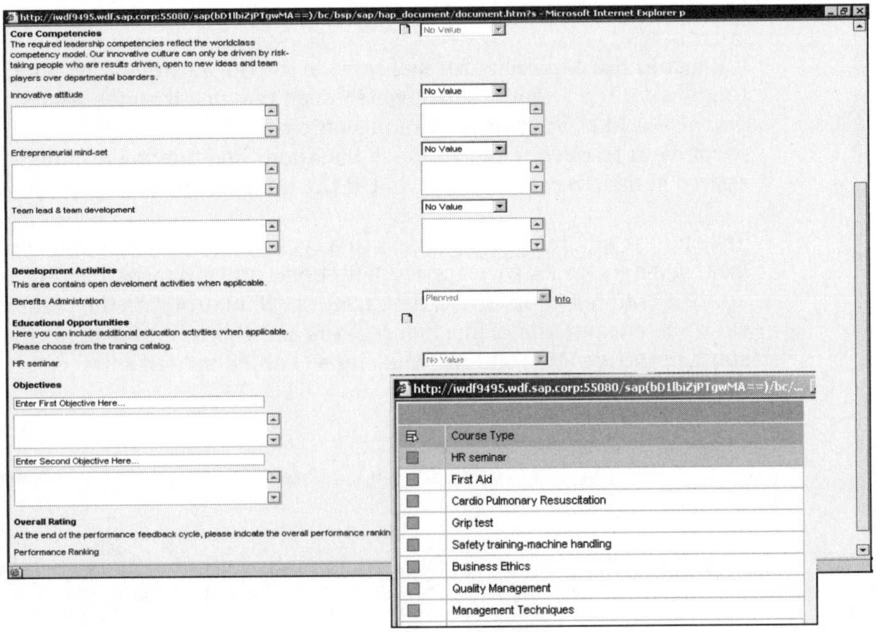

Figure 3-5:
Self-service selection of a training course.

All this self-service isn't hard to do: It merely requires that you use services to build your business processes, identify who needs access to view and update what data, and provide that access.

Preconfigured Business Scenarios

ERP has always offered a set of business applications that model and reflect your business processes. Today's mySAP ERP delivers generic and industry-specific scenarios. Here's how scenarios work:

A business process step is a basic business task or transaction. Business process steps are the building blocks for business processes; several individual process steps strung together create a business process. For example, one business process step might be to cancel an order.

So you add several related steps and you create a business process that gets you to a defined business outcome. Business processes are usually carried out within one organizational department and are typically supported by at least one application such as mySAP ERP or mySAP Customer Relationship Management (mySAP CRM). Examples of business processes include vehicle delivery and cash receipt.

So what's a scenario? A business scenario carries out end-to-end business processes and can even span processes across multiple organizational units and applications, both inside and outside your enterprise. Business scenarios solve customers' key business issues. An example of a business scenario in the automotive industry is order-to-delivery, which strings together all the steps along the way from a customer placing an order to the delivery of a shiny new car.

How can you tell the difference between a business process and a scenario? The criteria used to differentiate between these two, as well as between processes and process steps, depend on your industry. Figure 3-6 illustrates a portion of something called the *scenario hierarchy*. It outlines the relevant processes and process steps for the industry-specific scenario order-to-delivery in the automotive industry.

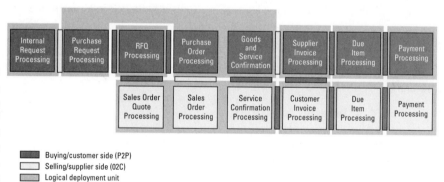

Figure 3-6: The anatomy of a business process scenario.

mySAP ERP delivers generic end-to-end scenarios such as

- **Procure2Pay** for the purchasing types in your company. This scenario involves steps such as purchase request processing, RFQ processing, supplier invoice processing, and payment processing.

- **Order2Cash,** which incorporates steps involved in processing customer orders, right through fulfilling the order, shipping it, and receiving and processing customer payments.

- **Hire2Retire** is the human resources scenario that features steps such as creating performance objectives, searching for training courses, promoting an employee, and posting a job opening.

One of the great things about scenarios is that they are flexible. Because scenarios call services from a central services repository in SAP NetWeaver (find out more about this in Chapter 7), you can easily rearrange the pieces of a scenario, or even outsource a piece. You save money because scenarios are already set up for you right out of the box. When you have to make changes, you save even more money because making any modification to those scenarios is fast and painless.

Gaining Productivity through Industry-Specific Scenarios

One cool benefit that SAP makes available to customers is industry scenarios and corresponding SAP industry solution maps. The scenario hierarchy is also reflected in these solution maps. These handy tools show the scenarios for a particular industry segment. You can drill down to see the detailed scenarios processes. The scenarios are grouped into business scenario groups that match an industry's high-level, mission-critical processes. You can find much more detail on industry solutions and solution maps in Chapters 7 and 11.

This provides a huge leap in productivity as ERP is already prepared for your specific industry and the way your people do business.

SAP has identified more than 25 industries and grouped them together into three industry segments: manufacturing, service, and financials and public Sector. Here's the complete list of industries:

Manufacturing Industries

- Aerospace and defense
- Automotive
- Chemicals
- Consumer products
- Engineering, construction, and operations
- High tech
- Industrial machinery and components
- Mill products
- Mining
- Oil and gas
- Pharmaceuticals

Service Industries

- ✔ Logistics service providers
- ✔ Media
- ✔ Postal services
- ✔ Professional services
- ✔ Railways
- ✔ Retail
- ✔ Telecommunications
- ✔ Utilities
- ✔ Wholesale distribution

Financials and Public Sector

- ✔ Defense and security
- ✔ Healthcare
- ✔ Higher education and research
- ✔ Insurance
- ✔ Public sector

Each industry has specific scenarios with solution maps and, in some cases, these maps are broken down even further. For example, the Media industry segment has the following four solution maps:

- ✔ Broadcasting
- ✔ Entertainment
- ✔ Newspapers and magazines
- ✔ Premium-content publishers

In Chapter 7, we explain how you can adapt and extend scenarios using *modeling,* a process that saves lots of time over writing and rewriting pages of code.

Sharing and Outsourcing

Your parents probably taught you to share and work well with others, right? Of course, they were right, and that's what this section is about: the ability to pool services that are used by several groups in a shared services center, and to utilize outside vendors to do work that would be more efficiently done outside of your company's walls.

Centralizing functions with shared services centers

The whole idea of shared services centers is that you take some piece of your business process scenario and make that piece available to many groups through one centralized function. For example, all the items and services that your company buys probably end up in an invoice-processing phase at some point. You might purchase consulting services through your HR department, paper clips through a centralized administrative group, and tons of steel through your manufacturing purchasing department. It doesn't make sense for each of those groups to have a piece of its process called invoice processing when all invoice processing could be handled in one group. That's the idea behind a shared services center, and it can make your people more productive.

Now you could create a shared service center by taking everybody dealing with a function right now in three locations and moving them to a single location (perhaps one with lower costs). But you could also create a virtual shared services center. Essentially, you are routing all the requests for that service from various business processes around the company to one virtual location, used by one group of people (whether they are all in the same office or not) who manage that piece of the process.

After a piece of a business process scenario shifts to a shared services center, when that piece of the work is completed, you can then loop back into each specific business scenario. For example, after an invoice is processed in a shared services center, payment information can be returned to be dealt with in a step that involves analyzing payment behavior at the end of the credit management process.

You could use a shared services center approach to consolidate a piece of a process in a lower-cost location, where, for example, salaries might be lower than in other regions of the country or world, or where facilities are less expensive to build, rent, or maintain.

Outsourcing the nondifferentiating parts

After you isolate certain business processes as shared services, you can easily outsource that piece of your business to a third party. Because you get best practices with mySAP ERP right out of the box in the form of business process scenarios, you can easily coordinate with an outside vendor to do those processes for you. These folks do this kind of work for a living, so they bring a better cost structure to the table.

In a Business Process Outsourcing (BPO) situation, you typically outsource the nonindustry-specific, nondifferentiating parts of your business to save money and free your people for other things. For example, many companies outsource payroll, transactional human resources, accounting, customer service functions, or travel planning. This task is the only thing that the third-party vendor does, bringing economy of scale and focus to the work at hand.

But BPO isn't a simple task. You have to figure out the best processes to outsource, find the right partner, and negotiate a contract that includes meaningful (and enforceable) service-level agreements (SLAs). When you get to the point of implementation, you need to carefully define the interfaces between your systems and the vendor's systems. Finally, you have to set up methods to monitor and measure performance to enforce the negotiated service-level agreements and ensure compliance with any government requirements, such as Sarbanes-Oxley (a U.S. act that became law in 2002, introducing changes to regulations of corporate governance and financial practices).

Besides using shared services centers, SAP helps your foray into BPO by providing integrated business solutions, such as mySAP Business Suite, on a BPO model. SAP also provides a network of certified BPO partners who can handle your outsourcing because they are totally integrated with SAP technologies and the ESA architecture (see Figure 3-7). The mySAP Business Suite, which includes mySAP ERP, is the choice of a great many BPO providers and their customers. SAP has worked hard to ensure that these BPO providers, such as Accenture, ADP Global Employer Services, IBM, and EDS, have the latest training on the latest SAP solutions.

To outsource or not to outsource?

How do you choose what to outsource? Here are some rules of thumb:

- ✔ Find areas that have repetitive activities, such as generating payroll checks.
- ✔ Look for processes that offer savings if done in bulk — for example, printing.
- ✔ Look for outsourcing opportunities that can remain invisible to your customers.
- ✔ Identify services that can provide a level of integration that helps you retain some kind of control.
- ✔ Look for relatively self-contained services that make for easier integration with your BPO partner.

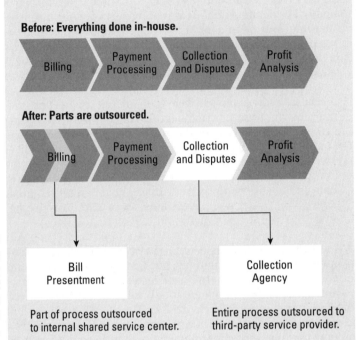

Figure 3-7:
Taking
pieces out
of the
process to
outsource.

Outsourcing: A case in point

As a pilot program for the SAP for Utilities solution portfolio, the Rottweil Municipal Utility Company decided to stick with its existing IT partner for processing invoices. In connection with implementing SAP Utilities (based on mySAP ERP), the company's own IT people realized that by working with an SAP-savvy third party, it could save money.

"Outsourcing is cost effective for companies of our size. We don't want to have to set up our own IT team for SAP," commented Heinz Wettstein, the SAP implementation project's manager at Rottweil. "Our IT partner has had the necessary experience for years. This solution presents us with calculable costs."

The ambitious goal of going live with several modules (Financial/Accounting, Assets Management, Controlling, Materials Management, Sales and Distribution, and Service Manage-ment) of mySAP ERP was a challenge. Prior to beginning the actual implementation work, SAP worked to optimize the utility's business processes and, on this basis, a set of specifications was drawn up in collaboration with all affected departments to define the internal and external requirements the system would have to meet. Understanding what both outsourcing partners and internal users would need made for a much smoother implementation that supported Rottweil's outsourcing initiative.

Making Things Run Smoothly with Automation

Think about how manufacturing plants around the world use robots and automated processes to produce huge quantities of everything from lipstick to washing machines: The list is endless. Without automation, producing all this stuff would simply not be possible. Wouldn't it be a good idea to apply the principles of automation to ERP? mySAP ERP goes a long way to help automate business processes and make your work easier.

Automation in standard business processes

Many standard business processes have to be done to keep an organization afloat. (We talk more about those standard processes in Chapter 2.) Automation can go a long way to helping these processes run faster and making your organization more productive.

For example, at the end of a fiscal period, reconciling all your company's billing is normally a time-consuming manual process. With mySAP ERP, you can significantly streamline the reconciliation by automating the process. The person handling this gets an overview of the entire closing process through a cockpit and uses the tools there to automate the closing of individual financial statements.

Using new technologies for data entry

You can save time and get more productive when you automate data entry as well as processes.

In addition to using Adobe Forms for automating data entry, you can go a step further with radio frequency identification (RFID) tags. You can use these tags to remotely read data about objects and even people. For example, you can tag stock in a warehouse so that it is consistently tracked, minimizing hands-on processing and ensuring that accurate, up-to-date stock information is available throughout the enterprise.

For more information about RFID technology, see Chapters 6 and 13.

Chapter 4

Gaining Business Insight

The buzzword *analytics* is a popular one in most corporate hallways today. What exactly are analytics? They are reports, graphs, charts, tables . . . in short, any summary or analysis of data that you hope will help you to figure out what you're doing right and what you're doing wrong.

Too often, the data that analytical tools use is off in some database that you may or may not have access to. If you do have access, you have to leave the work you're doing, log in to some special database, and generate a report. If you don't have access, you might get analytics delivered to your desk in the form of a monthly paper report. Too often, that report arrives today when you needed it last Thursday, when you could have made a strategic shift in your supply chain that could have prevented a manufacturing disaster.

In this chapter, you find out about the many ways that mySAP ERP can deliver analytics right within the context of your business processes. With mySAP ERP, you get information when you need it in a form that is relevant to your work, and you can act on it right away.

Tapping into the Potential of Analytics

Businesses live on data. If that data is timely and accurate, it's priceless. If it's late and inaccurate, it can cost you a bundle in lost sales and productivity. With mySAP ERP, SAP has rewritten the book on analytics, allowing you to share data across all layers of your business and improve decision-making within every area of your enterprise. SAP Analytics for ERP is tucked into mySAP ERP and provides both strategic (used for higher-level planning) and operational (more business process–related) analytical tools.

With a single platform, you can now put to work a unified set of applications to help you analyze data and make decisions fast. Your finance, human resources, supply chain, and other corporate functions can jump on the analytics band-wagon, gaining both insight into where your business is headed in the future and day-to-day process support.

Getting it right

So what would it look like if you could get your analytics act together? With effective analytics delivery, you could

- ✔ Give the right information to all employees regardless of their roles
- ✔ Take advantage of *predictive analyses.* These applications take a look at existing data and help you to project possible futures to guide you to better business choices
- ✔ Make use of real-time data to proactively set your company strategy
- ✔ Spend more time working with actual analytics results and less time con-structing data models to generate those analytics
- ✔ Achieve first-mover advantages, targeting the right customers, investing more intelligently, and optimizing your pricing for services and products

Best of all, you would get all this data in the context of your specific indus-try's business processes in real time, allowing your business to be much more flexible and competitive than it is today.

Ineffective analytics: What's the cost?

On the other hand, if you don't get your analytics act together, you pay a big price:

- ✔ With poor or delayed feedback, you can't take action to correct prob-lems quickly.
- ✔ Decisions are delayed or made on your gut feeling rather than on the basis of solid data.

✔ Information is available only to a small, elite group, whereas the people driving the business processes are left in the dark.

✔ A lack of real-time insight means that when opportunity knocks, you're not there to answer because you're running around trying to find a report.

✔ People spend their time as human integrators (see Figure 4-1). This means that people are spending valuable time trying to gather and piece together information out of the context of their everyday work.

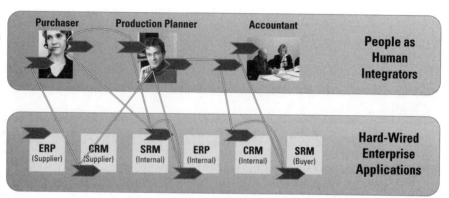

Figure 4-1:
Employees become human integrators of data with inefficient analytics delivery.

Enterprise analytics: The way of the future

Enterprise analytics is a combination of strategic and operational tools that offer a single information set managed by SAP NetWeaver Business Intelligence (SAP NetWeaver BI). Everybody sees the same information, and it crosses all kinds of boundaries all around your organization, including people's roles, business processes, and various stockpiles of data (see Figure 4-2).

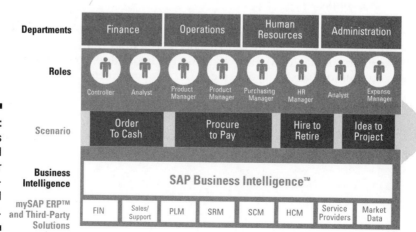

Figure 4-2:
Analytics spread across your organizational boundaries.

SAP took the analytics that existed as an isolated capability, somewhere out there in IT land, and embedded those analytical tools and dashboards right within business processes in mySAP ERP. Suddenly, analytics are in the hands of the people who really need them, *when* they need them.

Empowering Business People

You're smart enough to know that there's a right way and a wrong way to do analytics. But where do you start?

What you need is to put analytics in the right place at the right time. That means giving control over analytics to the people who need them in the context of the work they do every day. So what, exactly, does that look like?

Embedding analytics in business processes

One snag with delivering analytics in the past was that it happened outside of your other work. You might be processing an order, only to find that you had to stop to get on the phone and call accounting for a client's credit status. Putting analytics in the same spot as your other work tools makes good sense. You can do just that using something called *embedded analytics*.

Delivering data to your dashboard

In Chapter 3, we talk about scenarios that pull together all the pieces of a business process. With embedded analytics, you can get the data you need right in the context of business processes. In Figure 4-3, you can see some logical places for analytics to appear in an ordering process, for example.

How is that information delivered? It appears in a personalized portal, like the one shown in Figure 4-4. This portal is a work center (we talk about work centers in Chapter 3). Here you have the information and tools you need to do your job based on your role in the company, including really useful analytics such as key performance indicators (KPIs), scorecards, and graphical reports.

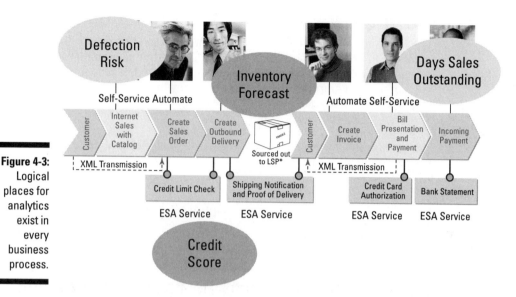

Figure 4-3:
Logical
places for
analytics
exist in
every
business
process.

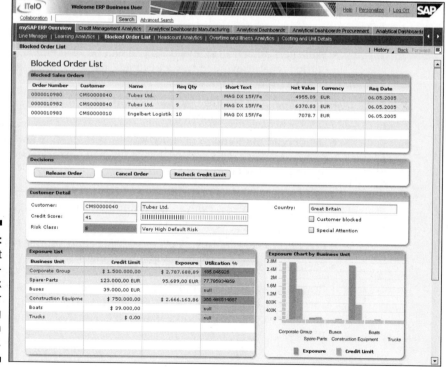

Figure 4-4:
A credit
manage-
ment work
center
delivering
analytics in
context.

Connecting roles with analytics

The information you see in your work center is based on your role, as we point out in Chapter 3. Roles are sets of policies that an administrator can assign to employees. These policies are tightly linked to the various things you do in your company. For example you may be a production engineer, employee, and manager, so you may be assigned three roles to give you what you need to get your work done.

Take a look at a few examples of the types of analytics that are delivered to people based on their roles:

- ✔ If you're the CFO, you might get

  - Top-line key performance indicators (KPIs) to get an overview of how well your operation is performing

  - Trend analyses to help you strategize upcoming opportunities

  - A total view of the enterprise that allows you to efficiently manage strategy and measure performance against strategic objectives, increase shareholder value, reduce financial risk, and integrate company finances with customer relationship management and supply chain applications

- ✔ The analytics toolkit for the VP of human resources would include

  - Skills and objective analyses so you can be sure employees are getting what they need to succeed and move forward in the organization

  - Compensation analysis to check whether your salaries and benefits are staying competitive

  - Headcount planning to perform real-time budgeting and planning, plan headcount, and ensure that individual performance measures are in sync with corporate goals

- ✔ A line of business manager (the person who is in the trenches running an area of your business, such as the manufacturing supervisor) would need

  - Inventory analysis, to stay on top of parts and supplies

  - Service-level analysis, to monitor efficiency and productivity

  - Purchasing analysis to monitor procurement costs, analyze inventory levels, look at processes that affect cash flow, or perform an analysis of how to source goods in a way that maximizes your profits

Part of the beauty of control centers and work centers is that data, including analytics, can be pushed to you based on your role in the company. If an analysis indicates an issue you should know about, the system sends you a report and an alert for action. Rather than you having to hunt down analytics, they find you when and where you need them.

Analytics for your industry

Analytics are specific for your role within the organization, but many roles are specific to a particular industry. For example, you are unlikely to find many plant managers in the banking industry or many molecular biologists in the railway industry.

mySAP ERP forms the basis of the SAP industry solutions, and the analytical information for mySAP ERP has been enhanced substantially with specific industry content. There are more than 100 analytical dashboards for more than 25 different industries, with more to come in the future. For example:

- ✔ SAP Analytics for retail helps store managers better understand and predict the performance of core activities, such as trade promotions, in order to make adjustments to processes and strategies quickly, avoiding costly delays.

- ✔ SAP Analytics for credit management allows financial service companies to display customers' credit information, buying behaviors, past purchases, and credit lines. This historical data can be stored in SAP and non-SAP systems or syndicated data sources such as Dun & Bradstreet. From inside the same application, users can increase or stop access to credit lines for a given customer or partner and even block or authorize individual purchases.

- ✔ SAP Analytics for tax management complements the SAP for Public Sector solution portfolio. This dashboard allows organizations to better monitor and understand the tax basis (where contributions are coming from in the context of historical tax collection) and take steps to reclaim amounts due.

- ✔ SAP Analytics for high-tech manufacturing allows managers and other employees at production plants and warehouses to get deep insight into order status, plant utilization, order backlogs, and restock levels. SAP partners have built SAP Analytics applications that bring together manufacturing execution system data with order supply chain and production data to give you very detailed views down to individual machines' uptime status and throughput capacity.

- ✔ Analytical applications within the SAP for Banking solution portfolio provide support for enterprise-wide reporting and strategic management, as well as help you to manage organization and financial products.

Making analytics actionable

In addition to putting analytics in business processes where your people live, ERP also helps you to make your analytics *actionable*. That simply means that when you get a graph showing some looming disaster, you also have the tools at hand to communicate about the problem and take action. Here's what happens:

- ✔ You get an *alert* in the form of an analytics report or graph.
- ✔ You *analyze* the data to determine what's going on.
- ✔ You *resolve* the issue by taking action.

What kind of action-packed tools do you have at your disposal? Look back at Figure 4-4. Notice the buttons labeled Release Order, Cancel Order, and Recheck Credit Limit? These are actions you take in your business process as a result of what your analytics tell you about your customer's credit.

So, say you're a credit manager. Every day, you have to make decisions about blocked orders. These are orders that, for one reason for another, hit a snag when winding their way through your processing system. Instead of navigating around the various neighborhoods of your system, you can build an analytical application that allows you to get the necessary information in one application, including past payment behavior and current credit usage. (Read all about how that works in the section "Tallying Up the Analytics You Get in mySAP ERP," later in this chapter.) Then, when you find the information you need, you don't have to head over to some other system to release or reject the order. Instead, you have applications analytics that allow you to take action right then, in the exact same environment and interface.

When knowledge and a way to act on that knowledge sit side by side, your business becomes much more efficient.

A comprehensive approach

A discussion of analytics wouldn't be complete without a discussion of SAP Strategic Enterprise Management (SEM). SAP SEM integrates the process of planning, reporting, analyzing, and responding to business change on a strategic level (as its name implies). SAP SEM helps you make the leap from the world of financial data, which tells the story of past performance, to the world of operational data, which takes a stab at projecting future financial results. Through SAP SEM, mySAP ERP not only provides the processes but also the software for all the management methodologies you need to lead your company into the future, such as Balanced Scorecards, Management Consolidation, and Risk Management.

SEM's key capabilities include

✔ **Strategy Management:** SAP SEM helps marry corporate strategies with business operations through the use of analytics with complex-sounding names like Balanced Scorecards (shown in the following figure), Value-Based Management Methods, Strategy Maps, and Value Driver Trees (these have nothing to do with automobiles or wood).

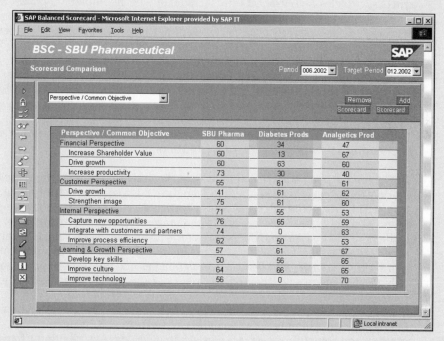

✔ **Performance Measurement:** SAP SEM keeps an eye on the performance of strategic success factors and overall business operations through performance scorecards. There are also integrated benchmarking capabilities that help you track what you had planned against what actually happens.

✔ **Business Planning and Simulation (BPS):** This is the part of SAP SEM that helps you to plan, budget, and forecast in collaboration with others across various locations and organizations. BPS offers "what-if" capabilities through scenario planning and dynamic simulation. As a result, you get strategic, operational, and financial plans that work together easily.

✔ **Business Consolidation:** You can consolidate actual and planned data while keeping an eye on legal and management issues.

✔ **Stakeholder Relationship Management:** This is the part of SEM that communicates strategies and investor information to major stakeholders and collects all their feedback via the Internet.

Outtasking the creation of analytics to the user

In the past, analytics were available to a small number of folks dwelling somewhere up on the executive floor. Eventually, information might filter down into the cubicles below, but it often arrived late or incomplete. It makes much more sense to get those analytics in the hands of the people who are deeply involved in business processes: the line of business managers and worker bees.

Analytics in mySAP ERP do just that, working hand in hand with Business Information Warehouse (SAP BW), the part of SAP's landscape that centrally stores your enterprise data, and SAP NetWeaver Business Intelligence, a set of tools for integrating data across the enterprise. This duo drives information to lines of business people through portals, as we talk about earlier in the chapter.

But beyond making analytics more widely available to people in the trenches, it also makes sense to allow them to take the design of analytics into their own hands. This frees your IT group, where bottlenecks might keep you waiting for weeks or months for a new report. In a managed self-service environment made possible by ESA and SAP NetWeaver, you enable every Tom, Dick, and Mary to create their own analytics as easily as they might create a presentation slide. Of course, with central access policies and controls, people can only create analytics relative to their areas of responsibility and authority.

Visual Composer, part of SAP NetWeaver, is an easy-to-use tool that you can put to work to assemble these analytics in the form of KPIs, hierarchies, queries, and semantic views in a process that's as easy as painting a flower in a drawing program (well, almost). In this case, however, what you paint is your personal vision of the world. Users can select a data source from a list (for example, a database of customer addresses), define interactions of various sources of data (perhaps mapping customer addresses to their latest billables), and essentially "draw" the images that you click on to call the data.

Read more about Visual Composer and SAP NetWeaver in Chapter 6.

Tallying Up the Analytics You Get in mySAP ERP

SAP NetWeaver Business Intelligence (SAP NetWeaver BI), SAP Strategic Enterprise Management along with the technical repository, and the SAP Business Information Warehouse are the trio that forms an analytical platform that gives you a single set of information throughout your enterprise.

mySAP ERP has 45 business process groups and 750 predefined KPIs and information cubes lurking within it. That's a lot of analytics power (see Figure 4-5) coming to you right out of the box. But, you're not limited to those options: You can use predefined content in mySAP ERP for your industry or create customized analytics for your specific needs.

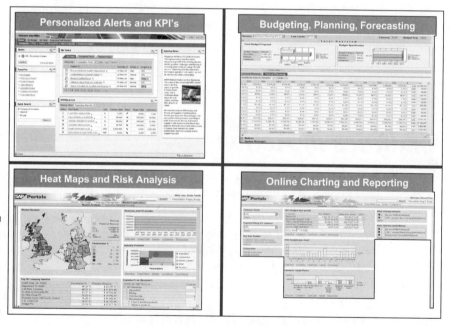

Figure 4-5: Various analytics tools in mySAP ERP.

Table 4-1 shows you the various types of analytics tools available to you within four main categories of mySAP ERP: Financial, Human Capital, Operations, and Corporate Services.

Table 4-1	Examples of Analytics in mySAP ERP
Category	*Analytics*
Financial	Budgeting & Planning; Performance Management; Business Consolidations; Balanced Scorecard; Credit Management; Cash Flow Analysis; Working Capital Analysis
Human Capital	Workforce Planning; Strategic Alignment; HR Performance Management; Cost Planning & Simulation; Organizational Planning
Operations	Maintenance Cost Planning; Inventory Analysis; Warehouse Analysis; Sales Planning Analysis; Procurement Monitoring; Service Level Analysis; Manufacturing Analysis
Corporate Services	Expense Analytics; Travel Cost Analytics; Project Analytics; Vacancy Analytics; Partner Performance Analytics; Contract Analytics; Hazardous Material Analytics; Hazard & Safety Analytics; Waste Lifecycle Analytics

Analytics in Action

How do these advances in analytics work out there in the real world of business processes? The following sections offer a few examples.

First, we step you through a process called express planning and show you how ERP-delivered analytics come into play. Then, we take you through a life-cycle costing example to show how you can use analytics to plan and monitor pricing and profitability of your products.

Expediting your budgeting with express planning

Planning and budgeting are as unavoidable in business as taxes and death are in life. If you have to deal with these tasks, wouldn't it be nice if the process was as streamlined and painless as possible?

Among the new analytics offered in mySAP ERP 2005 is the express planning process. This process takes you step by step through planning and budgeting. The advantage of express planning is that a manager can plan for the coming fiscal year using sophisticated software that requires absolutely no training. The entire process contains embedded analytics that provide users with reports on the current state of the planning process.

You can configure the analytics that are built into this process to work any way you like. You can also replace them with other analytical services, for example, services specific to the budgeting process in an industry with lots of assets such as a trucking fleet, where plan data is compiled from maintenance plans and historic maintenance activities. Because the planning process is a model and not hard-coded, it makes configuration changes and modification comparatively easy and much more cost-efficient.

See Chapter 6 for more about how modeling makes IT changes easier.

Here's an example of the steps in the express planning process and how a manager might use them:

1. **Review the current situation.**

   The manager reviews the master data to determine whether the right equipment, employees, and so on have been assigned to their respective cost centers (see Figure 4-6).

Figure 4-6: Reviewing data about various aspects of your business.

2. **Review strategy and targets.**

   The supervisor then reviews the pertinent corporate strategy that applies to her area within the company.

3. **Enter goals and tasks (see Figure 4-7).**

   After reviewing the strategy, the supervisor breaks the big picture into specific objectives for her group.

4. **Enter planned data.**

   After the manager has completed the preliminaries, the planning process begins. The user is presented with a list of areas to address. In this example, the manager is asked to enter plan data for third parties, equipment, internal orders, other costs, and risks. If the manager selects "Employees" (see Figure 4-8), she is confronted with a list of cost centers that she can select one by one. From there, the manager is presented with a list of organizational units — the different positions — that are involved with that the cost center. There is also a table that automatically calculates planned costs based on this data and shows the previous year's budget against the projected future budget.

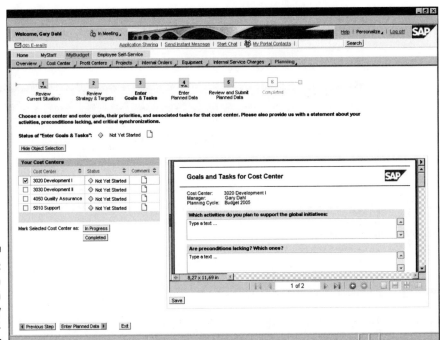

Figure 4-7:
You can break down goals by cost center.

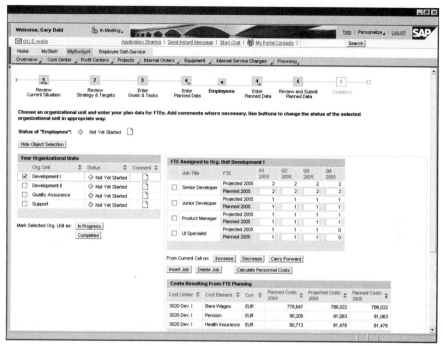

Figure 4-8:
Planning
employee
cost
projections.

5. **Review and submit planned data.**

The manager can review all the plans and change any value that needs changing. After she has completed this step, she can submit the plan electronically.

The plan is now completed. The manager submits her plan to her supervisor and is now subject to happy approval or dreaded rejection. In the case of rejection, the manager has to revise the plan and adopt any changes.

This whole process is triggered via e-mail, meaning that everybody who participates in the planning exercise always knows what he has to provide to make it happen and when every deliverable is due.

Analytics in the plant

Today, companies are being challenged to lower manufacturing costs. Regulations are pushing companies to meet quality standards. A plant manager has to stay on top of a lot. These folks are often overloaded with data, but they still don't have quick access to all the information they need about orders, labor, machines, and materials.

Plant managers need to tap into key performance indicators (KPIs) that raise an alert if some aspect of the operation is out of balance. To that end, SAP Manufacturing provides manufacturing intelligence dashboards; these are portals that push analytics to managers so they can analyze the problem and find solutions using collaborative tools. These role-specific dashboards allow managers to monitor and manage manufacturing performance and act quickly to make changes.

Dashboards provide manufacturing personnel with sophisticated analytics and reporting tools that help them recognize trends, be alerted to potential problems, analyze situations, and identify opportunities to improve performance. Folks can monitor critical metrics using their own custom reports or KPIs from an SAP-predefined library. They can even drill down through each KPI to analyze the cause of a problem and solve it. In addition, when they receive real-time alerts, they can trigger business processes in mySAP ERP to resolve the issue.

With advanced integration, an enterprise could be set up to have data from a third-party shop floor manufacturing system pop up in the plant manager's work center by integrating the third party into mySAP ERP via SAP NetWeaver.

Playing by the rules: Compliance challenges

These days, many industries face the challenge of compliance with various government and industry regulations. Staying in compliance, quite simply, could mean the difference between keeping your enterprise out of legal hot water and penalty-free and becoming tomorrow's business-disaster headline.

Regulations requiring compliance run the gamut (see Figure 4-9) from the Kyoto Protocol for environmental protection to cross-border trade compliance to corporate governance stipulations set by the Sarbanes-Oxley Act and the Revised International Capital Framework, known as Basel II. Requirements of the latter include having your CEO and CFO certify financial reports and internal control reporting requirements.

Management today has to rely on first-class compliance analytics that give an overview of how the company is measuring up. Compliance information is available from all sorts of applications within mySAP ERP, such as financials, environment, health and safety, and more. Audit systems, whistle-blower components, and internal controls are all built right in.

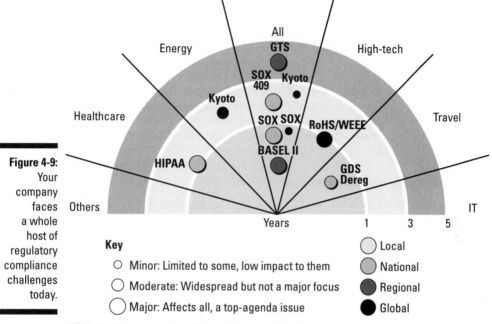

Figure 4-9:
Your
company
faces
a whole
host of
regulatory
compliance
challenges
today.

Key

○ Minor: Limited to some, low impact to them

○ Moderate: Widespread but not a major focus

◔ Major: Affects all, a top-agenda issue

◯ Local

◯ National

◉ Regional

● Global

HIPAA: Health Insurance Portability and Accountability Act
SOX: Sarbanes-Oxley Act
BASEL II: International Convergence of Capital Measurement and Capital Standards: A Revised
Framework (Basel Committee on Banking Supervision)
GDS DEREG: Deregulation of the Global Reservations Systems
RoHS/WEEE: Restriction of Hazardous Substances Directive/Waste Electrical and Electronic
Equipment (Producer Responsibility) Regulations

Here a few of examples of SAP analytics tools and the types of regulation they pertain to:

✔ Global Trade Services for cross-border trade regulations

✔ SAP xApp Emissions Management, Kyoto Protocol

✔ SAP management internal capabilities, Sarbanes-Oxley Act

Take a look at how SAP analytics support two of these challenges, the Kyoto Protocol and the regulations for electronic waste and hazardous substances.

Complying with Kyoto

Russia formally ratified the Kyoto Protocol, which is aimed at curbing global emissions of greenhouse gases, on November 16, 2004. That ratification triggered a 90-day countdown to bring the international climate treaty into force.

The United Nations protocol became legally binding in February 2005, committing the 30 industrialized countries that have backed it to cutting their greenhouse gas emissions to nearly 5 percent below 1990 levels. They have until 2012 to achieve this decrease.

SAP xApp Emissions Management (SAP xEM) helps companies deal with these requirements in several ways. The application helps companies comply with emissions regulations worldwide with analytics and reporting tools, while increasing their revenue by tracking the trading of emissions credits (incentives for companies meeting emissions targets). The application also helps manage capital investments that companies make to stay in compliance.

Keeping high-tech in line

Electronics manufacturers face a growing number of new and complex regulations governing the usage and disposal of hazardous substances used in electronic products. The European Union (EU), for example, has come up with two new stringent environmental regulations that impact all products sold in the EU.

As a result, high-tech manufacturers have to diligently and proactively identify violations and risks, manage and report on enormous amounts of data, and collaborate seamlessly across departments and with partners and customers. And as the regulatory environment evolves, companies need ways to continuously update compliance lists to reflect new requirements. Such far-reaching changes come with a steep price tag, but compliance is not an option: Everybody has to comply to avoid fines, lost sales, and diminished brand value.

When you combine the SAP environment, health, and safety functionalities (part of mySAP ERP) with the TechniData's Compliance for Products application, you get support for business processes such as sustainability reporting, compliant product design, labeling, dangerous goods management, centralized master data management, and business-to-business collaboration. With preconfigured integration into back-end systems and full integration with mySAP ERP, customers can move toward compliance without having to build pricey system interfaces.

Managers' lives become easier when they can use a management cockpit that places all compliance information at their fingertips. In addition to providing access to a central database for managing and controlling environmental product compliance, the cockpit allows compliance managers to develop material-level composition lists. They can use these lists to analyze individual products for environmental risks. Employees can generate a comprehensive list of parts, constituent materials, and any pure substances used as products progress through development. They can then compare this data to a list of banned substances and materials and ensure compliance throughout the development process.

Industries banking on analytics

So mySAP ERP offers many different types of analytics. But, as we have seen, the analytics capabilities of mySAP ERP can be extended to industry solutions. SAP already supports more than 25 specific industry solutions with analytical functionality. We now look at the specific analytics functionality offered with mySAP ERP and the SAP for Banking solution portfolio.

Analytical applications within the SAP for Banking solution portfolio provide crucial process support for business strategies thanks to integrated tools for financial accounting, cost controlling, risk management, asset-liability management, and profitability analysis. These applications can also help banks address legal compliance challenges. With this support, you can streamline the handling of portfolio and market data, improve the speed and quality of both internal and external reporting, and more easily comply with changing regulatory requirements such as international accounting and financial reporting standards. These applications help banks

- ✔ **Effectively consolidate, plan, and do accounting:** SAP for Banking includes comprehensive consolidation functions that operate on multi-dimensional data structures. For example, you can define organizational units such as companies, business areas, or profit centers to support a matrix organization.

- ✔ **Address compliance rules head-on:** Banks face an increasingly complex set of national and international regulations that require ever-more detailed information about their business structures and key performance indicators.

- ✔ **Handle risk management more effectively:** With the analytics in SAP for Banking, you can analyze and control risk for all your trading and nontrading products.

- ✔ **Enhance profitability through better measurement:** Includes features for profitability management that can help you analyze the profitability of various distribution channels, organizational units, products, and clients.

Chapter 5

Keeping IT Flexible

. . . .

. . . .

In the preceding chapters, we talk about how service-enabled mySAP ERP helps your enterprise differentiate itself, makes your people more productive, and helps you gain business insight. The last piece of the puzzle is how this all helps the people who live in your IT world to connect with your MBA and accounting types.

That's what this chapter is about. We explore the way that services help IT speak business's language by making business processes granular, and how best practices out of the box provide solutions while leaving room for flexibility when it comes to custom applications development.

Creating a Common Language for IT and Business

Throughout this book, we talk about the need for a common language between IT and business people. This is such an important concept that we're going to revisit it for a moment in a little more detail.

Syntax, meet semantics

Here's an analogy: If you have teenagers, think about that relationship. Do you understand them? Do they understand you? Of course not. Even though you speak one language (for the most part), you have different experiences and you have different expectations.

In the business world, there's business-speak and technology-speak. In the past, it was painful to try to translate from one to the other. Here's an example: Anne is a product manager with an MBA. She uses a computer, but doesn't really want to understand how it works. Anne tends to think in terms of return on investment, sales goals, and fiscal quarters (see Figure 5-1). If she needs to install a new computer application, she calls the IT guy or gal and lets that person deal with it.

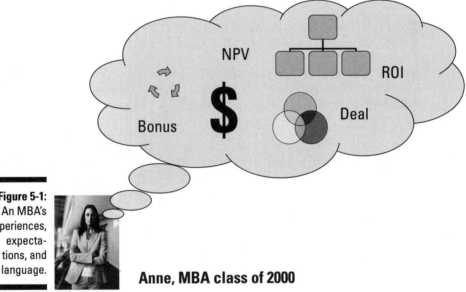

NPV

ROI

$

Deal

Bonus

Figure 5-1:
An MBA's experiences, expectations, and language.

Anne, MBA class of 2000

Joe, a senior accountant, lives for cost centers, neat spreadsheets full of formulas, and number-crunching (see Figure 5-2). Joe may understand how to enter a formula in Excel and how to get a cost report from SAP, but when it comes to installing a new piece of software on his computer, he's at a loss. Joe knows how much a new desktop workstation costs, but he couldn't set one up to connect to the network if you paid him.

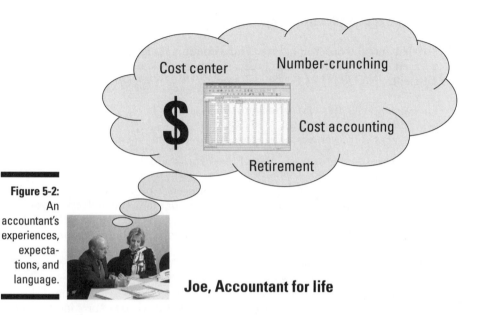

Figure 5-2:
An
accountant's
experiences,
expecta-
tions, and
language.

Joe, Accountant for life

Tom, the IT guy, thinks in terms of firewalls, virtual private networks, and scalability (see Figure 5-3). Tom's only experience with business types is when they mess up a request he's put in for five new PCs or demand that a new server be up and running in a ridiculously short time. Don't these guys know that technology takes time to configure and deploy?

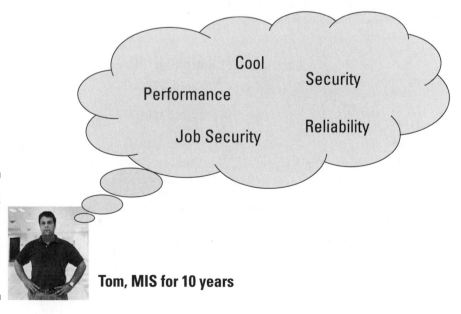

Figure 5-3:
An IT
person's
experiences,
expecta-
tions, and
language.

Tom, MIS for 10 years

Not one of these folks really understands the jargon or perspective of the other.

So what can you do? You have to find a common language for everybody in your enterprise landscape. So take a step back and consider language for a moment.

Spoken language has two aspects to it:

✔ Syntax is the sentence structure, grammar, and vocabulary

✔ Semantics relates to the meaning of words and phrases

Before you can get everybody understanding each other's semantic meaning, you have to get them speaking the same grammar and vocabulary, so you need to start at the level of syntax. If the business person thinks in ROI calculations and the IT person thinks in programming code, there's a disconnect.

Enterprise services to the rescue. Enterprise services have a clearly defined syntax based on Web service conventions (see Chapter 1 for a primer on Web services and XML). Semantics is the area where enterprise service jump ahead of Web services. Enterprise service semantics in this case are provided by the service names and the selection definition for service parameters. Service names follow strict rules (see Chapter 7 for more about service naming). The parameters for service names are carefully chosen to only include commonly understood business parameters. So, business people understand what's going on, and IT people can easily provide the technical piece needed to solve a problem.

ERP's enterprise services, then, become the common language for IT and business (see Figure 5-4).

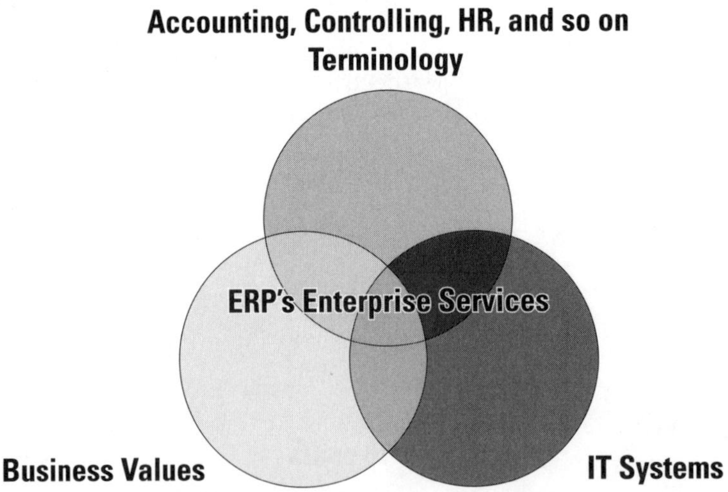

Accounting, Controlling, HR, and so on Terminology

Figure 5-4:
ERP's enterprise — where IT and business people come together.

ERP's Enterprise Services

Business Values

IT Systems

Enterprise services get granular

One of the goals of ESA is to provide the common language and interfaces to technology that business people understand. This happens when transactions are transformed into enterprise services. Those services have to be defined with a granularity that's meaningful to business people and professional experts such as accountants and HR professionals.

Granularity simply refers to the level of detail exposed at the interface. This means you have to correctly define services so that they relate to the individual steps of a business process. If you define these steps in just the right granular way, they can be more easily and flexibly rearranged and modified.

Having the right granularity means that you make only the parameters that are necessary from a business perspective visible to users. That means that all the techie stuff that deals with systems, such as security, transaction controls, database layout, and so on, never shows up in the enterprise service interface. The enterprise service then becomes the interface between business and IT.

Enterprise services are IT tools, and so Tom the IT guy is comfortable with them. Enterprise services, however, are associated with a business activity. That means that Joe the accountant understands how a service that helps him calculate ROI is valuable, and Anne is hip to the value of a service used to call up customer order history. The fact that services are both great tools for IT to work with and they are easily understood by business people and professional experts is what makes enterprise services so powerful.

Enterprise services understand industries

Just as your teenager and you have different backgrounds, different industries come from different perspectives. They speak different languages; every industry is in its own little jargon-dominated world.

That's where SAP industry scenarios come to the rescue. Enterprise services are defined in the context of an industry, so they are instantaneously meaningful and useable in your own little corner of the business world.

SAP provides scenarios for more than 25 industries, broken down into processes and, at the detail level, into enterprise services.

How IT Works in a Service-Enabled World

What does a service-enabled world look like from an IT perspective? We're glad you asked. . . .

Developing enterprise software

If you look at the systems in almost any large company, you can see different layers of technology stretching back almost all the way to the early days of mainframes. Even when antique devices such as punch cards are no longer visible, the architectures that they used, such as batch processing, are still in place. It's as if the modern IT department is being haunted by the ghosts of technology past. Punch-card readers spinning magnetic tapes and disk drives the size of washing machines still cast a shadow on the way IT works.

Things are no different when you look at the history of enterprise software. Mathematicians and software engineers from SAP and other companies have worked on ERP solutions that have grown as available technology grew, so there are many layers of solutions in place.

One of the fundamental drivers of SAP's success is that the company faced complex problems head on from day one. SAP never solved just one problem at a time. Its products always solved all possible different versions of the same problem, including customizing for various vertical industries and specific issues at individual companies. That's why enterprise applications are so difficult to build.

Enterprise applications are complex because they are general-purpose systems for solving specific problems. Buying an enterprise application is not like buying a car or a refrigerator; enterprise applications aren't a final solution when they arrive at your company. They must be adjusted to meet your specific needs. In fact, enterprise applications are more like a configurable toolkit for building exactly the car or refrigerator you want.

You can meet the specific situations at one company by setting the right values for all the possible different choices. For example, many companies have products that they sell to make money. On this level of abstraction, the processes are the same. But now look at a consumer products company such as Colgate, which offers many brands and even more products. Colgate has vast production facilities, just-in-time shipments, and retail sales to juggle. On the other hand, consider a company like ExxonMobil, which needs to manage oil fields, tanker fleets, refineries, and gas stations. Its business processes are fundamentally different on the detailed level, but both of these companies run successfully on SAP.

In walks business content

SAP calls settings and methods of configuration that you can apply to mySAP ERP *business content.* Most SAP products come with a huge collection of pre-configured settings for customers to choose from so they don't have to rein-vent the wheel each time and create each setting manually. This content is essentially business best practices that you get right out of a box.

One of the cheapest ways to close the gap between the enterprise application that comes out of the box and exactly what your company needs is to use packages of business content that make the enterprise application meet a specific situation or need. This makes IT's life much easier. It's like having a component for a car accessory ready to install. If you want satellite radio, you use a kit to install it in your car.

For example, the equivalent preconfigured content for an enterprise applica-tion might be an interface for a portal that allows employees to update their own addresses. The business content would be a set of screens, a workflow between them, and other settings that offer a ready-made capability to allow employees a self-service system. The self-service information may differ, but the infrastructure of employee information is there to give you a head start.

The more business content that is available, the easier it is to make an enter-prise application do exactly what your company wants it to do. SAP has hundreds of different packages of best practices business content for all its products.

But every company has some specific, differentiating business processes that may need something beyond industry best practices from a box. Another way to make an enterprise application meet your needs is for the application to have the flexibility to allow you to create your own business content. When your needs are so specific that you have to resort to custom development, services may allow you to pick and choose and build what you need. And if that approach isn't good enough, writing code can always get the job done.

As flexible as it is for developers who must get into custom development, one of the main goals of SAP NetWeaver is to ensure that making an enterprise application that works for your company involves business content and ser-vices, rather than custom programming.

Figure 5-5 shows a value/investment matrix. As we discussed in Part I of this book, every company has standard business processes that don't set your business apart from the competition. In this area, you are under constant pressure to reduce costs. Best practices help you to do just that.

On the other hand are high-value, differentiating business processes. This is where you have to invent your own best practices. This requires an investment on your part, but enterprise services and modeling significantly reduce this investment.

You have to make sure that you don't spend your valuable investment dollars in the lower-right quadrant of the matrix shown in Figure 5-5, which would just be a waste of money.

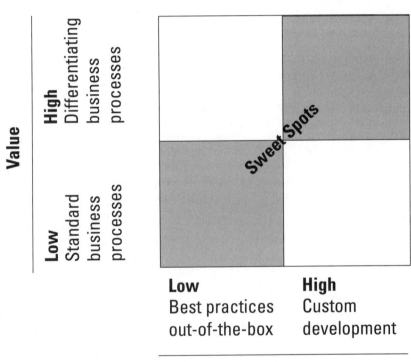

Figure 5-5:
Evaluating best practices versus custom development work.

Using Abstraction to Hide Complexity

If there is a silver bullet, a secret to creating great enterprise applications, it is the proper use of abstraction. If you understand abstraction, for the most part, you've got a handle on SAP technology and can impress people at the drop of a hat.

Abstraction consists of a process of mapping multiple pieces of data to a single piece of abstract data based on similarities in the various pieces. For example, many different database products that may be from Oracle, IBM, or Microsoft may map to the abstraction *database*.

The two sides of abstraction

Almost all abstractions have two sides: a simple model of what someone needs to know, and the complex mess underneath that is managed by the technology delivering it. When you push the power button on your computer, the power surges through the microchips and disk drives, and all sorts of programs start loading, but the screen only shows you the simple result of all this stuff (usually a blue sky, a green field, and some weird music). That is what most abstractions are like: Push or click something simple, and you start a chain of complex events that produce something a user can actually use.

The idea is that the user of the abstractions gets to think of the problem in very simple terms because the implementers of the abstraction (in this case, SAP) manage the complexity behind the scenes and reduce the problem to the smallest terms possible. SAP essentially went crazy creating abstraction all over the application stack. This is very good news for both end users and IT people.

Which database is under there, anyway?

One of the first abstractions SAP created allows seamless access to data. The current version, Open SQL, allows SAP to write its programs in one way using routines for data access provided by Open SQL. At development time, the programmer (the user of the abstraction) never has to know whether there is an Oracle database or an IBM database or a Microsoft database underneath. At run time, the Open SQL layer magically knows which database is present and translates the request into the right form. The programmer, however, can remain blissfully ignorant of what's going on behind the scenes.

SAP gives you the freedom to pick your own databases (and operating system and hardware platform). This allows you to pick and choose the combination that offers you the best total cost of ownership and flexibility. If you have licenses and skilled support people already in place, don't reinvent the wheel — use 'em!

It's important to note that all abstractions have to exist both at development time, when the behavior of the system is defined, and at run time, when the programs execute and the task of the abstraction is being carried out. That's why most of the abstractions used in enterprise applications have components to support both development and run-time use of the abstraction.

Taking abstraction further

But SAP didn't stop there. Besides Open SQL, SAP has abstractions for every part of an enterprise application. Here's a list of the abstractions in today's SAP solution:

- SAP NetWeaver Application Server
- Web services
- SAP Web Dynpro
- SAP NetWeaver Portal
- SAP NetWeaver Mobile
- SAP NetWeaver Exchange Infrastructure
- SAP NetWeaver Master Data Management
- SAP NetWeaver Business Intelligence
- SAP NetWeaver Developer Studio
- SAP Solution Manager

Some of these deal with providing a programmer with a way to write code so that it runs on many different platforms. Some support access and integration. Others allow various applications to talk to each other. But they all make an IT person's life simpler.

Enterprise services are the latest leap forward in the abstractions that have come from SAP in the past and have proven to be a powerful asset to businesses around the world.

Summing Up the IT Service-Enabled World

Three things sum up how SAP NetWeaver, in a service-enabled world, supporting enterprise products such as mySAP ERP, helps you manage technology:

- ✔ **Standardization:** For the SAP NetWeaver Application Server, for Web Dynpro, and for Web services, open standards play an important role in defining SAP functionality.

- ✔ **Granularity and abstraction:** Keeping the underlying technology out of the user's sight while offering flexibility in highly granular service design provides great control over your business processes.

- ✔ **Modeling:** Finally, at every turn, in products and toolkits, modeling is taking a more prominent role, showing that the SAP way of conquering complexity through abstraction is alive and well.

We discuss modeling in more detail in Chapter 7.

If you look at what is different about SAP NetWeaver compared with the abstractions used in SAP R/3, the rise of modeling may be the most striking difference, even more important than the rise of standards.

Modeling is important because it provides a way to conquer even more complexity than simple abstractions. In *modeling,* a set of simple abstractions of components is used to define the universe of a program being developed. Then a model is created by defining connections between those components. Web Dynpro, for example, has a whole set of components that define common user-interface elements such as buttons and text boxes.

The models, which are stored as metadata, are then read by a special program that then generates all the Java or ABAP code needed to create an application that works just like the model says it should.

The most ambitious foray into executable models is the SAP Composite Application Framework (SAP CAF). (Read more about SAP CAF in Chapter 9.) This is an environment for modeling entire applications, not just the user interface, from application and platform components exposed as Web services.

Another new frontier for SAP NetWeaver are languages for BPM. Such languages hold the promise to make the configuration of how programs work much easier. Because things are presented in business terms, perhaps one day these languages will allow business analysts instead of programmers to control most of the logic. SAP is participating in standards efforts for specific types of BPM languages like BPEL4WS, a joint effort by Microsoft and IBM to merge their two previous efforts at creating such a language. If the standards-creation efforts succeed, such a language could be used in every SAP application including mySAP ERP, as well as every SAP NetWeaver component.

Part II
Getting Under the Hood: The Underlying Technology

The 5th Wave   By Rich Tennant

"Oh, an Oz—wide ERP system has been discussed, but it's not as impressive as the giant, floating, disembodied head of the Wizard keeping an eye on everything."

In this part . . .

*J*ust as a word processing application sits on top of an operating system such as Microsoft Windows, mySAP ERP rests on top of a technology platform called SAP NetWeaver. To understand the full potential of mySAP ERP, you need to appreciate its power. The chapters in this part introduce you to SAP NetWeaver, look at how it behaves in designing and running applications, and go further into how you work with services. Finally, we look at the world of composite applications; using these, you can orchestrate functionality from several applications to make technology better support your business processes.

Chapter 6

Meet SAP NetWeaver

· ·

· ·

*E*verybody's gotta have a vision. For Columbus, it was finding a better route to Asia by sailing west. (Of course, turns out, the New World was in his way.) For Galileo, it was inventing a telescope to view the planets and discover satellites around Jupiter. For you, maybe it's making sense of all the technoid gobbledygook your company has to deal with day in and day out so that you and your IT people don't end up old before their time.

If so, you'll be glad to hear that, at its core, SAP NetWeaver is an ambitious vision for improving information technology, including the software and hardware that runs the world of business. But SAP NetWeaver is not just a vision: It's a set of tools and methodologies that can take your company where it needs to go. And finally, it's the technical underpinning of mySAP ERP.

So, What Exactly Is SAP NetWeaver?

SAP NetWeaver is a super-sized serving of technology and tools made up of products and concepts that are useful to the corporate decision maker and the technologists who work together to solve huge information challenges.

SAP NetWeaver offers a platform that allows your organization to integrate all your systems and integrate with third-party systems. In addition, SAP NetWeaver acts as a platform on which you can build applications. The goal of all this is not to just pile up technology in your back office; SAP NetWeaver's purpose is to enable you to be more flexible so that you can adapt when the inevitable changes come along. Whereas technology used to be the stumbling block to making changes, it now enables the solution.

Some of the things you can do with SAP NetWeaver include

- ✔ Creating portals that give each user exactly what he needs from all your applications
- ✔ Providing a unified view of information from every part of your company and delivering it to employees just when and how they need it
- ✔ Knitting processes that are distributed in bits across many applications together into one streamlined interface

And because it is based on the latest technology and approaches to business processes, SAP NetWeaver also increases flexibility and enables change throughout your enterprise. Not bad, huh?

Orchestrating a Technology Symphony

Sometimes it seems like brain surgery is child's play next to grasping the world of enterprise resource planning (ERP). SAP NetWeaver is such an ambitious undertaking, with so many dimensions, that it is hard even for experienced IT professionals to quickly understand its structure and potential. But here's a starting point: Think of SAP NetWeaver as essentially an orchestra of technologies with many programs and toolkits, each adding its own voice to the composition to allow you to design, deploy, and modify business processes. These are capabilities that either didn't exist before or, if they did, nobody could afford them.

What's in it for me?

So, if a capability enables you to do something, how, exactly, do you use that capability to get your work done? The answer is that SAP paid attention to how people really do their jobs and designed its products to make technology easier for people to use. Here are the key benefits of SAP NetWeaver:

- ✔ **Flexibility in business strategies:** SAP NetWeaver helps you be flexible about making changes to your IT infrastructure. For example, using SAP NetWeaver, you can deal with outsourcing, centralizing or decentralizing, consolidating, and integrating of IT when those dreaded mergers and acquisitions hit. With SAP NetWeaver, you've got what it takes to effectively execute, measure, and refine your corporate strategies.

- ✔ **Innovative business processes:** SAP NetWeaver is the power behind the throne for ready-to-go, innovative, industry-specific software products, such as mySAP ERP. These are the products that allow your company to recompose your existing systems so you can give birth to innovative business processes.

- ✔ **Improved integration:** SAP NetWeaver keeps down your total cost of ownership and frees IT people to focus on the future. When you hook up with SAP NetWeaver, you can take advantage of all your existing IT investments, whether they come from SAP or somewhere else. SAP NetWeaver also builds in integration knowledge that keeps you from having to spend a mint for consulting services. After it's in place, SAP NetWeaver also keeps the cost of change down.

- ✔ **Reduced TCO:** With SAP NetWeaver, you can get more value from your existing IT investment. It provides a business-focused infrastructure, meaning that SAP NetWeaver talks the language of your business, not some technology jargon. This make continuous business-process evolution and change less painful. SAP NetWeaver minimizes the risk and cost of introducing new business processes because existing systems essentially remain unchanged.

- ✔ **Improved development:** Because you can compose new business processes on top of your existing systems, developing new applications is way less difficult than it used to be. This is done using a service-oriented architecture based on Web services, Java, and other industry standards.

- ✔ **Savings across the entire IT landscape:** SAP NetWeaver technology components are integrated in a single technology platform, which is always better than crossing over a jumble of multiple platforms. SAP NetWeaver comes preconfigured with business content. This keeps complexity at bay and supports standardization and consolidation in your IT department. SAP NetWeaver technology components also integrate happily with SAP applications, which reduces custom integration.

- ✔ **Better business performance:** SAP NetWeaver helps companies pull together and analyze information across their organizations, so they get the insight they need to make the right changes. SAP NetWeaver supports all stages of your business, from getting the information you need to improving your business processes.

- ✔ **A really good user experience:** With SAP NetWeaver, companies can extend their business processes to include all employees, suppliers, and customers. Solutions built using SAP NetWeaver also provide a seamless user experience by using a role-based portal interface.

> ✔ **Making the best use of best practices:** With SAP NetWeaver, you can take existing people skills and build on current practices or compose new functions that meet your needs. SAP NetWeaver supports communication, knowledge management, and collaboration across your existing corporate systems.

Here are just a few of the reasons why SAP NetWeaver is so unique:

✔ Supports change by allowing flexibility in the IT infrastructure

✔ Provides the flexibility, visibility, and control to effectively execute, measure, and refine corporate strategies

✔ Allows companies to recompose their existing systems to support innovative industry-specific business processes

✔ Reduces TCO across the IT landscape and frees resources to focus on growth

✔ Reduces the cost of change while leveraging existing IT investments, including both SAP and non-SAP software

✔ Makes it easier for companies to outsource selected functions, centralize or decentralize operations, consolidate operations, and integrate IT after mergers and acquisitions

SAP NetWeaver 101

When in doubt about the meaning of words, most folks usually revert to the dictionary. So, we start your SAP NetWeaver education with a little definition.

SAP NetWeaver is a set of capabilities that are provided by many different SAP products constructed to work with each other to make people, information, and business processes work together across technologies and organizations, all based on services.

Granted, it's a mouthful. So, for you visual learners out there, here's an SAP solution map for SAP NetWeaver that describes all its capabilities. Figure 6-1 shows the most common way that people explain what SAP NetWeaver does.

What you're looking at are the "IT practices" supported by SAP NetWeaver. You can meet business process requirements by implementing crucial IT practices with a flexible, step-by-step approach. You can address your immediate IT needs first because the platform components are tightly integrated. You can then expand over time with a cost structure you can live with.

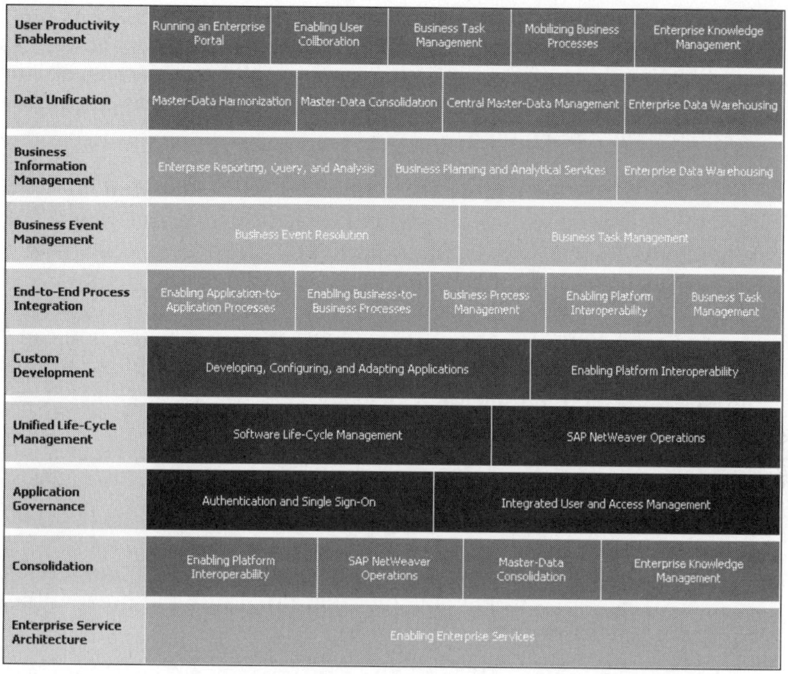

User Productivity Enablement	Running an Enterprise Portal	Enabling User Collaboration	Business Task Management	Mobilizing Business Processes	Enterprise Knowledge Management
Data Unification	Master-Data Harmonization	Master-Data Consolidation	Central Master-Data Management	Enterprise Data Warehousing	
Business Information Management	Enterprise Reporting, Query, and Analysis		Business Planning and Analytical Services		Enterprise Data Warehousing
Business Event Management	Business Event Resolution			Business Task Management	
End-to-End Process Integration	Enabling Application-to-Application Processes	Enabling Business-to-Business Processes	Business Process Management	Enabling Platform Interoperability	Business Task Management
Custom Development	Developing, Configuring, and Adapting Applications			Enabling Platform Interoperability	
Unified Life-Cycle Management	Software Life-Cycle Management			SAP NetWeaver Operations	
Application Governance	Authentication and Single Sign-On			Integrated User and Access Management	
Consolidation	Enabling Platform Interoperability	SAP NetWeaver Operations	Master-Data Consolidation	Enterprise Knowledge Management	
Enterprise Service Architecture	Enabling Enterprise Services				

Figure 6-1: The SAP NetWeaver solution map.

Bringing all the instruments together

So now you understand something about the pieces of SAP NetWeaver and what goals the folks at SAP had in mind when building it. But what, exactly, does this thing do?

To understand that, you have to grasp the importance of a thing called *prepackaged integration*. Making applications work together is vitally important to most companies. That's where services and prepackaged integration come in — both are integral parts of SAP NetWeaver and, naturally, heavily used by mySAP ERP.

Prepackaged integration simply means that all the products in SAP NetWeaver were built to work together out of the box and to work with mySAP ERP. The integration was done at the factory, when the products were created, not after the fact. This represents a huge savings in both money and time when it comes to making applications work together. In the past, companies spent gobs of money just to make programs work together that weren't designed to. SAP NetWeaver eliminates this financial hemorrhage from your IT budget.

Another benefit of prepackaged integration is that SAP NetWeaver comes ready to work with the entire mySAP Business Suite collection of enterprise applications, not just mySAP ERP. These applications arrive at your office ready to plug into many of the products in SAP NetWeaver, which saves you yet more time and money.

It's important to remember that none of this prepackaged integration prevents integration with products and tools from other vendors. This flexibility simply makes it cheaper and easier to connect SAP systems with each other as well as to connect with non-SAP systems.

So, with the concept of prepackaged integration in mind, you can begin to grasp exactly what can be done with SAP NetWeaver: integrating existing applications and building new ones.

Most people who have used SAP NetWeaver will tell you that it can do absolutely anything, but in more practical terms, here's how it's actually being used out there in corporate-land:

- ✔ Companies create portals that bring together functionality from mySAP ERP as well as from many different programs and present them in one consistent, easy-to-use interface.

- ✔ Companies use SAP NetWeaver to create one consistent version of any company's vital data by collecting it from many different applications.

- ✔ Companies use SAP NetWeaver to start a process in one application and then provide one user interface as the process continues through other applications, or even through other companies' systems.

Because companies create these applications based on prepackaged integration, the applications cost much less to extend and maintain. The bottom line is that these advanced development tools enhance productivity and increase savings.

In an orchestra, each instrument has a different role. The composer or arranger assigns parts to flutes, tympanis, and trumpets. The rhythm generally stays with the percussion crowd. The violins and French horns may carry the melody along. But during the concert, all instruments add to the harmony of the piece.

The areas that SAP NetWeaver focuses on work the same way. Each is a powerful instrument that can make many different kinds of IT music, but each also has one thing that it does particularly well. Each uniquely talented component has the most value when playing well with others to solve a problem.

Giving SAP NetWeaver the Once-Over

If you want to get anywhere, you have to know what road to take. With SAP NetWeaver, you get a logical freeway that leads to Enterprise Services Architecture and ultimately gives you increased business flexibility.

SAP NetWeaver helps you handle the following areas:

✔ User productivity enablement

✔ Data unification

✔ Business information management

✔ End-to-end process integration

✔ Custom development

✔ Unified lifecycle management

✔ Application governance

✔ Consolidation

✔ Business event management

✔ Service-oriented architecture design and deployment

Just in case you don't know what each of these is, we describe them in the following sections.

Making Users Productive

Web-based portals and mobile interfaces help IT organizations come to the aid of users and groups to improve their productivity. They do this by providing all kinds of collaborative tools, better management of data (called *knowledge management*), and personalized access to applications and data that people need to do their work. The really important IT activities are enabled by the SAP NetWeaver Portal component in combination with the SAP NetWeaver Mobile component. See Figure 6-2 for an overview of user productivity in SAP NetWeaver.

Figure 6-2:
Enabling
user produc-
tivity in SAP
NetWeaver.

Running an Enterprise Portal	Enabling User Collboration	Business Task Management	Mobilizing Business Processes	Enterprise Knowledge Management
▶ Implementing a Global Portal (Federated Portal) ▶ Implementing a Multitenant Portal ● Providing Uniform Content Access	● Collaboration In Virtual Rooms ● Ad hoc Collaboration ● Administering Collaboration Services	● Central Access to Tasks ● Support for Offline Processes	● Running Mobile Applications with an Online Connection ● Enabling Mobile Applications for Occasional Connection	● Content Integration and Management ● Content Creation, Publication, and Access ⊘ Enterprise Search ● Documentation, Manuals, and Training Materials Management

Running an enterprise portal

With the very nifty portal technology, you can develop, configure, and operate an enterprise portal. An enterprise portal contains an external-facing
portal (meaning that people outside of your organization can view the
portal), and it can enable business-to-business (B2B) activities with business
partners as well as information sharing via Web communities. With SAP
NetWeaver, you can perform a variety of procedures, including

✔ Implementing a global portal.

✔ Implementing a multitenant portal. (With this feature, you can host multiple companies or tenants using the same instance of SAP NetWeaver,
reducing your hardware investment and enabling outsourcing.)

✔ Providing uniform content access.

Some user productivity examples

Employee self-service is one of the most popular ways to use mySAP ERP. In
this sort of deployment, all the services that a company offers its employees,
from making human resources information about health care and pension
plans available, to simple modifications like changing an address, all happen
in one place. This can save lots of money by reducing the burden on the HR
staff, who otherwise have to answer all of these questions one at a time.

Another popular self-service use is an external portal in which a company
enables all its suppliers to keep track of shipments, invoices, and payments
through a Web site, which saves the receiving and accounts payable departments a lot of time, paperwork, and headaches.

Like the arrival/departure screen at an airport, portals are also a central access point, the one place people go for important information. By harmonizing the look and feel of different types of applications from different vendors, you make your users much more productive, and along the way, you save lots of money.

Enterprise knowledge management

It's a good idea to provide an integrated work environment for your information workers. In this kind of environment, these workers can create, publish, manage, and search all kinds of information. Because information is power, this is a good thing.

With SAP NetWeaver, IT organizations can perform procedures such as the following, which help your information workers get that much-desired integrated work environment:

- ✔ Content integration and management
- ✔ Content creation, publication, and access
- ✔ Enterprise searches
- ✔ Documentation, manuals, and training materials management

Enterprise Knowledge Management allows you to store, categorize, and search through structured and *unstructured documents,* such as word processing files, presentations, spreadsheets, and all the other documents you shuffle around on a daily basis. Needless to say, finding information you need quickly helps save you time and money.

Helping folks to work together

We should all help each other out, and SAP NetWeaver supports that kind of cooperation. If you're sitting at your desk, you can regroup tasks that occur in various locations into coordinated activities and then execute tasks quickly from a central location using a single user interface. Here's what you can do to collaborate with others when you have SAP NetWeaver:

- ✔ Collaborate in virtual rooms
- ✔ Spontaneously collaborate
- ✔ Administer collaboration services

See Chapter 3 for more about how users make use of portals through control and work centers.

Unifying Data

When you put SAP NetWeaver in place, your IT organization can ensure that all master data (including user-defined data and data related to customers, suppliers, and employees) is accurate and free of those pesky duplicate records. You give internal and external users and applications a lot of flexibility in accessing one set of data across the board. See Figure 6-3 for an overview of data unification in SAP NetWeaver.

Figure 6-3:
Data unifica-
tion in SAP
NetWeaver.

Master-Data Harmonization	Master-Data Consolidation	Central Master-Data Management	Enterprise Data Warehousing
● Interactive Master-Data Harmonization ● Automated Master-Data Harmonization	● Interactive Master-Data Consolidation ● Automated Master-Data Consolidation	● Central Master-Data Management	● Modeling the Enterprise Data Warehouse (EDW) ● Running the Enterprise Data Warehouse (EDW)

Unification of data is made possible by SAP NetWeaver components such as SAP NetWeaver Master Data Management (SAP NetWeaver MDM), SAP NetWeaver Exchange Infrastructure (SAP NetWeaver XI), and SAP NetWeaver Business Intelligence (SAP NetWeaver BI). Here's how this works:

✔ SAP NetWeaver lets you consolidate master data by searching for master data across linked systems, identifying identical or similar objects spread across local IT systems, consolidating master data, and providing ID mapping. All this means that you get consistent information all around your company that you can use to analyze your business activities and generate reports.

✔ You can consolidate and harmonize master data from different systems. During consolidation, you can search for master-data objects across linked systems, identify identical or similar objects, cleanse objects, and more. All of these activities help you keep data consistent and tidy all around your organization.

✔ You can centrally manage master data and support data consistency across all locations in a global company.

✔ You can create and manage a single centralized repository of product content, with support for premium search capabilities and publishing of product information to searchable Web catalogs or paper catalogs.

Managing Business Information

When it comes to business information, the lifeblood of most organizations, SAP NetWeaver performs another neat trick. Using SAP NetWeaver, IT organizations can increase the visibility and reach of all your enterprise data and help people at all levels and locations take raw data and mold it into integrated, meaningful information that they can act on. Business information management is made possible by SAP NetWeaver components such as SAP NetWeaver BI, SAP NetWeaver XI, and the knowledge management functionality of SAP NetWeaver Portal. See Figure 6-4 for an overview of business information management in SAP NetWeaver.

Figure 6-4:
Business
information
manage-
ment in SAP
NetWeaver.

Enterprise Reporting, Query, and Analysis	Business Planning and Analytical Services	Enterprise Data Warehousing
● Enterprise Reporting, Query and Analysis ● Excel Integration ● Ad hoc Query ● Information Broadcasting ▶ Modeling Business Intelligence Data with SAP NetWeaver Visual Composer	● Business Planning ● Analysis Process Design	● Modeling the Enterprise Data Warehouse (EDW) ● Running the Enterprise Data Warehouse (EDW)

Enterprise reporting, query, and analysis

Using SAP NetWeaver, your IT organization can deliver reports and other analytics to people at all your locations, helping people to make sense of enterprise data. People can analyze patterns and trends and put business intelligence to good use with information from all your departments and divisions, ranging from back-end internal systems to external supplier and customer networks.

SAP NetWeaver helps you perform the following procedures:

✔ Integration with Excel to display SAP reports in that familiar spreadsheet format

✔ Ad hoc queries

> ✔ Information broadcasting
>
> ✔ Modeling of business data with the SAP NetWeaver Visual Composer tool

Planning and analyzing your business

Almost everything goes better if you have a plan. You can perform state-of-the-art planning and predict and react to changing market conditions in time to make a difference. Using SAP NetWeaver, you can build planning applications that are tailored to your specific needs for strategic or operational planning.

Putting data in warehouses

SAP NetWeaver helps you to create and operate an enterprise-wide data warehouse. This isn't like your typical warehouse; it has no shelving or forklifts. This data warehouse is made up of information. Using SAP NetWeaver, you can both model and run an enterprise data warehouse.

Integrating processes end to end

Another thing that SAP NetWeaver makes possible is that IT organizations can make a whole lot of applications and business partners' systems work together consistently to perform business processes. These different systems can exchange information and execute transactions smoothly, just as if they were a single system. Process integration is supported by SAP NetWeaver components such as SAP NetWeaver Exchange Infrastructure (SAP NetWeaver XI) and SAP Auto-ID Infrastructure. See Figure 6-5 for an overview of end-to-end process integration in SAP NetWeaver.

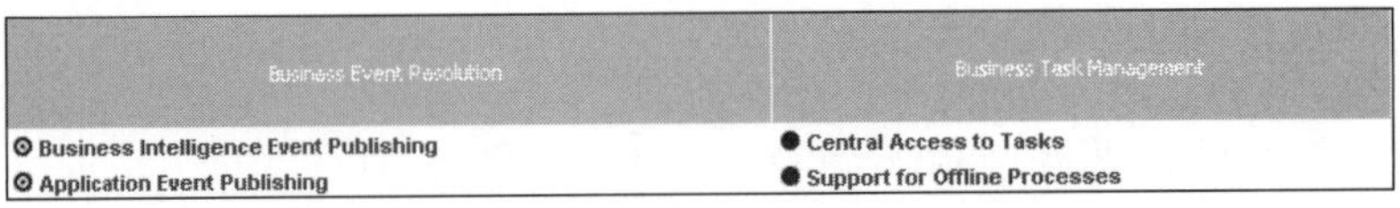

Figure 6-5:
End-to-end
process
integration
in SAP
NetWeaver.

Business Event Resolution	Business Task Management
⊙ Business Intelligence Event Publishing	● Central Access to Tasks
⊙ Application Event Publishing	● Support for Offline Processes

Making business-to-business processes work

Have you ever wanted to seamlessly connect your own business processes with those of your partners? SAP NetWeaver's communication and process-integration capabilities extend beyond the borders of your company and allow you to integrate your systems with those of your business partners.

 Discover more about how SAP NetWeaver makes integration possible in Chapter 8.

SAP NetWeaver helps with the following:

✔ Business partner integration using industry standards

✔ Small-business partner and subsidiary integration

Enabling application-to-application processes

It doesn't matter whether you have one application from one vendor and another from its competitor: You can easily connect SAP and non-SAP applications within your enterprise. You do this by syncing the process flow between the applications using message-based and standards-based process integration.

Business process management

Business processes are all over your company. You can model business processes for those really important roles within your business. SAP NetWeaver supports process blueprinting, system implementation and integration, and process execution. Specifically, SAP NetWeaver enables you to

✔ Use and adapt predefined content

✔ Automate processes

Enabling an RFID infrastructure

Today, RFID (radio frequency identification) is hot. This great technology allows you to scan a huge container of products and find each and every tagged item, without ever opening the box. SAP NetWeaver can connect RFID technology directly to software to sense and control automated signals in real time. This means that inventory or package-delivery information can be hooked right into your ERP system seamlessly.

Customizing Development

When it absolutely, positively has to be done your very own way, custom is the way to go. With SAP NetWeaver, your IT organization can take advantage of existing investments in technology and skills, by creating new enterprise-scale applications that help your company stay ahead of the competition. Custom development is supported by the following SAP NetWeaver components: SAP NetWeaver Application Server (SAP NetWeaver AS), SAP Composite Application Framework (SAP CAF), and SAP NetWeaver Developer Studio. The following sections explain how this all works. See Figure 6-6 for an overview of custom development in SAP NetWeaver.

Enabling Application-to-Application Processes	Enabling Business-to-Business Processes	Business Process Management	Enabling Platform Interoperability	Business Task Management
● Appplication-to-Application Integration	● Business Partner Integration Using Industry Standards ● Small Business Partner and Subsidiary Integration	● Usage and Adaptation of Predefined Content ● Process Automation ● Combining Embedded and Unbounded Processes	● Enabling Coexistence of Several Portals ● Ensuring Application-to-Application and Business-to-Business Integration ● Providing Web Services Interoperability ● Managing Heterogenous System Landscapes ● Developing Applications Compatible with SAP NetWeaver	● Central Access to Tasks ● Support for Offline Processes

Figure 6-6: Custom development in SAP NetWeaver.

Developing, configuring, and adapting applications

SAP NetWeaver's model-driven environment gives you all you need to develop, configure, and adapt user interfaces for SAP-delivered applications. You can also develop, model, and configure custom composite applications. SAP NetWeaver helps you to

✔ Create applications using Web Dynpro for Java

✔ Leverage Java 2 Platform, Enterprise Edition (J2EE) standards for port-
ing and adopting applications

✔ Create business applications using the ABAP programming language

✔ Create applications using Web Dynpro for ABAP

✔ Create applications using SAP NetWeaver Visual Composer

✔ Create portal applications using the .NET portal development kit

✔ Develop mobile applications for occasional connections

Enabling platform interoperability

Like your mother said, sharing is good. You can share content with non-SAP
portals and get yourself set up to operate with non-SAP software and technology platforms. You can also support interoperation with non-SAP solutions
on a business-process level. Using SAP NetWeaver, you can

✔ Enable several portals to coexist

✔ Ensure application-to-application and business-to-business integration

✔ Provide Web services interoperability

✔ Manage heterogeneous system landscapes

✔ Develop applications that are compatible with SAP NetWeaver

Unified Lifecycle Management

Although we often wish somebody would manage our lifecycles, we're usually on our own. However, with SAP NetWeaver, your IT organization can
automate the lifecycle of applications. By managing an application's lifecycle,
you can ensure that your operation never falters and that your company
reacts quickly to change. Lifecycle management is supported by SAP
NetWeaver components such as SAP Solution Manager and SAP NetWeaver
AS. See Figure 6-7 for an overview of unified lifecycle management in SAP
NetWeaver.

Developing, Configuring, and Adapting Applications	Enabling Platform Interoperability
● Creating Applications Using Web Dynpro for Java ● Porting J2EE-Based Applications to SAP NetWeaver ● Creating Business Applications Using ABAP ▶ Creating Applications Using Web Dynpro for ABAP ● Creating Applications Using SAP NetWeaver Visual Composer ● Creating Portal Applications Using the .NET Portal Development Kit ● Developing Mobile Applications for Occasional Connection	● Enabling Coexistence of Several Portals ● Ensuring Application-to-Application and Business-to-Business Integration ● Providing Web Services Interoperability ● Managing Heterogenous System Landscapes ● Developing Applications Compatible with SAP NetWeaver

Figure 6-7:
Unified lifecycle management in SAP NetWeaver.

Governing Applications

With SAP NetWeaver, your IT organization can maintain just the right level of security and quality to keep all your precious intellectual property and information assets safe. What's really cool is that you can do this without compromising flexibility, user productivity, or collaboration with customers and partners. Application governance is made possible by SAP NetWeaver components such as SAP NetWeaver AS, SAP NetWeaver XI, and SAP NetWeaver Portal. See Figure 6-8 for an overview of application governance in SAP NetWeaver.

Software Life-Cycle Management	SAP NetWeaver Operations
● Implementation Support ● Software Maintenance	● Monitoring SAP NetWeaver ● Administering SAP NetWeaver ● Adaptive Computing ● Data Archiving

Figure 6-8:
Application governance in SAP NetWeaver.

Integrated user and access management

You can create a centralized user administration facility and consolidate the user management technology you already have in place. SAP NetWeaver helps you to integrate user and access management, including a third-party directory server.

Authentication and single sign-on

You can get control of your lightweight directory access protocol (LDAP) directory and integrate different SAP systems into a landscape where your employees use a single sign-on to get what they need. With SAP NetWeaver, you can provide the following:

> ✔ Authentication using a directory with single sign-on (SSO) integration using SAP logon tickets
>
> ✔ A single sign-on based on Security Assertion Markup Language (SAML)

Consolidating All Your Systems

SAP NetWeaver helps you to deal with all the stuff you have stuffed into your system from different vendors and technologies. SAP NetWeaver does all this by using a single technology platform based on a service-oriented architecture and by flexibly spreading the wealth of computing power according to changing user needs. Consolidation is enabled by SAP NetWeaver components such as SAP NetWeaver Portal, SAP NetWeaver BI, SAP NetWeaver MDM, and SAP NetWeaver XI. See Figure 6-9 for an overview of consolidation in SAP NetWeaver.

Figure 6-9:
Consolidation in SAP NetWeaver.

Authentication and Single Sign-On	Integrated User and Access Management
● Authentication Using a Directory with SSO Integration Using SAP Logon Tickets ⊘ Single Sign-On Based on Security Assertion Markup Language (SAML)	● Integrated User and Access Management that Includes a Third-Party Directory Server ● Integrating User Management and Access Management

User-interface consolidation

You can bring all your applications together by providing a single user interface. Start by providing an internal portal that links application functionality, and then make the portal available externally to suppliers, distributors, and customers.

Information consolidation

Bringing together all the information that drives your business is a really important thing. You can consolidate information to provide complete, end-to-end, reliable, and open business intelligence. SAP NetWeaver lets you perform sophisticated master-data consolidation, harmonization, and distribution of data to connected applications.

Process consolidation

SAP NetWeaver lets you reduce integration and maintenance costs by using an integrated tool set to build your own integration procedures. These procedures are created by using the appropriate messaging interfaces, mappings, and routing rules.

Adaptive computing

Solving complex software issues isn't the easiest thing in the world, but by flexibly distributing intensive computing activities across various server systems, you can increase efficiency and reduce costs. You can also assign hardware resources on the fly to meet specific application needs.

Business event management

With SAP NetWeaver, your IT organization can support an event-driven architecture. Business events are assembled from a wide variety of systems so that information gets to decision makers in the context of a relevant business process. The decision makers solve the problem: voilà, event resolution! Event resolution is enabled by SAP NetWeaver components such as SAP NetWeaver Portal, SAP NetWeaver XI, SAP NetWeaver BI, and SAP CAF. See Figure 6-10 for an overview of business event management in SAP NetWeaver.

Figure 6-10: Business event management in SAP NetWeaver.

Enabling Platform Interoperability	SAP NetWeaver Operations	Master-Data Consolidation	Enterprise Knowledge Management
● Enabling Coexistence of Several Portals	● Monitoring SAP NetWeaver	● Interactive Master-Data Consolidation	● Content Integration and Management
● Ensuring Application-to-Application and Business-to-Business Integration	● Administering SAP NetWeaver	● Automated Master-Data Consolidation	● Content Creation, Publication, and Access
● Providing Web Services Interoperability	● Adaptive Computing		◉ Enterprise Search
● Managing Heterogenous System Landscapes	● Data Archiving		● Documentation, Manuals, and Training Materials Management
● Developing Applications Compatible with SAP NetWeaver			

Business task management

Business task management (BTM) with SAP NetWeaver helps get the right tasks to the right people and provides the means to complete tasks on time and with the best results. SAP NetWeaver helps people coordinate, monitor, and adapt their own tasks and the tasks they assign to coworkers, including tasks that involve filling out forms. Organizations can provide

- ✔ Central access to tasks
- ✔ Support for offline processes

Service-Oriented Architecture Design and Deployment

With SAP NetWeaver, you can invest in a service-oriented architecture that helps you consolidate and standardize your basic processes and leverage existing investments. All this means that you can compose new, distinctive business processes flexibly and at low cost. Service-oriented architecture design and deployment are essentially enabled by every single component of SAP NetWeaver. See Figure 6-11 for an overview of ESA in SAP NetWeaver.

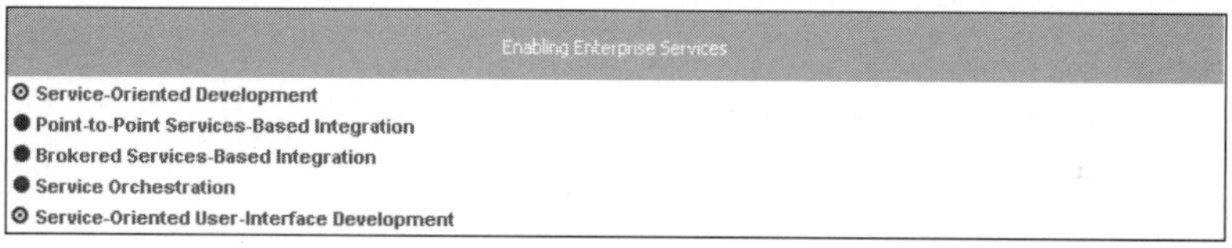

Figure 6-11:
Enterprise
Service
Architecture
SAP
NetWeaver.

Enabling Enterprise Services

- ⊘ Service-Oriented Development
- ● Point-to-Point Services-Based Integration
- ● Brokered Services-Based Integration
- ● Service Orchestration
- ⊘ Service-Oriented User-Interface Development

You can easily design, implement, build, and run applications based on Web services. With SAP NetWeaver, you can enable

- ✔ Service-oriented development
- ✔ Point-to-point services-based integration
- ✔ Brokered services-based integration
- ✔ Service orchestration
- ✔ Service-oriented user-interface development

Guided Procedures: Focus on Activity

Guided procedures are features designed to make your life easier when working with multiple applications. Guided procedures help you set up and execute collaborative business processes. These processes seamlessly integrate back-end system transactions and services into the context of a business process.

Enterprises that want to streamline work often face the following challenges:

✔ Too much time and money is lost in inefficient, often paper-based, execution of processes.

✔ Form-based paper processes are often distributed manually to one or more IT systems.

✔ Business process workflows aren't set up for easy ad hoc collaboration.

✔ Employees without specialized software skills lack a flexible tool to set up and execute business processes in their daily work.

To overcome these challenges, companies have to provide their employees with access to all information and processes that enable them to take informed, timely, and appropriate action.

User-friendly user interface

Users demand a work process molded around people, rather than a business transaction. It makes a lot more sense if collaborative activities happen within the context of the corresponding business scenario in a way that helps employees to work and collaborate. ERP functionality, such as transactions and analytics, and collaborative services can be integrated as needed to support features in context. The result is a software product with guided procedures that gives you value way beyond traditional applications.

Guided procedures

SAP xApps is a new generation of packaged composite applications, a breed of information technology that enables you to continuously improve and innovate. The SAP xApps portfolio aligns people, information, and processes to let you execute enterprise-wide strategies with greater ease and efficiency.

Guided procedures center around an intuitive user interface that enables even technically challenged users to create or change scenarios. With guided procedures, all your back-end transactions or services can be quickly and easily combined with workflow and communication steps. This results in a map of business processes in a wizard-like interface. The combination of these steps with interactive forms makes it possible to integrate offline and online steps within business processes.

Interactive form integration

However well you define a process, you may sometimes have good reasons to stray from the routine methods; for example, if Joe in the next cubicle over asks for help, a step could be delegated to the team assistant or sent over to the boss for approval. Guided procedures focus on improving employee productivity by streamlining tasks that occur frequently with a powerful and flexible tool for defining and managing workflows. At the same time, versatile old guided procedures are as well suited to everyday work processes, such as arranging meetings and booking travel, as it is to longer-term work procedures.

Guided procedures integrate with existing enterprise-wide employee directories, ensuring that you select the right person for each task. At each step of a particular process, the relevant team members are automatically alerted about the jobs assigned to them. Additional messages and any relevant documents can be attached. As a bonus, you can make changes to the user interface at any time. For example, if a process becomes too complex to manage, it can be split into a number of smaller subtasks.

The user interface allows you to track the status of each activity so that you can monitor whether work is getting completed on time. The person in charge can quickly identify any inefficient areas and kick off corrective measures. In this way, you can speed up day-to-day work, while encouraging the ongoing, collaborative improvement of a process.

Designing Processes and Managing Solutions: SAP Solution Manager

SAP Solution Manager is not technically part of SAP NetWeaver, but it has graciously handed its customers the same tools for managing the lifecycle of an application that it uses to manage its own products. For 30 years, SAP has developed, installed, configured, and upgraded software in heterogeneous, multiplatform environments. And it's no slacker in development, either.

With SAP Solution Manager, you can keep track of the versions of installed code, separate local customizations from the core product, get an installation and packaging framework for components of an application, and take advantage of a systematic approach to patches and upgrades.

SAP Solution Manager also provides a framework for configuration and management of an application in a high-availability environment. This means that it provides monitoring of the mySAP Business Suite solutions, SAP NetWeaver components, and applications from other vendors. It also reaches inside applications to monitor the processes going on inside. By all of these means, SAP Solution Manager helps improve the productivity of your operations staff and reduce maintenance costs.

How might you use SAP Solution Manager? A good example would be to manage the upgrade of any of the mySAP Business Suite solutions using the best-practice process templates and automatic detection of required upgrades based on your existing software. You could also use SAP Solution Manager to package and distribute a custom application that you're rolling out to all the data centers of your enterprise.

Discover more about how SAP Solution Manager works in Chapter 11.

So, how does SAP Solution Manager manage the three-ring circus of development? It uses services from SAP support such as EarlyWatch, which gives notice of important upgrades, combined with business content about best practices for implementation and a monitoring system, along with an issue-tracking and project-management framework specifically designed to support complex IT operations.

SAP Solution Manager is the installation and upgrade program for mySAP Business Suite solutions, SAP NetWeaver components, and all the applications you build using them.

What Can SAP NetWeaver Do for You?

The point of integration technologies is to help companies win in today's brutally competitive marketplace. No matter how cool all of these technologies are, if they don't help you make more money, save more money, and beat the competition, they probably aren't worth your precious time and IT budget.

A key question you should be asking, then, is "How does SAP NetWeaver help your business win?" A detailed answer to this question differs from company to company, but a basic set of principles can explain how SAP NetWeaver enables companies to build competitive advantage.

Unified testing

The whole set of SAP NetWeaver components has been tested and validated together by SAP — something that is simply not possible for *all* the potential combinations that could occur when you're dealing with random releases of different components.

One platform powering all SAP solutions

In 2005, the following SAP applications are built upon and ship with the synchronized SAP NetWeaver '05 technology base: mySAP ERP, mySAP Supply Chain Management (mySAP SCM), and mySAP Supplier Relationship Management (mySAP SRM), among others.

The results? Reduced complexity and the synchronizing of, for example, SAP BW with your mySAP SCM solutions, or your mySAP CRM and portal solutions, or your mySAP SRM solutions and the SAP XI. The need for different sets of adapters and plug-ins simply goes away and everything is conveniently streamlined.

It's just better for customers

Bean-counters, take note! This approach offers numerous administrative, TCO, and QA benefits, including

- All of these SAP NetWeaver components are now based on the same version of SAP NetWeaver AS (Release 6.40) and so share a common technical foundation. This simplifies a wide range of infrastructure activities, including administration, monitoring, and user and security management. Everything can use the same operating system release, as well as the same DBMS release. Reduce complexity in an IT landscape and you reduce TCO.

- Many parts of SAP NetWeaver can be run within a single physical server if a small configuration is sufficient, thus reducing the number of systems and databases for you to administer.

✔ Many parts of SAP NetWeaver can be run within one management entity, the SAP NetWeaver AS system, with its shared database, shared central services, common external IP address, and so on. An SAP NetWeaver AS system can be a single small box running just one instance of the SAP NetWeaver AS, but it can also scale up to multiple big computers with many instances of the SAP NetWeaver AS that run together as one logical (albeit huge) unit.

Whether you're working with SAP NetWeaver today, or with one of the next few versions, each shares certain key advantages for businesses that we discuss in the next sections.

Technology and Data: The Great Equalizers

In today's world, the availability of technology and information is a great equalizer. Everyone has access to oceans of data, and technology keeps getting cheaper and better. If the secret sauce for beating the competition is better processes, the ugly truth is that the recipe doesn't stay secret for long. Your company's competitors quickly figure out, using technology and information, how to imitate your best practices and catch up.

On top of that, business conditions change awfully fast. In this new century, boom and bust cycles have compressed. Information moves faster and markets are more and more efficient, putting the squeeze on everybody. (Just do a quick count of ulcers among high-level managers and you'll see what we mean.)

So in this environment, what is the sustainable advantage? What you need to win is the ability to adapt processes as rapidly as business conditions change. Adaptable businesses innovate faster and beat competitors to market. Companies that spend their time and resources innovating are more profitable, and they provide their shareholders with a greater return on equity.

You heard it here, first.

SAP NetWeaver Enables Business Process Evolution

It's amazing how often companies understand what they have to do to change their processes, but the rigid and costly nature of IT prevents them from making those changes. SAP NetWeaver changes this equation by breaking the IT bottleneck.

One theme that runs through our descriptions of all the SAP NetWeaver components is the way that each component can be adapted to account for changes. Whether it is modeling, or configuration, or just a beautifully designed product that helps manage complexity, each SAP NetWeaver component is ready to evolve as your business does. SAP has a general theory of how applications should be constructed to be flexible that is called *Enterprise Services Architecture* (ESA). ESA is what enables SAP NetWeaver to amplify the power of the mySAP Business Suite solutions.

So what does this mean for you? It depends on who you are:

- ✔ **CEO:** SAP NetWeaver allows flexible implementation of business strategies so that companies can adapt rapidly to changing business conditions.

- ✔ **IT professional:** SAP NetWeaver empowers IT types to drive innovation into business processes across the entire enterprise by taking an existing IT infrastructure that enables work and turning it into an enabler of change. (CEOs like things like that.) SAP NetWeaver is also built to evolve with ease, which makes change cheaper and less risky.

- ✔ **CIO:** CIOs and their fellow travelers use SAP NetWeaver as the platform of choice to better align IT with their business and to support business process evolution. TCO (total cost of ownership) is made up of the cost of applications, tools, and what it takes to integrate it all together. The prepackaged integration of SAP NetWeaver drives TCO as low as it can possibly go, helps reduce complexity, and still allows you to integrate with non-SAP systems.

- ✔ **Developer:** For developers and architects who love gadgets, SAP NetWeaver represents the ultimate whiz-bang toolkit. SAP NetWeaver is by far the most advanced platform for business computing in terms of model-driven development, business-process management, and abstraction at all levels. By becoming an expert in SAP NetWeaver, developers learn cutting-edge technology and lead change at their companies.

Chapter 7

Bringing Services to Life with SAP NetWeaver

*T*wo big goals of enterprise computing today are to reduce the cost of your standard business processes and to enable you to launch business innovations with a lower investment. To do that, you have to find a bridge from technology to business strategy. That's where SAP NetWeaver comes in.

SAP NetWeaver is the technological underpinning of mySAP ERP. Understanding exactly how SAP NetWeaver allows you to model business processes and define services that get your work done is important to your understanding of the potential of ERP.

In this chapter, you read all about how services are stored, organized, named, and assembled into solutions. You also discover some of the techie aspects of creating services, namely something called *Web Service Description Language* (WSDL), which is the language used to build services. Finally, we explore an approach to applications development called *modeling*.

Working with Services

As you may have gathered by now, ESA-enabled ERP is all about services. In the following sections, we dig into the concept of where your local services are "kept." Services are not just kept in your own enterprise system; services are universal. If you want to find a service offered by someone else (such as a business partner like a bank or shipping company), you need to understand how all services are named and have an understanding of how services are organized.

A home for services: The service repository

Deep within SAP NetWeaver lies the service repository, where all services live. It's like a dormitory for services. The repository can hold thousands of services related to ERP and your business processes. mySAP ERP 2005 shipped with a few hundred services, and there will be hundreds more in early 2006. Because you just can't get enough services, even more will follow in years to come for ERP, mySAP CRM, mySAP SCM, and so on.

Finding a service with solution maps

When you talk about getting an ERP solution, the discussion doesn't start with technology such as ESA and SAP NetWeaver. It starts by looking at your business objectives. From there, you need to define the business processes that support those objectives and then identify the services that support those processes.

To help you get from the business process to an individual service and even to the technical specification of that service (the so-called Web Service Description Language), SAP provides you with business scenario–driven industry solution maps (see Figure 7-1). These maps outline the processes in a solution (such as ERP or CRM) or the processes in an industry (such as chemicals or the public sector).

Here's an example. Say that your business needs better financial information about its customers. You want to create a simple Web page where the customer service representative can enter the customer's name and get a list of the current balances on the customer's account, all credit notes issued to that customer, payments received, and so on.

End-User Service Delivery				
Analytics	Strategic Enterprise Management	Financial Analytics	Operations Analytics	Workforce Analytics
Financials	Financial Supply Chain Management	Financial Accounting	Management Accounting	Corporate Governance
Human Capital Management	Talent Management	Workforce Process Management		Workforce Deployment
Procurement and Logistics Execution	Procurement / Supplier Collaboration	Inventory & Warehouse Management	Outbound and Inbound Logistics	Transportation
Product Development and Manufacturing	Production Planning / Manufacturing Execution	Enterprise Asset Management	Product Development	Life-Cycle Data Management
Sales and Service	Sales Order Management	Aftermarket Sales and Service / Professional Service Delivery / Foreign Trade		Incentive & Commission Management
Corporate Services	Real Estate Management / Project Portfolio Management	Travel Management	Environment, Health & Safety	Quality Management
SAP NetWeaver™	People Integration	Information Integration	Process Integration	Application Platform

Figure 7-1: The mySAP ERP Solution Map.

Just where do you find the services to support this new application? Start with a solution map. This lays out all the business processes in an organization.

This example involves generic financials functionality, so the ERP Solution Map fits the bill. Figure 7-1 shows a solution map, which is created from within the Solution Composer.

Because you want financial information about your customer, you click the line labeled *Financials*. The solution map drills down to show the processes supported by the Financials functionality (see Figure 7-2).

mySAP ERP
Financials

Financial Accounting

General Ledger
Accounts Receivable
Accounts Payable
Fixed Assets Accounting
Bank Accounting
Cash Journal Accounting
Inventory Accounting
Tax Accounting
Accrual Accounting
Fast Close
Financial Statements
Parallel Valuation

Figure 7-2: The Financials functionality in mySAP ERP.

All the financial information about your customer would be in Financial Accounting, and more specifically, in the general ledger. Click the General Ledger link, and a list of all the services available is displayed (see Figure 7-3).

You Are Here: Home > Accounting Document Processing > General Ledger Processing Enterprise Service

📟 **General Ledger Processing Enterprise Service**
Enterprise Service

Availability
⊙ Future Focus

See also
■ Where used
■ Enterprise Services Index

General Ledger Processing Enterprise Service

Enterprise Service Operations

General Ledger Account Attributes Query Response ⊙	Retrieve the GL Account Details like Chart of Accounts, Currency, Tax Code
General Ledger Accountfor Company List Query Response ⊙	Retreive GL Accounts for a Company Code
GLAccount Annual Balance Query Response ⊙	Service reading the closing balance of a G/L account for a chosen year. The balance is the amount resulting from the difference between the debit and credit side of an account.
GLAccount Current Balance Query Response ⊙	Service reading the closing balance of a G/L account for the current year. The balance is the amount resulting from the difference between the debit and credit side of an account.

Figure 7-3:
List of services for General Ledger.

In the list of services that are available under General Ledger, the following services that you need to complete your process are available

- CustomerAccountCurrentBalanceQueryResponse service, which looks up a customer balance.

- CustomerAccountBalancedItemsQueryResponse, which lists the clearing transactions made to a customer account in a given period. Clearing entries (for example, payments) and the items that they cleared (for example, invoices or credit memos) are displayed together.

Deducing the functionality of the services from the way they're named is pretty simple. In fact, the naming conventions for services are critical because they help you find and use the services.

Naming services

Naming services isn't quite like naming your bouncing baby girl. (What *was* Madonna's mother thinking?) On the contrary, the naming and design rules for ESA services are founded on a very solid rationale. With naming rules, you get

- ✔ Efficient interaction with Solution Manager

- ✔ Consistent inventory of services

- ✔ Recognition of identical or similar services

- ✔ Harmonization of service inventory

- ✔ Maximized reusable services

The first step in defining a service is to look at the business requirement that drives the service. In this example, if you want to see the outstanding balance of a customer, the name of the transaction is CustomerAccountCurrentBalanceQueryResponse.

The *CustomerAccountCurrentBalance* part of the service name is fairly easy to understand, but what does *QueryResponse* mean? For each service, the naming reflects not only what you get but also how the service is used. In this example, the service sends a query and requires a response; hence *QueryResponse*.

Other services may provide a notification or actually perform a function such as change or add a new order to the system, so the service name would reflect that function.

Here's another example of how this service naming works. A Customer Credit Fact Sheet presents all credit- and collection-relevant customer data to the user at a glance. The Credit Fact Sheet may be needed, for example, by people in roles such as Sales Manager, Credit Manager, or Collection Clerk. The Credit Fact Sheet requires information from a credit management application, as well as information from accounting (specifically payment behavior, payment history, and sales volume).

The name of this service is CustomerCreditFactSheetQueryResponse, which could be broken down into more specific services: DunningLevelCustomer CreditFactSheetQueryResponse (in which dunning equals payment history, for the nonfinancial among you) and SalesVolumeCustomerCreditFactSheet QueryResponse, for example.

What's handy about this naming convention is that it expresses things in business terms, not programming terms. That makes services easy to locate and call from the services repository, whether you're an IT person or a guy sitting at a desk. It's another example of the way that mySAP ERP helps everybody around the water cooler speak the same language.

A Web Service Description Language Primer

In this section, we switch perspectives to that of the person who is setting up all of these services, rather than the person using them. To get into some of the more techie stuff about services, you need to see how services are called via the Web Service Description Language (WSDL). First, we tell you what WSDL is, and then we show you how it works.

WSDL revealed

Think of Web services as a flexible and configurable plug and socket for applications, just like the plug that you use to connect your computer to a wall outlet.

When one application wants to allow other applications to connect and access some of its functionality or data, it describes the way that its plug works by using a standard form called *Web Service Description Language* (WSDL). Other applications take a quick look at the description and then plug in.

After the connection is made, WSDL also describes commands that control the flow of information over the connection. The information moves back and forth as messages formatted in XML, a standard language that can describe almost any data format.

Like HTML and HTTP, Web services are based on a standard definition that is not controlled by any one company. That's one of the reasons that Web services became so popular so quickly. Another reason is that Web-service connections between applications are much cheaper to create and maintain than earlier approaches to making those same connections. Unlike some of those earlier methods, Web services are reusable, which means that one Web service can be used by any number of other applications. And, one application can provide many different Web services.

An example of WSDL in action

Here's how WSDL works with enterprise services on the nitty-gritty technical level. The pleasant surprise here is how relatively simple this all is, compared to previous application programming interfaces (APIs). That simplicity results from stating things in business parameters, rather than in programming code.

A WSDL definition typically contains the following key pieces of information:

- ✔ A description/format of the input messages
- ✔ The semantics of the message being passed to the underlying systems
- ✔ A description/format of the output messages
- ✔ The endpoint for the service, that is, the service's URL

Take a look at a very simple example. Say you are creating a service that allows customers to check the availability of a seat on a plane. First, you need to define the input criteria; in this case, this is the input the system needs in order to check the availability of a seat. The name of the service follows the standard naming convention, so it is called FlightSeatAvailabilityQuery_In.

Using the integration builder tool of SAP NetWeaver (see Figure 7-4), you can easily define the overall service.

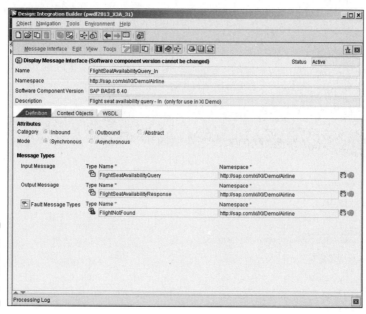

Figure 7-4:
Defining the
overall
service.

TIP

Note in Figure 7-4 that there is a column labeled *Namespace*. Enterprise services are all grouped together in so-called *namespaces*, which are a closed set of names or a place where a set of names is stored. Namespaces are typically identified via a URL. You can use namespaces to resolve naming conflicts.

Namespaces are comparable to a directory in Windows that helps you organize files. In this example, a namespace called `http://sap.com/xi/XI/Demo/Airline` acts like a directory, available to any customer. You place a specific Web service in this namespace called FlightSeatAvailablityQuery.

So far, so good. So what's going on in the underlying code? There are three operations in this particular namespace (see Figure 7-5):

- ✔ **An input message,** containing input parameters (the way you specify how to go about gathering data) for the operation.

- ✔ **An output message,** containing output parameters (how you make the results of an operation available to users) for the operation.

- ✔ **A fault** (no, we're not laying blame here), which describes what's returned in the case of an exception. In programmers' lingo, an *exception* is a problem or set of conditions that causes the microprocessor to stop in its tracks and use a different routine to deal with the problem.

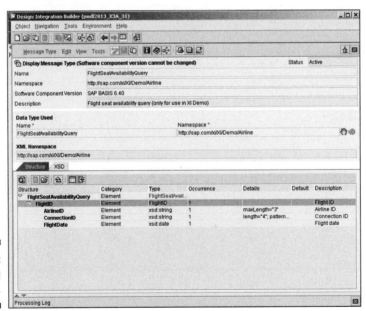

Figure 7-5:
Defining
the input.

You input an airline ID, the connection ID (the flight number), and the date of the flight. The exact formats are defined in the *Type* column (see Figure 7-6).

All this is easy to define; the difficult part is to convert this into WSDL. Using the WSDL tab shown in Figure 7-7, you can automatically generate the WSDL.

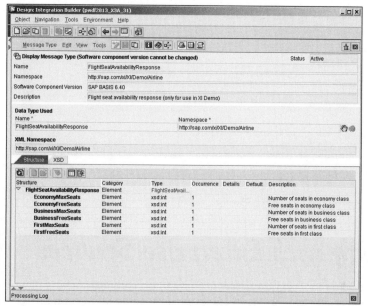

Figure 7-6: The output data.

What becomes of this WSDL file? When someone wants to set up a system to use a service, he requests the WSDL file, which tells him the location of the service and the function calls, and how to access these calls. Then he uses the information in the WSDL file to form a SOAP (Simple Object Access Protocol) request to your computer.

WSDL is complex, and folks have developed numerous tools to create the WSDL files. Specifically, SAP has developed the integration builder tool of SAP NetWeaver to make the generation of this code as simple as possible.

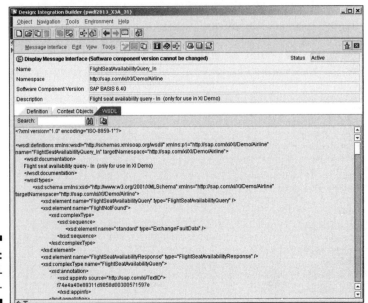

Figure 7-7:
The WSDL
data.

Modeling with Enterprise Services

Modeling for computers has nothing to do with fashion and glamorous folks walking down runways. In computer terms, *modeling* refers to a whole new way to create applications that doesn't involve yards of spaghetti code. It's so simple, it makes the process practically child's play.

Modeling basics

Modeling means turning data sources, relationships, interface elements, and so on into visual objects and icons that you can move around a page. You can use modeling to manage the technical complexity underlying ERP functionality. Modeling describes what a program should do by defining relationships between simplified components, rather than piling up mounds of code. For a user-interface modeling system, for example, the components used for modeling might be buttons and text boxes. After the relationship between the components is described (or modeled), the description (called a model) is then used to generate the program.

In most model-driven environments, a little traditional code has to be written here and there, but most of the application is generated by the model. This means that when it comes time to fix or improve the program, you have much less complexity and code to understand and maintain. Trust us: This is a huge leap forward in reducing your total cost of ownership (TCO). If you don't believe us, just ask your IT person. Plus, code generated by these tools tends to have fewer bugs and requires less upkeep than code written the old-fashioned way.

To institute a model-driven approach, SAP created a new programming model, along with the basic building blocks that programmers use to create programs. The new model bridges Enterprise Services Architecture and SAP NetWeaver so that programmers have a ready-made pattern for matching the way you design applications (Enterprise Services Architecture) with the tool you use to build them (SAP NetWeaver). The way that this new programming model comes to life is through the SAP Composite Applications Framework (SAP CAF), the SAP NetWeaver tool for building composite applications.

This programming model has its very own goals, which are to

- Increase the use of modeling in application development to create relationships between services so that you can create applications automatically, instead of programming each one by hand. This speeds development and makes programs easier to change.

- Increase the number of reusable components in an application. One set of tools would be used to manage master data in all applications, for example. You might create a tax engine to perform tax calculations. Commonly used functions could be carried out with shared components and standard approaches.

- Use the portal as the interface for all products.

- Accelerate user interface (UI) development by using patterns — reusable combinations of components and processes that appear over and over again when you're creating applications. Patterns are a great way to give programmers a head start in creating applications.

- Employ business-process management tools to control and customize the behavior of programs. This means that you get a clearer separation between process control and business logic.

- Use one nice, consistent approach across all applications to address such challenges as reporting, integrating desktop applications, and accessing data.

- Adopt a single approach to storing all different kinds of data.

At its heart, this new programming model maximizes the amount of each program that is made up of reusable components, anticipates as many potential variables as possible, and provides a standard method for dealing with them. The result of such a model is a new kind of software that is far less costly to develop and far easier to change and maintain.

Patterns, models, and frameworks

A few decades of experience have shown how applications should be constructed. The way different types of software work, including many user interface designs, is fairly similar in key ways: They follow certain patterns.

Programmers have recognized this and developed so-called *software patterns* that work in concert with models and frameworks. Patterns, models, and frameworks — what the heck are those? Don't worry: In the following sections, we explain it all.

Starting with a pattern

Think about the software programs you use every day. Many programs have menus along the top; you click the menu and a list of commands is displayed for you to choose from. These commonly occurring types of user interfaces are examples of *patterns*. The concept of patterns is really pretty simple. They provide a way to do something that includes general steps that are frequently the same, and specific choices that change based on the specific action.

Another example would be the search pattern: In a section of your application window is an area for your input. This could be a simple text box like the one displayed on a Google Web page or a more form-like structure, such as the one you use when you book your flight to Hawaii. You click a Search button to get your search results. When you know how to operate one search engine, you know how to use them all.

Patterns are a win-win deal: They make a programmer's job easier because there is less code to write, and they make users happy because the users know what to do in many situations and what results to expect.

SAP developments tools, such as the Composite Application Framework (CAF) or Visual Composer, simplify your life by making heavy use of patterns, especially in the area of user interfaces. A developer selects a pattern, which does most of the work of creating the application, and then fills in the details of the kind of field that each record should contain and how the information should be displayed.

Forget code?

"What about code?" you may ask. Does this approach make programming languages obsolete? No. Coding in languages such as Java is still part of building an application with the SAP CAF, but it plays a much smaller role. The SAP CAF uses the patterns (models prepared in advance that are ready to be configured with metadata) along with other metadata to generate the code that eventually becomes the program. Handwritten code is then used to create application-specific objects and services that are controlled by more metadata that is then plugged into patterns by using the SAP CAF.

Putting models to work

Modeling is the second magic bullet that SAP provides for developers. It turns out that you can think of most applications as involving the basic elements of user interfaces, including roles, processes, objects, services, and, in the case of composite applications, underlying systems.

SAP allows developers to specify the behavior of an application by defining relationships between the elements. This means picking and choosing between high-level elements, such as roles or processes, and linking them to data. Then developers can link data to screens, and so on. (When we say high-level, we mean that these elements have a lot of functionality included in them already. This functionality is described and controlled by what is called *metadata,* which is a fancy way of saying data that describes what a program should do.)

The reason that this is called *model-driven development* is that the program is created by changing a description (metadata) of what the program should do. This metadata is used to generate the code that lies under the covers.

So how do patterns and models fit together? You can think of patterns as predefined models. If you look at the search pattern, you find that it has four elements: a UI (user interface) element for your input, a Search button, a data source that can be queried, and a UI list element where the results appear (also called output). The relationship between the four elements is predefined: When the button is clicked, the program gets the data from the input field(s) and sends it as a query to the data source, which returns a list of results that are handed over to the output element in the UI.

Erecting a framework

OK, here's the next technical concept: An environment that enables you to do model-driven development and to use patterns is called a *framework*. A good example of such a framework is the SAP CAF.

To a developer, the SAP CAF is actually a big modeling environment that allows you to define a program in terms of a standard set of model elements that are grouped together into patterns. (Remember patterns, which we describe in the previous section?) Developing the application is generally much faster, and maintaining it is much cheaper because a model is usually easier to update than code.

In this discussion, we emphasize the use of patterns in the user interface. But it's important to recognize that patterns can be used at any level of the application where you discover a common structure. The way that certain parts of the application logic work, the way that data is retrieved from a database, or the way that processes are implemented may be done using patterns. Using process patterns, as it turns out, is one of the most productive ways to speed application development.

Visual Composer: The modeling whiz kid

Simply put, SAP NetWeaver Visual Composer enables you to happily drag and drop objects that represent data sources and interface elements to create content for a portal. Assume you're a manager who wants a personal portal page that displays the monthly sales totals for each salesperson on your team. Using Visual Composer, you simply drag a portal page into your workspace (called the storyboard) from an interface elements list. Then you fill that storyboard with contents from the sales information database. You can build queries without knowing a whit of query language, simply by assembling icons and elements from various lists.

Even if you're programming-phobic — say a business consultant, analyst, process expert, or writer of a *For Dummies* book — you can use SAP NetWeaver Visual Composer to make a diagram of just what you want a page to do. Then this clever application not only presents the content, but also creates iViews (reusable and configurable portions of a page in a portal) that come ready to be deployed. In a nutshell, SAP NetWeaver Visual Composer is about as easy as sketching out what you want on a napkin and getting it delivered to your desktop in minutes.

The latest and greatest

Visual Composer is constantly evolving. For example, in the latest version, you can add fields that are specific to different user groups. A team leader requesting vacation time may want to delegate his work to a substitute while he's off in Barbados. The Vacation screen for team leaders (yes, there's a Vacation screen) could be changed to add a permanent field called *Substitute*.

You can add validation to a defined field so that a little message pops up if a user requests a particular item. Following our vacation example, if you request special leave, a little message could pop up reminding you that you have to get a manager's approval.

Say that you've requested special leave that goes beyond the number of vacation days you have left. You could create an additional field on the fly labeled *Reason for Leave* to give you space to explain the request.

In the near future, Visual Composer is slated to update features that will allow easy interaction with touch screens, advanced printing services, and a generation of pop-up windows. (Don't worry: These pop-ups are the good kind.)

One of the chief benefits of this approach is that it dramatically reduces the amount of time that the IT department has to spend on content assembly and maintenance. Instead, this is left to the business experts. While these folks may not know the first thing about how to code, they completely understand the business process they're trying to model.

Entire business processes, and not just content, can be modeled in this way. Essentially, you can create multiple pages that track a process in depth by creating iViews and bundles of iViews on a similar theme (called *business packages*). No programming required.

Do-it-yourself modeling

Have you ever tried to buy something online and had something about your order that was really weird? Maybe you wanted the standard size but in an nonstandard color? Suddenly, the whole ordering process fell apart. That's because you asked the system to make an exception to all the prepro-grammed guidelines somebody fed into it.

Traditionally, in technology-land, exceptions to a routine procedure you've predefined are hard to handle. ESA and SAP modeling tools, however, make exception handling much easier.

Here's an example. Say you ordered something within the Procure2Pay business process. When the package arrives, you open it, only to find that somebody shipped you the Jx-HHG69 rather than the Jx-HKG67. The next step in the system may be to submit the invoice, but you need to do something exceptional, namely, return the package and adjust the record in the system.

In the past, this would involve getting on the phone to somebody in purchasing, shipping, or accounting — or all three. With ESA and modeling tools, you can handle it all by putting together your own solution (which is referred to as WrongPackage2ReturnDelivery).

Using Visual Composer, you can

✔ Browse the enterprise services that live in the services repository. In this example, the following services might come in handy: Purchase OrderDetailsByRequester, PurchaseOrderDetailsByTrackingNumber, ReturnGoodsReceipt, and GetReturnAddress.

✔ Connect the services with easy-to-use UI templates.

✔ Compile the whole shebang. Voilà! You've built your own solution that can be run in the SAP NetWeaver Portal.

ESA Is Open to Working with Other Tools

Because Web services offer open standards (meaning standards that have a publicly available set of specifications so they can be used by anybody), ESA is open, too. That openness allows it to work with a variety of non-SAP technologies quite happily.

Microsoft and SAP: Logical bedfellows

Microsoft is committed to open standards, just as SAP is. Microsoft has made some of its products open-source so that they can cozy right up to Web services. This makes several Microsoft products a perfect match for ESA-enabled ERP.

How Microsoft opened the door to open-source

Microsoft has made Office products open through something called IBF (Information Bridge Framework). A *framework*, in object-oriented developer-speak, is simply a reusable design structure that you can use to make building applications easier. The main goal of IBF is to make users of Office products more productive, which it does by allowing Office to consume (or use) Web services.

SAP provides Web services through its ESA-enabled ERP; IBF is what allows Office products to connect with ERP functions.

Mendocino closes the loop

Mendocino is a set of employee and manager self-service applications that connect Office and ERP. To help you understand how it works, here are some ways you might use Mendocino in your business:

- ✔ **Time management:** You can use the Outlook calendar to streamline time reporting to an enterprise time-reporting program (see Figure 7-8).

- ✔ **Budget monitoring:** This allows you to get SAP budget reports in your Outlook inbox and work with them offline. You can be proactively alerted to time-critical budget information.

- ✔ **Leave management:** This lets you receive leave requests via your Outlook calendar.

- ✔ **Organization management:** With this tool, you can get up-to-date info about employees via mySAP ERP HCM using Microsoft Office InfoPath forms. (InfoPath is a set of tools you can use to create dynamic forms that are used to gather and share data across your business processes.)

- ✔ **Personnel change requests:** Reports can be sent from mySAP ERP HCM through Excel or Outlook to keep you up to date about promotions, bonuses, new positions, and more.

All the Office programs can be integrated with your enterprise applications and data. You can customize the Microsoft Research pane so that it is specific to your ERP-related data, for example. All Office applications have easy connectivity with e-mail to exchange documents. You can deliver business analytics through Excel and smart documents in Word.

See Chapter 3 for more about Mendocino.

Visual Studio: One size fits all

SAP is a leader in several things, and one of them happens to be model-driven development.

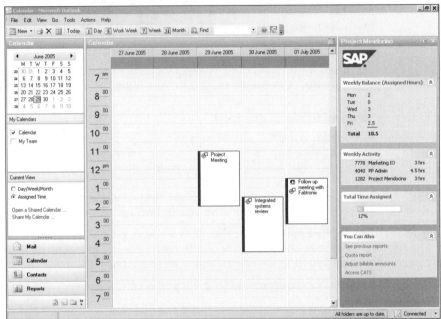

Figure 7-8:
Taking a
peek at
Project
Mendocino.

See the section "Modeling with Enterprise Services," earlier in this chapter, to refresh your memory about modeling.

Some folks use something called Unified Modeling Language (UML) as a general-purpose modeling language. It's the one-size-fits-all approach. But SAP chose to go with domain-specific languages expressed in eXtensible Markup Language (XML) to support various forms of automation. Domain-specific languages have built-in assumptions about the context of your application. For example, SAP models business applications, but other folks model computer games or telephone networks. Domain-specific languages are smarter. As a consequence, they offer a faster, less expensive, and more reliable approach to application development.

SAP uses domain-specific languages as the basis of its modeling tool, Visual Composer. The purpose of this is to model business applications powered by enterprise services.

PDF forms

Adobe is another technology giant committed to open standards through Web services. This means that it's easy to use interactive PDF forms in the world of service-enabled ERP.

Specifically, SAP has integrated Adobe Interactive PDF forms into SAP NetWeaver. An application such as mySAP ERP HCM can use these electronic forms to submit requests and handle reporting. With Adobe Interactive PDF forms, you can stay in complete compliance with all the requirements established for paper forms. Electronic forms are easy to back up for recordkeeping, and you can e-mail them or use them from mobile devices.

Using these interactive forms, financial-services providers, for example, can easily create interactive loan applications complete with customer names and addresses, and even include mortgage rates based on the customer's credit score and geographic region. Applicants complete the forms at their convenience and return them. The digital forms then automatically update the enterprise's application with new information. This avoids costly and often error-prone manual data entry.

Using these virtual forms, your enterprise can get more efficient and reduce the total cost of SAP ownership. That's because you can leverage business-critical information in extended forms-based processes to

- ✔ Reach customers with dynamic, personalized, intelligent processes in the common currency of business: forms and documents
- ✔ Collaborate more effectively with partners and share information in forms and documents more securely and intelligently
- ✔ Improve internal efficiencies through automated form processes
- ✔ Provide an auditable form process history and help to ensure that documents aren't tampered with to meet demanding regulatory requirements
- ✔ Maintain and protect document integrity through advanced user controls and document security

You can read more about Adobe integration in Chapter 3.

Other Web service–compliant tools

Any development tool and programming language that can understand Web services can be used with ESA-enabled ERP. Of course, this means that your programmer won't get the full benefits provided by the SAP NetWeaver tools, but he can use the tool that's familiar and easy to use.

Tools from Microsoft, IBM, BEA, Borland, and Eclipse and programming languages including Java, C/C++, Visual Basic, C#, Python, PHP, and PERL are just some examples of this handy interoperability.

Chapter 8

SAP NetWeaver Up and Running

In This Chapter
▶ Understanding the concepts of the ESA-enabled ERP platform
▶ Using Web services over HTTP
▶ Figuring out business and technical protocols
▶ Exploring the XI run-time

*I*f you've read any of this book up to this point, you know that services sound like the best idea since indoor plumbing. They make you flexible, more productive, and more focused on your business than on the technological underpinnings.

But just in case you're the curious type who wants to know more about those technological doodads, this chapter looks a little more closely at how services work and what happens when you call one.

To use a service, such as "Cancel Order," you first have to call it. Calling a service, also referred to as *invoking* a service, brings it to life. This involves some highly technical stuff like run-time architecture, interaction semantics, transactional behavior, and sessions. (Don't worry: We try to make this discussion as painless as possible.)

Figuring Out ESA Run-Time Architecture

Run-time has nothing to do with your morning jog. *Run-time* refers to all the things that go on when a system (in this case, SAP NetWeaver) is actually in operation. (This is in contrast to *design-time,* which refers to all the things that happen when a system is being designed and coded.)

To understand how Web services communicate, you need to understand protocols. A *protocol* is a set of rules for the communication of two entities. If the entities happen to be two people on the phone, the protocol involves greetings and introductions, followed by a bit of chitchat and topped off by goodbyes.

If the two entities are computers, it's not very different. The computers and the programs open a connection (greet and introduce each other), exchange some data (chitchat), and end the connection (say goodbye). Of course, instead of words and phrases, they use zeroes and ones to communicate.

Enterprise services are described and stored in SAP NetWeaver's XI service repository. At design-time, when the service is modeled and implemented, SAP NetWeaver generates a piece of code called a *proxy*. You can generate proxies in Java and ABAP. These proxies connect all that back-end functionality to the interface of the enterprise service.

As shown in Figure 8-1, when an application, a PDF form, or whatever invokes an enterprise service, the associated proxy is called. The invocation can be done through a Web service interface or via the XI run-time. We explain the inner workings of these two protocols and their differences later in the chapter.

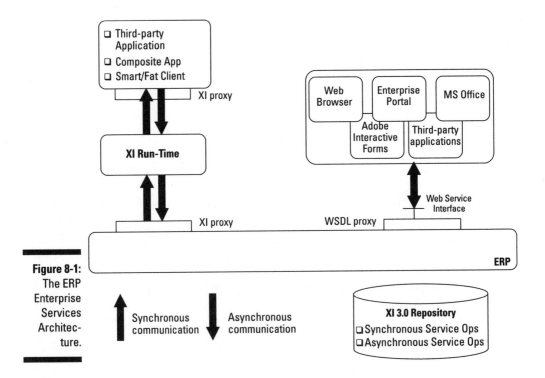

Figure 8-1:
The ERP Enterprise Services Architecture.

You can take this one step further into the realm of the technical: Proxies *parse* the XML messages. To parse means to take the data out of the message in small chunks so a program can act on the information it provides. In an SAP system, this is done via an SAP proprietary interface called the Business Application Programming Interface (BAPI). The results of the calls are then translated back into XML by the proxy. (For the programmers out there who might be wondering, the back-end functionality is mostly written in ABAP, a programming language invented by SAP.)

Business and Technical Protocols: Synchronous versus Asynchronous

All of these little interactions that go on when you invoke a service have their own behavior; these behaviors are also known as the *interaction semantics* of enterprise services. Interaction semantics come in two types: synchronous and asynchronous.

Protocols can exist on different levels and be either business or technical protocols. Here's how they differ:

- ✔ A business protocol is between two business entities, for example, a seller and a buyer.
- ✔ A technical protocol exists between two computers; for example, the protocol could be HTTP.

Interaction semantics can be applied to business protocols as well as technical ones. We take a closer look at the business protocols first.

Business protocol interaction semantics

Essentially, whenever you expect an immediate response to a request (for example, if you run a query for a set of data), you are using synchronous business semantics. When you don't expect an immediate response (for example, when you click the Submit button to send a purchase request for your boss to review), that's asynchronous.

The business process that an enterprise service is designed to handle is eventually executed over a technical protocol; this is where the two different semantic types come into play. So we start by looking at the interaction semantics of the technical protocol.

More than you ever wanted to know about technical protocol interaction semantics

Web services use HTTP, which is a synchronous protocol. This means that a request and the response to that request are combined in the same interaction, as shown in Figure 8-2. You may be saying, "So what?" Well, the client process (or thread) is typically blocked while the service is being invoked. When the server is unavailable, the invocation fails.

Figure 8-2:
A request and response hang out together in synchronous transactions.

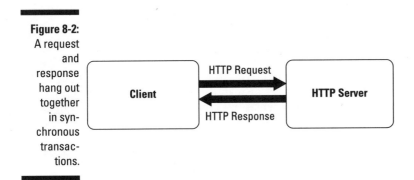

Whether you realize it or not, you experience this frequently using your Web browser. For example, say that you want to book a hotel room online. You invoke (call) a service on the hotel-booking Web site. This service is invoked via HTTP. While the system "thinks" about your request, you can't do anything in your browser window, so you just sit there and wait or go get a soda (this is the client process being blocked while the service is invoked). After you have your soda and the server returns, one of three things happens:

- ✔ Your booking is confirmed.
- ✔ The room wasn't available on that date.
- ✔ There was a technical problem, for example, the hotel reservation back-end system wasn't available or the connection to that system was down. In this case, you might see one of those dreaded error messages, as shown in Figure 8-3.

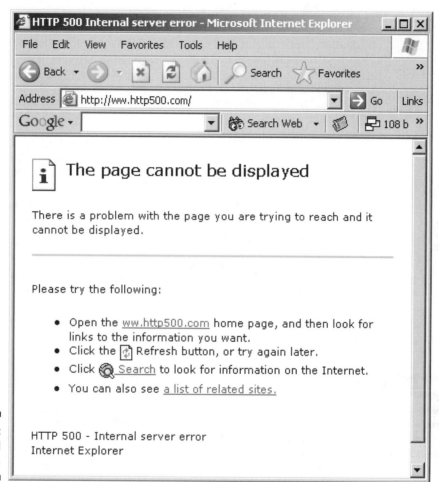

Figure 8-3:
An internal
server error.

The first option is fine and dandy and lets you move on to other things.
The second option requires that you choose another date or room type
and repeat the process. The third option sends you back where you started
to try the request again or wait until later when the system decides it wants
to cooperate.

Enterprise services that are executed as Web services work the same way,
except that, instead of a person calling the service, the program calls it.

But this brings up a major drawback of HTTP. What should the application, form, or whatever do when an enterprise service is called and something unexpected happens that leads to an error? If the programmer didn't build in a response, nothing happens. This is clearly a shortcoming of the protocol.

However, the simplicity of the protocol has its advantages: The programmer doesn't need to know anything about the server other than its URL and the XML message format, which you can easily obtain from the SAP NetWeaver XI service repository.

In contrast, the XI run-time uses an asynchronous interaction model based on message queuing. This is also known as *store-and-forward.* In our hotel booking example, if the third option occurs, it makes a huge difference if you're using asynchronous, store-and-forward semantics. With asynchronous semantics, you don't have to retry your request. The retry mechanism is baked right into the protocol (in this case, the XI run-time).

As shown in Figure 8-4, when a client sends a request, it places the request in a local queue. This queue attempts to send the request to the next XI hub (a *hub* is a program that connects an inbound queue with an outbound queue). The hub itself has both receiving and sending queues. If the hub is unavailable, the message stays in the receiving queue and the client process keeps trying to send the message to the hub.

Figure 8-4:
Holding a
request in a
local queue.

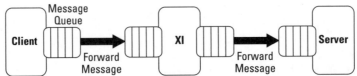

What does all this mean? It means that in the asynchronous model, the client logic is *not* blocked after a request is sent to the queue. If the service isn't available, there simply is no impact on the client. This reliability comes at a performance price, however: Queuing and dequeuing take time.

Furthermore, you need some piece of code within the client. This code, known as the *client-side proxy,* handles the queuing and dequeuing. This creates some constraints when your client is a Web browser, PDF form, or anything written in a programming language other Java or ABAP.

Web services are synchronous, and the XI run-time is asynchronous.

Hubba, hubba

For our purposes, a *hub* is a program that connects an inbound queue with an outbound queue. But that's not all. Having a hub between your two endpoints adds additional value by

✔ Automatically converting parameters from one format into another (called *format transformations*).

✔ Automatically determining the routing of your call (called *parameter mapping*). You could have many server endpoints (for load-balancing reasons, for scalability reasons, or for logistical reasons); the hub determines which server it should send your request to.

The XI run-time provides both of these features.

Going deeper: Enterprise service interaction semantics

Enterprise services have both a technical and business protocol aspect that can get a little confusing, so bear with us. Enterprise services have business interaction semantics that are implemented by a technical protocol, which in turn has its own interaction semantics. Still with us?

Take a look at some examples for the business aspect of enterprise services:

✔ "Get all purchase orders from yesterday for more than $100,000" is clearly synchronous. I make the request and expect to get a list of purchase orders immediately, not next week.

✔ "Hire Joe Smith as director of Product Management" is clearly asynchronous because I don't expect to sit around at my computer while HR makes Joe an offer and processes a pile of paperwork, and he drives in to start work next Monday. What I really do is to kick off a complex process and feed in some initial data, such as name, starting date, compensation, and so on.

The interaction semantic of the business operation does not determine the interaction semantic of the underlying technical protocol. This means that a synchronous business operation can be executed over an asynchronous technical protocol and an asynchronous business operation can be executed over a synchronous technical protocol.

So now we have a couple of possibilities:

✔ An enterprise service with synchronous interaction semantics, as shown in Figure 8-5, using a synchronous Web service or using the asynchronous XI run-time

✔ An enterprise service with asynchronous interaction semantics, as shown in Figure 8-6, using a synchronous Web service or using the asynchronous XI run-time

Enterprise Service with synchronous interaction semantics, for example, "Get All Purchase Orders from yesterday for more than $100,000."

Implemented over Synchronous Technical Protocol	Implemented over Asynchronous Technical Protocol

Get all purchase orders from yesterday for more than $100,000

Get all purchase orders from yesterday for more than $100,000

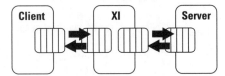

Figure 8-5: Synchronous business interaction semantics.

Return all those purchase orders

Return all those purchase orders

Now what?

Obviously, the most straightforward solution is to use synchronous technical protocols for synchronous business interactions and asynchronous technical protocols for asynchronous business interactions.

However, as we explained earlier, you can also implement synchronous business interaction semantics with an asynchronous technical protocol and vice versa. And you may have good reasons for doing that.

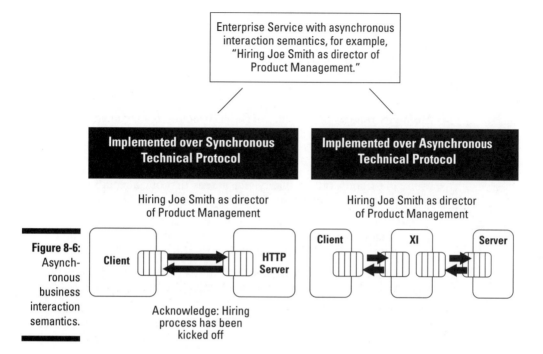

Figure 8-6: Asynchronous business interaction semantics.

For example, you may have a set of enterprise services with synchronous as well as asynchronous business semantics, but with some client configurations, including HTML user interfaces and PDF forms, you have to use synchronous Web services. (Don't ask why. Just trust us on this one. You have no options.)

Understanding the differences helps you make the run-time decision that's right for your situation.

Getting a Handle on the Transactional Behavior of Services

We'll start off with a few techie terms. A *transaction* is a single activity in a computer system, such as the act of entering a customer order. Enterprise services exhibit something called *transactional behavior*, reflecting the fact that a service is essentially a single business transaction. The behavior of transactions is referred to as the *semantics of transactions*. (Remember, semantics equals behavior.)

Transactions are defined by four properties referred to as ACID (Atomicity, Consistency, Isolation, and Durability). Transactional behavior is closely associated with the underlying database(s):

- **Atomicity** refers to the ability of the transaction management system to guarantee that either all the tasks of a transaction are performed or none of them are.

  For example, a transfer of funds can be completed or it can fail for a multitude of reasons, but atomicity guarantees that one account won't be debited if the other is not credited as well.

- **Consistency** refers to the database being in a legal state when the transaction begins and when it ends. This means that a transaction can't break the rules, or integrity constraints, of the database.

  For example, if an integrity constraint states that all accounts must have a positive balance, any transaction violating this rule is aborted.

- **Isolation** refers to the ability of the application to make operations in a transaction appear isolated from all other operations. This means that no operation outside the transaction will ever see the data in an intermediate state.

  For example, a bank manager can see the transferred funds credited to one account or the other, but those funds will never be credited to both simultaneously, even if she runs a query while the transfer is being processed.

- **Durability** guarantees that after the user has been notified of a transaction's success, the transaction will persist, and not be undone. This means that it will survive system failure because the database system checks the integrity constraints and there's no need to abort the transaction. Typically, all transactions are written into a log that can be played back to re-create the system to its state right before the failure. A transaction is deemed committed only after it is safely entered into this log. For example, after the money is in your account, it stays there until you starting spending it.

The ERP enterprise services are mostly atomic transactions; this makes using them simple, as shown in Figure 8-7. You don't have to worry about ACID properties and special protocols: You just call the enterprise service and it is executed or not; if it's not executed, an exception is raised.

Transactions come in types

If you're an IT type, you might want to note that there are two types of transactions:

✔ Atomic transactions, which have no subtransactions.

✔ Distributed transactions, which may involve multiple subtransactions executed in different

systems. These require complex mechanisms (for example, a two-phase-commit protocol) to ensure transactional behavior.

If you're not an IT type, there's absolutely no need for you to know what a two-phase-commit protocol is, so just move on!

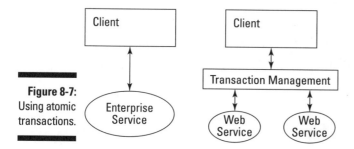

Figure 8-7:
Using atomic transactions.

Simplifying Sessions

It's time for a few techie definitions (aren't you glad?). In computing terms, a *session* occurs when data is shared between a client and a server over some period of time and across interactions. A good example of a session is an electronic shopping cart. You put books or other goodies into and out of the cart until you eventually proceed to the checkout.

Stateless refers to a client/server system that does not share data between different interactions.

The process of managing a session is, quite logically, known as *session management*. When you use sessions, you have to make the session-management mechanisms known to the client so that the client can then be coded to make use of them. This makes the client side much more complex.

Similar to transactional behavior and the Web service protocol, the design principle for session management is "Keep it simple, stupid." If you have no sessions and all enterprise services are stateless, you are keeping things about as simple as you can, as shown in Figure 8-8.

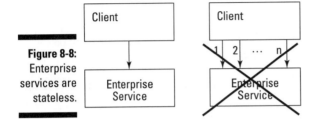

Figure 8-8:
Enterprise
services are
stateless.

Stateless is very simple, but it comes at a price: You have to send all the necessary data every time you invoke a service because nothing is kept on the server.

Seamless Security

Security is a really important thing when you're running enterprise software. The topics of particular importance when you're calling enterprise services are

- **Authentication:** Establishes the identity of the client and the server
- **Authorization:** Controls access to data and functionality based on the identity of the client (and the parameters of the call)
- **Encryption:** Scrambles the message so that nobody but the designated receiver can read it

The following sections describe how this trio works to keep your data secure.

Authentication

You may use a few methods to identify yourself to others: your passport, driver's license, or green card. In the same way, there are many ways to establish the identity of the client of an enterprise service. The most common ones include certificates or the popular combo of user ID and password.

Most of us are familiar with user IDs and passwords because we spend half our lives typing them in (and the other half forgetting them). The interesting aspect in the context of enterprise services is that you're dealing with a client system, which is typically a third-party or composite application that has its own authentication systems. The client needs to be known to your ERP system. There are two ways of doing this:

- ✔ Use the SAP NetWeaver single sign-on mechanism in the client application. SAP NetWeaver's single sign-on automatically maps an identity between different systems so you only have to log in once.
- ✔ Map the client IDs and passwords to ERP identities. ERP identity is the enterprise service caller's identity.

Certificates are also known as X.509 certificates. (You can impress your IT guy by casually mentioning this someday.) You probably use certificates all the time. For example, when you deal with your bank over the Internet, certificates are flying around like mad because your bank uses (we hope!) HTTPS, the secure version of HTTP. When HTTPS shows up for the first time in the URL field of your browser, it establishes a secure session. In the process, the bank's server authenticates itself to your browser so that you can be assured that you are dealing with your bank and not with some con artist who is only pretending to be your bank.

X.509 certificates use a mechanism based on a combination of public and private keys that establishes the identity of an entity, such as the Internet server of your bank. They can also be used to authenticate clients. Certificates are issued by so-called *certificate authorities,* which are trusted entities such as Verisign that verify your identity before issuing a certificate.

X.509 certificates are intrinsic components of HTTP's secure sibling, HTTPS. HTTPS mandates the use of certificates for authenticating servers and enables the use of certificates to establish client identities.

Authorization

After you establish the identity of a caller with authentication, the ERP system has to figure out what the caller should be allowed to do and see. Enterprise services use ERP authorization mechanisms that provide the identity of the caller to the ERP system.

Roles, as we explain in Chapter 3, play an important part in providing access rights. They make an administrator's job much easier because the access rights are defined within polices for a specific role. The user gets the access rights along with his role. When a user changes roles in the company, simply assign the new role, and the access rights are instantly updated.

By decoupling users and access rights through roles, you also make the security audits for enterprise systems much easier and transparent. This is particularly important in the context of compliance with Sarbanes-Oxley and other regulations.

Encryption

In your house, you may keep your neighbor from eavesdropping by shutting the windows and turning up the stereo. The two most common ways to secure messages that you send via a computer network from eavesdropping are to use virtual private networks (VPNs) or to establish secure communication channels over the public Internet. You are probably familiar with both approaches from your corporate e-mail and intranet access. Either you create a VPN connection via special software installed on your laptop (often involving a device that generates a random number that identifies you to your server), or you access your corporate e-mail by using an HTTPS connection to the Web that interfaces with your company's e-mail server.

Enterprise services work in a similar way. If someone calls your services from outside your corporate intranet, she may establish a VPN and become an extension of your intranet. Alternatively, she can use an ID and password or X.509 certificates in conjunction with HTTPS to invoke enterprise services. The client identity is established, and the messages are encrypted and sent over the public Internet.

Taking a Closer Look at Web-Service Run-Time Architecture

Web-service run-time architecture (something of a mouthful, we grant you) is simply the way a Web service is designed to respond when you call that service. Web-service run-time involves a client and a server, which both use HTTP or HTTPS to exchange some XML-formatted message.

Figure 8-9 shows the Web-service run-time architecture for enterprise services. The server provides a Web service via an HTTP (or Web) server. The format of the input and output messages is defined in WSDL and can be found in the enterprise service repository. All a client needs to know is the URL and the XML format.

The beauty of all this is that the client can be written in any programming language, including Java, Perl, PHP, C/C++, or Visual Basic, and can be run on any operating system and hardware platform. This is the power of open standards and a keep-it-simple interaction model.

Take a look at how our two earlier examples, "Get all purchase orders from yesterday for more than $100,000" and "Hire Joe Smith as director of Product Management," get invoked as Web services.

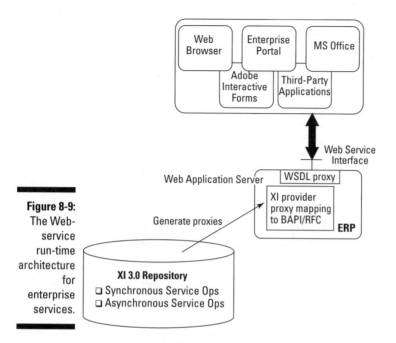

Figure 8-9:
The Web-
service
run-time
architecture
for
enterprise
services.

"Get all purchase orders from yesterday for more than $100,000" is a straight Web service call that contains all the necessary input parameters and returns an XML message with the requested purchase orders.

"Hire Joe Smith as director of Product Management" is a Web service call that includes within the XML input message some essential parameters such as name, start date, compensation, and so on. The HTTP call returns and the output message acknowledges the kick-off of the hiring process.

Discovering XI Run-Time Architecture

The final piece of the services puzzle is the asynchronous XI run-time. The XI uses a different technical protocol than the synchronous Web service infrastructure.

Remember that the XI run-time uses message queues, which ensure that messages are delivered regardless of whether the server is available at the time of the invocation. That's a great feature, but, as with all great things, it comes at a price: You need to have a specific piece of code in your client. This code, known as the *XI client-side proxy,* is generated by XI at design-time when you build the service. XI can generate proxies in Java and ABAP.

Although this isn't a big deal, it makes some usage scenarios very hard to implement — and in some cases even impossible. For example, if the application that is trying to invoke enterprise services is written in C++ or PHP, a popular Internet scripting language, a proxy in Java or ABAP is of little use.

If you have a Java or ABAP client, you can make good use of the XI run-time. The client puts the message in the local queue. From there, the message is sent to the XI run-time and then on to the server, where it is received by the XI server-side proxy. A response travels the same path, but in reverse.

Figure 8-10 shows the XI run-time architecture for enterprise services.

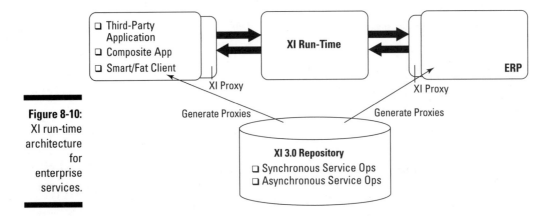

Figure 8-10:
XI run-time
architecture
for
enterprise
services.

Take our example services, "Get all purchase orders from yesterday for more than $100,000" and "Hire Joe Smith as director of Product Management," and you can see how they get invoked using the XI run-time.

"Get all purchase orders from yesterday for more than $100,000" is made up of a request and response. The request contains all the necessary input parameters and is sent from the client to the server. The response is another message that contains all the output parameters, also sent through the XI run-time. With the response, the server is the sender and the client the receiver.

"Hire Joe Smith as director of Product Management" is only a single message sent through the XI run-time from the client to the server. Given the reliability of the XI run-time, the client can rest assured that the server received the message and will act on it.

Chapter 9

Composites: Extending mySAP ERP

*W*hen you go to a Web site like Amazon.com, Google, or eBay, you get a single user experience. What does that mean? All the features and products you're looking for come at you with a consistent look and feel. Although the systems in the background are incredibly complex, the user interface is very simple: You can buy books with one click at Amazon, and the Google user interface is a simple text box and search feature. If you need further information, such as book reviews or search options, it's usually only a click away.

Still, the complexity behind the scenes is enormous. For example, when you buy a book online, various features are working behind the scenes to make the experience as seamless as possible: product catalogs, your personal buying history, a feature that lets you check on availability, a shopping cart, pricing and shipping information, book rankings, a used-book inventory, promotion and discount offers, reviews and recommendations, and your account data (including your shipping address, different payment methods, logistics/scheduling, packaging options for multi-item orders, and so on). But you don't see all that stuff: You just see an easy-to-use interface for ordering a book.

Composites keep this type of complexity behind the scenes by providing a single and easy-to-use interface comprised of multiple applications and systems. In this chapter, we give you an up-close and personal look at what composite applications can do to make your life simpler.

What Are Composites?

Like most companies, you probably have vertical functions such as sales, HR, and manufacturing. Traditionally, ERP provides applications with functionality that integrates data and processes within those different functional areas (see Figure 9-1).

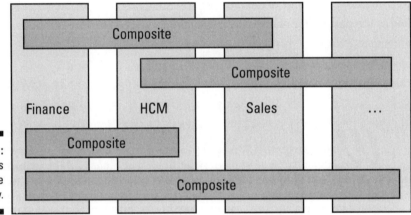

Figure 9-1: Composites integrate horizontally.

The whole new breed of composites provide end users with a seamless experience by leapfrogging across functional areas and integrating all kinds of data and systems. But just what is a composite?

The simplest way to explain a *composite* is as a Frankenstein's monster kind of creation, constructed primarily by building on parts of existing applications. But unlike Frankenstein's monster, the parts of the existing applications are not removed piece by piece. They serve the existing application and the composite at the same time. For example, composites can combine analytical information in the form of dashboards, embedding enterprise services in workflows and processes.

The personality of a composite

Composites generally have certain characteristics, such as

✔ Provide end users with a seamless intelligent experience irrespective of functional, data, and system boundaries

✔ Provide a single and intelligent user experience that doesn't force the end user to think about the underlying technology

✔ Break functional and system boundaries by viewing the enterprise as a whole

✔ Force enterprise-wide collaboration of systems and human beings

✔ Largely assemble a solution from existing multisource content

✔ Don't require a programmer to modify them, but are adaptable by nontechnical business users

This has been theoretically possible for years through the use of an *Application Programming Interface* (API), which allows one program to use the functions and data of another program. As a practical matter, however, APIs are linked to a particular programming language, don't adhere to any standard, aren't self-describing (which means that they can't tell other applications what they are about), and are used mostly to integrate one application with another. These limitations have made the reality of composites harder to achieve than bringing poor, dead Frankenstein to life.

As we discuss in Chapter 2, to be able to compete in the market, you need to innovate and to have an IT infrastructure (people, systems, and techniques) to implement and support those innovations. Composites do exactly this. SAP and its partners provide ready-to-use composites, but you can also build your own using tools, methodologies, patterns, technology, and application functionality provided by SAP.

Enterprise services to the rescue

Enterprise services change everything. Enterprise services are based on *Web services* technology and provide a way for one application to talk to another application that is language-independent and based on open industry standards; specifically, XML and HTTP. Furthermore, the Web Services Description Language (WSDL) defined in XML provides a Web service with the ability to describe itself so that both programmers and other programs can easily figure out what a Web service has to offer.

In the world outside of SAP, when people talk about *composites,* they mean building new applications out of existing applications using Web services instead of APIs to allow other programs to use their functionality.

But SAP is a world unto itself, so when SAP talks about *composites,* a whole lot more comes into play: SAP provides the architecture, the technology, the modeling tools, the application content through enterprise services, and the functionality.

Here are the four pillars SAP's composites stand on:

- **Enterprise Services Architecture:** The blueprint for how all the enabling technologies and applications come together in a coherent design. ESA defines how enterprise services are constructed from application functionality using Web service technology. The granularity of services plays an important role. We discuss the importance of granularity of enterprise services in helping both business people and IT people to understand them in Chapter 2.

- **SAP NetWeaver:** The platform (that is, all the technology underpinnings) on which you can construct composites. Besides the creation of enterprise services, which is not really that hard with XI tools, SAP NetWeaver provides solutions to difficult problems that come up when creating composites. SAP NetWeaver Portal, for example, solves user-interface problems such as disparate application interfaces, training gaps, and ease of use. SAP NetWeaver Master Data Management helps manage distributed master data. All the other components solve crucial issues so that, as much as possible, any composite built the SAP way comes from handy existing toolkits.

- **SAP modeling tools:** Model-driven development dramatically simplifies the creation of composites because there's absolutely no coding involved. Depending on the type of complexity you're dealing with, SAP provides two sets of modeling tools: CAF and its Guided Procedure layer, and Visual Composer. You find more detail about each of these in Chapter 7.

- **mySAP ERP and mySAP Business Suite:** A huge collection of functionality that is just sitting there, waiting to be reused by composites. Other vendors' applications can be used in composites as well. Right now, you can access quite a bit of the functionality of mySAP ERP, mySAP Business Suite, and other underlying solutions through enterprise services. More functionality will be Web-service enabled with new versions of each enterprise application.

The SAP modeling approach makes composites much easier to build and far less costly to update and maintain because the sort of business content that is created during modeling is much easier to modify and maintain than custom code.

Now, with all this thinking, applications, and technology firepower, composites have become more than just an interesting theory; composites harmonize beautifully with the architecture, the technology platform, the modeling tools, and the application content and functionality.

Making a difference in your business

At this point, you're probably sitting there in your office or cubicle wondering, "How will SAP NetWeaver and composites change my business?"

To understand how composites can change the way you do what you do, you need to understand the three ways of creating composites:

- **Custom-built (do-it-yourself) composites:** These are applications you build yourself by using the SAP's modeling tools, CAF guided procedures or Visual Composer, and perhaps a little help from SAP consultants or another systems integrator.

- **Composites in mySAP ERP or mySAP Business Suite:** These applications are used to enhance or extend the functionality of mySAP ERP. The composites approach could be used to create a new application that uses functionality from many different mySAP ERP solutions, or to use bits of one application to add its functionality and flexibility to another program. Industry-specific solutions provided by SAP are built and delivered this way.

- **SAP xApps:** These applications are packaged composites, meaning that they are created, sold, and supported as separate products. SAP xApps are created both by SAP and by partners who use the functionality in SAP NetWeaver and mySAP ERP and mySAP Business Suite. The functionality is expanded and assembled to solve unique challenges. SAP xApps are frequently focused on helping companies adopt innovative ways of doing business. Because xApps are ready to go and easy to deploy, they can save you time, effort, and money.

The Nature of Composites

A popular ice cream retailer may have 31 flavors, but why should life be so complicated? SAP has categorized composites into just three simple groups. This breakdown helps you to apply the appropriate technologies and create successful business cases for them. The three different flavors are composite applications, composite processes, and composite views, as shown in Figure 9-2.

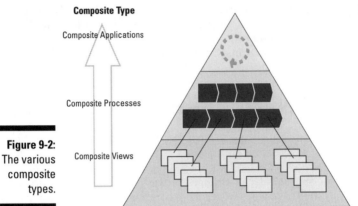

Composite Type

Composite Applications

Composite Processes

Composite Views

Example

xCQM - xApp managing the costing and quotation in the high-tech and similar industries

Express planning - A process that supports the entire management of a planning and budgeting process

Multisource budget planning page that combines plan numbers with external content from, for example, contract management system to project a maintenance revenue stream

Figure 9-2:
The various composite types.

Here's the rundown on what these three types have to offer and what technologies you need for each.

Getting comprehensive with composite applications

Composite applications are the heavyweights in the world of composites. They reuse functionality, processes, and transactions from more than one existing application to administer or manage a new business process spanning various functional areas such as HR, accounting, and so on.

This integration of multisource, multifunction content leads to a single user experience in one handy interface (for example, by providing you with reports side by side with a way to take action) that makes people much more productive.

Getting a perspective on composites

Things can mean different things to different people. For example, to a kid, ice cream is a treat. To an adult, it's a cholesterol attack. Different people have different perspectives on technology, too, depending on how they use it. Here are a few ways to look at composites:

 ✔ **Architectural perspective:** A composite application is a stand-alone application that sits on top of existing applications, has its own data model, and supports very complex business logic.

✔ **User-interface perspective:** A composite application may contain a number of visual and interaction features such as dashboards, guided procedures, embedded analytics, collaboration rooms, and so on to deliver an intelligent end-user experience.

✔ **Business case perspective:** Given the complexity of a composite application, it requires a fairly high investment and presents a higher-risk investment compared to other composite types. As a consequence, composite applications are less often developed by customers but are typically delivered as part of mySAP ERP or mySAP Business Suite, or as an xApp by SAP or an SAP partner.

✔ **Deployment perspective:** When a composite is delivered by SAP or a partner, it is highly configurable, rapidly deployable, and adaptable.

A good example of a composite application is Enterprise Risk Management. In certain obvious areas, your business is at risk, for example, in how well you deal with hiring people, finances, sales, and so on. A composite application could bring all the risk factors in your business together into a single application. Processes would wrap around this content, giving you the ability to monitor your risk and take action on it from one location. Tools such as Guided Procedures and interactive forms could support this application.

So, what would this look like? If you are the HR manager who has to staff a new plant, you run the risk of being unable to hire and train 1,000 people in time to open the plant (called *onboarding,* in corporate lingo). A composite application could show you all kinds of red flags (we're 999 people short!) and data (992 hires are in the pipeline and about to come through) to give you the full onboarding picture. This provides you with the tools you need to take action, such as signing off on the plant opening or getting your HR manager on the phone pronto.

Reusing components with composite processes

You can create a composite that brings together functionality and processes from various systems to focus on a specific business process. It's called a *composite process.*

The result of a composite process could dramatically reduce the number of hand-offs, redundant data entry, navigation time, process-cycle time, customer dissatisfaction, and more.

Composite processes also mean different things to different people:

✔ **Architectural perspective:** From this point of view, a composite process is an application essentially sitting on top of existing applications. It uses few new business objects but does use complex business logic. The process also has the ability to take advantage of the Guided Procedure design pattern to make working with these business objects and the associated business logic easier.

✔ **User-interface perspective:** A composite process is a process that you can augment with new composite attributes, such as a dashboard that you can use to monitor process status, embed content, and so on.

✔ **Business case perspective:** A composite process requires a medium investment compared to other composite types. Composite processes are either delivered as part of mySAP ERP or mySAP Business Suite, or built by the customer to satisfy his specific needs.

✔ **Deployment perspective:** When delivered by SAP, the composite process is packaged as part of an existing application and is highly configurable, rapidly deployable, and adaptable.

For example, SAP has embedded a new composite process into mySAP ERP called express planning. Express planning allows you to manage the whole planning and budgeting cycle that we all look forward to every year. This process collects bottom-up planning information from line managers and completely bypasses the spreadsheet hell that causes so much pain for planners and managers in many companies (see Figure 9-3).

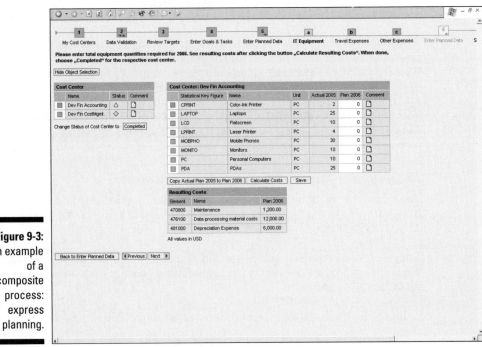

Figure 9-3: An example of a composite process: express planning.

Integrating content with composite views

A composite view is where you get a single page that incorporates content from multiple sources in one user interface. This provides the end user with a comprehensive view of that corner of the world (see Figure 9-4).

Here's how different people view composite views:

- **Architectural perspective:** A composite view uses simple business logic.

- **User-interface perspective:** A composite view adds in some composite bells and whistles such as embedded analytics that provide a richer user experience.

- **Business case perspective:** A composite view requires a low-level investment compared to other composite types. Composite views are either delivered as part of mySAP ERP or mySAP Business Suite, or built by the customer to satisfy his specific needs. For example, SAP delivers tons of composite views built right into mySAP ERP.

- **Deployment perspective:** When delivered by SAP, the composite view is packaged and deployed as part of an existing application. Its configurability, however, is limited.

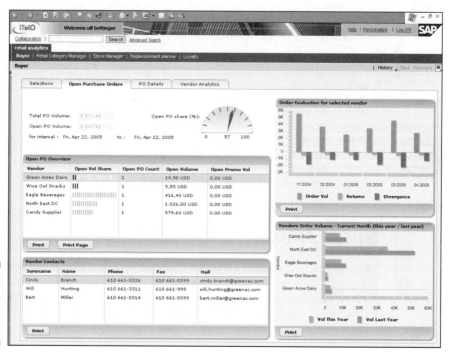

Figure 9-4: A composite view: PO Dashboard.

For example, Figure 9-4 shows a composite dashboard that provides information on vendors and associated purchase orders, all delivered through a single portal. The information comes from a variety of systems including CRM and ERP.

Fitting Together Composite Applications

So far, you've seen the big-picture moving parts of composite applications and how composites are differentiated by their complexity and associated technology.

Now it's time to look at just how composite applications get created. To make things easier for you, SAP has identified a number of patterns and provides software that helps you in designing composites.

Composites can be categorized into groups that have similar characteristics; specifically, they have a similar process structure or flow. This is what SAP calls a pattern for composites. The pattern itself is supported by software components and modeling tools such as CAF guided procedures or Visual Composer.

See Chapter 7 for more about modeling and the SAP tools.

In the following sections, we introduce and explain the following patterns:

- ✔ Guide2Result
- ✔ Request2Response
- ✔ Event2Resolution

SAP has not only identified patterns for composites, but also offers about a hundred business scenarios for these patterns.

Here are how three of these patterns work.

Guide2Result

Say that you just started a new job. You need to go through several steps to get yourself set up for work. For example, you need to order a computer and various supplies, sign up for a corporate credit card, sign up for benefits, and so on. You can use a Guided Procedure to step you through these processes in wizard-like fashion. The beauty of this is that you can move from step to step across systems, pulling what you need from various sources seamlessly (see Figure 9-5).

Figure 9-5:
From start to finish, a Guided Procedure steps you through a process.

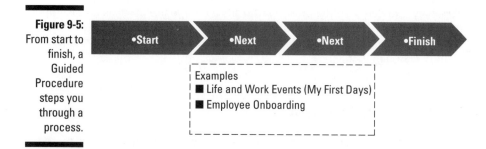

The Guide2Result pattern consists of a starting point and a sequence of steps that lead the end user to a defined result. The composite application guides the end user through the process. Each of the steps can be connected to different back-end systems, but that is invisible to the user.

Typically, the Guide2Result pattern is a composite process and is implemented using SAP's CAF guided procedure, often in conjunction with interactive forms.

Request2Response

We have to request a lot of things in our day-to-day work. We request vacation or leave time; we request a change in a project; we request services or support; and on and on. When you make a request in an SAP environment, you call services from various sources to capture data. Using interactive forms from Adobe, you can take that information, send the form for approval, and update master databases. Figure 9-6 shows the flow of this type of pattern.

Figure 9-6:
From generating a request to getting a response, you can gather data from anywhere.

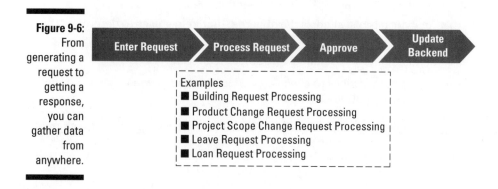

As the name suggests, the Request2Response pattern consists of a request (for example, by an employee or a business partner) and a response by the appropriate decision maker. The composite application executes the necessary workflow to get a response.

Typically, the Request2Response pattern is a composite process and is implemented using SAP's workflow, often in conjunction with interactive forms and the universal work list. The role concept of mySAP ERP is used to identify the right decision maker.

Event2Resolution

Say you're the manager of a department and you have to keep an eye on the travel expense budget. You can set things up so that, when you come within five percent of your total expense budget, an event is triggered. The event alerts you that you'd better keep a lid on travel costs for the rest of the quarter. To resolve the situation, you may take various actions, such as canceling some trips or denying pending travel requests (see Figure 9-7).

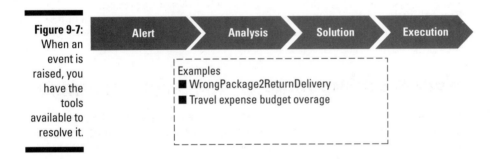

Figure 9-7:
When an event is raised, you have the tools available to resolve it.

The Event2Resolution pattern consists of

- An alert that is generated by the composite

- Analytical tools, such as dashboards, that help a user to determine the cause of the problem

- Simulation tools to help create solution alternatives

- Enterprise services to execute the decision you've made based on the proposed solution alternatives

Depending on the complexity, the Event2Resolution pattern can be a composite application, composite process, or composite view. For example, a credit management scenario (introduced in Chapter 7) is a composite view, whereas an enterprise forecasting tool is a composite application.

SAP xApps: Delivering on the Innovation Promise

SAP xApps are composite applications that are packaged as stand-alone applications and are delivered by SAP or SAP partners. They are composite applications delivered as separate products.

What do xApps need to work?

These xApps require the underlying functionality of mySAP ERP or mySAP Business Suite and use SAP NetWeaver as a technology platform. Additionally, xApps can leverage enterprise applications from other vendors, using SAP NetWeaver integration capabilities based on the integration infrastructure of SAP NetWeaver XI and SAP NetWeaver Master Data Management.

For example, SAP xApp Resource and Program Management (SAP xRPM) requires a skills-management system from SAP or another provider, but SAP xRPM does not contain related HR components. These must come from SAP or some other vendor's HR application. SAP xApps don't care what vendor provides the underlying functionality, as long as it's there.

Saving money up-front and along the way

Because composites are created through modeling rather than through a programming language, you can easily modify them without affecting the underlying components that you're repurposing.

Most of a composite is controlled through *business content,* which is basically a description of what you want to get done. This means you can adapt solutions to the needs of your company's infrastructure and reduce deployment costs because you're not getting in there and tinkering with hard-coded interfaces. When SAP delivers new ways to upgrade or extend a composite, you don't have to upgrade your current applications or existing composites. You can introduce new functions more cheaply and without messing up what's already in place.

Composites increase the return on your investment in applications because they take your existing applications and find all kinds of different uses for them. Frequently, this has the result of bringing the data or features of one application to a whole new population of users. It can also mean solving new problems at lower costs because you aren't starting from scratch, but from the functionality provided by your same old favorite programs. In either case, composites tap into the value from your installed base of applications.

Increasing flexibility

The whole idea of a custom application is that it fits your unique requirements — sort of like getting a suit made to order, right? So, the process should be flexible. It is.

The same modeling approach to building applications allows you much more flexibility when customizing composites to meet your exact needs. Changing the structure of the models is much easier and less prone to error than changing or developing custom code in a programming language such as Java.

Taking one from vendor A, one from vendor B . . .

SAP NetWeaver has *mapping capabilities* that enable you to integrate applications using XML so that one application can to talk to another, all for a fraction of the cost of development and maintenance of traditional methods. Also, if you don't have to continually build from scratch, you don't have to worry about maintaining a lot of custom code.

SAP and its merry band of partners provide connectors to the most common non-SAP systems that you might need to integrate, even if they're not yet XML-enabled. Even legacy applications can be integrated with SAP solutions, just for the one-time cost of Web services enablement. Instead of replacing your existing applications, you can get a bigger bang out of your existing solutions.

Going to market, to market

Ever sit around waiting to get a system up and running because a vendor is bringing out a new version of its application next month (or so it promises)? Because composites are independent of the release cycles of the individual applications that lurk under them, they are faster to develop and deploy. This means that you don't have to wait around until the next version of an application comes out — you can just go ahead and build what you want, when you want it.

The same goes for SAP. If SAP sees a need, it can create a composite application for that need right away. You get current and timely solutions to critical situations that just can't wait around to get some attention.

Zeroing in on your industry

Do these things work whether you're in the toy-manufacturing business or aerospace industry? Yes, and here's one big reason why.

SAP uses composites to develop solutions that address industry-specific business scenarios, using both generic and industry-specific components. For example, an intellectual property management solution is being developed to meet the specific requirements of the media industry. SAP or specialized independent solution vendors (ISVs) can provide similar applications.

So whether you build toy rockets or real ones, you're likely to find something to help your business take off (pun intended).

Because SAP xApps have all of mySAP Business Suite and all of SAP NetWeaver as a starting point, they can go where other applications fear to tread and do things that were impossible with technology and applications in years past. For this reason, SAP xApps are frequently focused on making a product that addresses an innovative process. Innovation often comes through industry-specific focus.

Automating it

Composites sit on top of not only mySAP Business Suite and enterprise applications from other vendors, but also on top of SAP NetWeaver and all its components. This means that problems that you couldn't solve with previous generations of technology just might be within your reach now.

SAP NetWeaver brings a lot to the table: advanced collaboration features, knowledge management, data warehousing and analysis, master data management, XML messaging, and more. SAP xApps already have automated processes that you could never effectively automate before, such as the end-to-end product definition process or mergers and acquisitions. You have far fewer limitations on what you can achieve than ever before.

SAP xApps bring benefits galore

It doesn't take a brain surgeon to figure out that if you can buy a solution out of a box, rather than spending tons of time building your own application, it's a good thing. But just in case you're justifying the purchase of SAP xApps to your boss and you have to throw reasons at him, go ahead and point out these three key benefits you get from SAP xApps:

✔ SAP xApps give you innovation at a lower cost. By providing packaged innovation through composites, SAP liberates you from your reliance on niche products or extensive modifications of existing applications. This approach lowers initial development and lifecycle maintenance costs.

✔ SAP xApps allow you to base your development on the very same platform SAP uses — the SAP CAF. That means you get support from SAP or its partners. This translates into both low initial cost of development and easy integration with SAP or non-SAP applications, and it keeps your IT costs in check.

✔ Because SAP xApps are built on SAP CAF, this speeds the development of both mainstream composites and SAP xApps by SAP industry business units, solution groups, and partners. Because SAP xApps aren't tied to the release cycles of underlying components, you can continue to introduce new functionality while using a more differentiated, less disruptive, and less expensive upgrade strategy.

A Case in Point: SAP xApp Cost and Quotation Management

So how does this xApp thing look in practice? In the highly competitive industry of contract manufacturing where profit margins are tight, the ability to acquire new business and maintain existing relationships with customers depends on your ability to respond quickly and efficiently to Requests for Quotation (RFQs).

Examining the challenges

The success and competitiveness of your manufacturing operation depends on your manufacturing and development expertise and the viability of your relationships with your suppliers. These two factors become essential for achieving profitability, but there are challenges to achieving this integration, including

✔ Quotation teams and manufacturing locations spread all around the globe

✔ The challenge of integrating existing IT systems and maintaining home-grown or third-party vendors

✔ The ability to obtain instant access to relevant data in light of ever-shorter response times

All of these challenges are critical hurdles that you have to leap over to get to an efficient quotation management process.

Enter xCQM

SAP's xApp Cost and Quotation Management (affectionately known as xCQM) is a new application designed to streamline the quoting process for contract manufacturers. The solution enables the creation of a quotation through the upload of a bill of material (BOM), automatic pricing of existing components, streamlined electronic Request for Quotation (eRFQ) processing for new components, and execution of consolidated costs reports.

The integrated end-to-end solution enables contract manufacturers to significantly improve the quality and turnaround time of their quotations and to focus on delivering value to new and existing customers, thereby increasing their quotation win rates (see Figure 9-8).

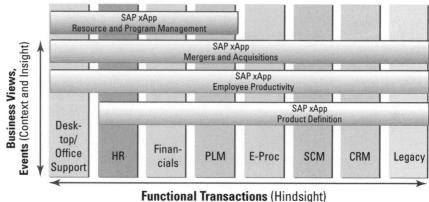

Figure 9-8: xApps integration crossing vertical silos.

The Cost and Quotation Management xApp includes the following enterprise services:

- ✔ CustomerAttributesQueryResponse gets attributes of a selected customer, such as an address.

- ✔ ProductGetStockRequirementsListQueryResponse gets stock information for a selected material.

- ✔ ProductDetailQueryResponse gets product details.

- ✔ PurchaseContractDetail gets pricing information from a contract.

- ✔ CustomerQuotationCreateRequest creates a quotation for a selected customer.

xCQM: Making the process flow

Take a quick peek at the architecture and the process flow of xCQM, and you can see how it is designed and implemented using ERP Enterprise Services.

Start by looking at the process flow from an end-user perspective. An account manager opens an opportunity (which is a business object with associated data), either created from ERP's Sales and Distribution module or manually. The opportunity already contains a set of information such as products to be quoted, quantities, start and end date, and so on. The account manager then selects the customer, and xCQM adds the specific customer's address. xCQM gets the address by simply invoking the enterprise service CustomerAttributesQueryResponse.

The account manager also has to run a background check on the customer (see Figure 9-9) to find out whether there are any credit holds on the account, delivery blocks, or other issues. This information is also provided by running the enterprise service CustomerAttributesQueryResponse.

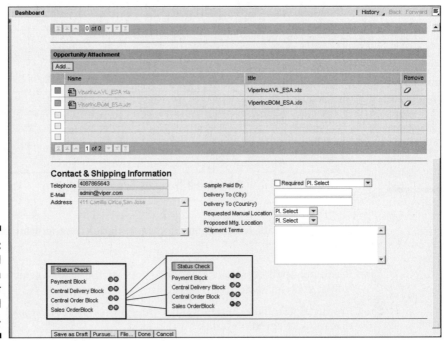

Figure 9-9: xCQM running a customer background check.

The next day, the quote team leader, Charlie, assigns a member of the quote team to this opportunity. The leader also enters the assigned costing activity using a dashboard.

When team member Heather finds out that she's the lucky one to handle the cost estimate for the material cost portion of this RFQ, she clicks the material cost link in the Quotation Worksheet, or QWS. This leads her to the costed bill-of-material, or BOM, view. From there, she can navigate to the exploded BOM view to take a gander at all the details.

In the exploded BOM view is a column called Stock. Heather clicks the column header and the enterprise service ProductGetStockRequirementsListQuery-Response is invoked again and again to call up the stock information for each item in the BOM. Then the service enters the information in the Quotation Worksheet for each line item.

Because a given material may have multiple prices, Heather may have to resolve a pricing conflict. She clicks on the conflict resolution icon in the exploded BOM for that material and uses the enterprise service ProductDetailQueryResponse to obtain and display additional data on the selected material (see Figure 9-10).

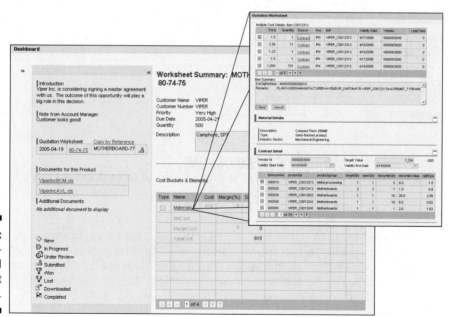

Figure 9-10: xCQM — material and contract look-up.

Heather could also find detailed information about the material prices in the customer's other contracts. She calls on the enterprise service Purchase-ContractDetail to conjure up the contract information.

Fast-forward to when the quote is complete. The account manager accesses an easy-to-prepare quote package for the product. From the quote package summary page, he gets the creation of a quote going in the back-end system using the enterprise service CustomerQuotationCreateRequest (see Figure 9-11).

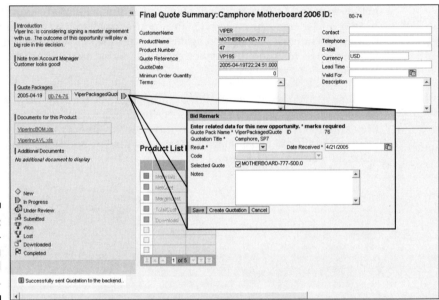

Figure 9-11:
xCQM —
returning
the finalized
quote.

xCQM: Architecture

Now that you understand what the application does, take a look at its architecture.

As shown in Figure 9-12, xCQM is the centerpiece application, a Java (J2EE, to be specific) application modeled with CAF. User access to the application is enabled through the SAP NetWeaver Portal, which also handles user management. You can also connect any lightweight directory access protocol-compliant (LDAP-compliant) corporate user database.

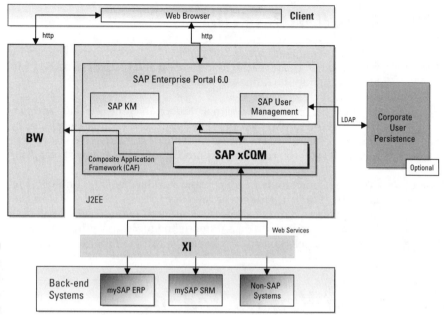

Figure 9-12:
xCQM
architecture.

Most of the functionality is provided via enterprise services from the ERP and SRM systems. The list of enterprise services, presented in the context of the xCQM process flow discussion in the previous section of this chapter, is shown in Table 9-1. Analytical services are provided through BW.

Table 9-1   List of ERP Enterprise Services Used by xCQM

Service	*Function*
CustomerAttributesQueryResponse	Gets attributes — for example, an address of a selected customer
ProductGetStockRequirementsListQueryResponse	Gets stock information of a selected material
ProductDetailQueryResponse	Gets product details
PurchaseContractDetail	Gets pricing information from a contract
CustomerQuotationCreateRequest	Creates a quotation for a selected customer

The Composite Team

Composite applications are one great big business opportunity for SAP partners. You can reuse all the functionality and content of mySAP ERP as well as all the other applications offered by SAP.

The best part is that now, with an ESA-enabled mySAP ERP and the modeling tools that SAP NetWeaver provides, you can very quickly and easily build composite applications. The intellectual barriers involved in understanding ABAP and BAPIs and the resulting required financial investment just disappear.

Your developers only need to know standard Web technology such as HTTP and XML. Enterprise services are easy to understand because they focus on your business functionality and content at just the right level of detail for building composites. The SAP modeling tools make the development of a composite itself a piece of cake (OK, a rather elaborate torte).

What Can You Do Today with Composites?

SAP provides a service to help you build an enterprise-specific ESA roadmap and help you identify the composites that you need. The details of this program are explained in Chapter 11.

SAP has made a large number of enterprise services available in a preview system, which is available through the SAP Developer Network SDN at www.sdn.sap.com.

Finally, take a look at the xApps that are available today by SAP and SAP partners and see which ones may fit your needs. Table 9-2 provides an overview of available xApps.

Table 9-2	SAP xApps and Packaged Composite Applications from SAP Partners
Product	*Description*
SAP xApps (Collaborative Cross Applications)	Packaged composite applications developed by SAP GBU X, as well as SAP IBUs, GBUs, and partners.
SAP xApp Cost and Quotation Management (SAP xCQM)	Turns business expertise and supplier relationships into revenue.

Product	Description
SAP xApp Resource and Portfolio Management (SAP xRPM)	Dramatically improves your ability to manage enterprise-wide project portfolios.
SAP xApp Product Definition (SAP xPD)	Translates your ideas into innovation.
SAP xApp Emissions Management (SAP xEM)	Enables energy-consuming and carbon dioxide–producing businesses to comply with environmental regulations.
SAP xApp Integrated Exploration and Production (SAP xIEP)	Optimizes the upstream oil exploration process.
SAP Global Trade Services (SAP GTS)	Drives regulatory compliance for international trade.
SAP xApp Emissions Management — TechniData	Helps corporations improve compliance to emerging emissions regulations world-wide and increase revenue through trading of emissions credits by flexibly aligning data and functions trapped in disconnected systems. SAP xEM helps you monitor, measure, document, and control emissions output with greater efficiency.
Manufacturing Performance Intelligence (MPI) by Lighthammer	Addresses the discovery, analysis, and closed-loop monitoring of opportunities and problems in manufacturing business processes.
PharmaConnect by EzCommerce	Helps pharmaceutical companies streamline the time-consuming, laborious processes involved with the administration of the Patient Assistance Program (PAP).
plannerDA by BristleCone	Integrates supply chain planning and execution on a planner's workbench for the consumer products and high-tech/manufacturing industries, providing a powerful tool for managing supply chain policies, resolving exceptions, and improving supply chain performance.

(continued)

Table 9-2 *(continued)*

Product	Description
Pricing Analytics by Vendavo	Increases corporate net margins by using unique pricing analytics to uncover areas where profits are won and lost.
ServiceFlow by Digital Fuel	Designed for enterprises and service providers that must control the cost, performance, and delivery of sourced services, ServiceFlow optimizes your organization's entire services and outsourcing lifecycle.
Visual Information for Plants (VIP) by NRX	Supports the unification of systems, workflows, and informational inputs and outputs in asset management applications such as performance reporting, work management, real-time process data, and reliability programs. It is designed for plant maintenance and equipment performance in asset-intensive industries.

Part III
Implementing Change

The 5th Wave   By Rich Tennant

"Stop working on the Priority Parking Spot Allocation program. They want to fast track the Coffee Pot/Cubicle Proximity program."

In this part . . .

If you're sold on the benefits of mySAP ERP and are eager to find out how to get the thing up and running, this part's for you! Chapter 10 discusses how to calculate your total cost of ownership and how to go about preparing your organization for change. Chapter 11 lays out a roadmap to help you put mySAP ERP in place, including several useful programs and tools to make the whole thing relatively painless. And Chapter 12 looks at SAP's future plans for mySAP ERP, so you can look ahead to even more improvements.

Chapter 10

Knowing What to Expect: Covering Costs and Managing Change

In This Chapter

▶ Making a business case for mySAP ERP

▶ Exploring the financial aspects of introducing mySAP ERP

▶ Taking on the challenge of change

*T*hroughout this book, we explore the challenges to business today and how mySAP ERP can help you address them. If we've convinced you and you're ready to put mySAP ERP to work in your organization, what should you do to get your ducks in a row? You probably have to justify mySAP ERP from a financial perspective to the powers-that-be in your corner of the world. To that end, in this chapter, we tell you about the tools and services available to help you impress even the most jaded CEO.

At this stage, you should also prepare yourself and your management to deal with impending change in your organization. Don't underestimate this: A mySAP ERP implementation touches just about everybody in your company and potentially your vendors, partners, and customers. At the end of this chapter, we give you some sound advice about dealing with change management.

The Financial Bottom Line of mySAP ERP

In Chapter 2, we cover the two major challenges businesses face today. Businesses have to find ways to

✔ Increase efficiency and reduce the cost of their standard processes

✔ Enable differentiating processes and foster innovation with low investment

But how do you know that implementing mySAP ERP will help you achieve these goals? What you need is a model. We're not talking about the people in fashion magazines; a financial model helps you imagine possible business futures.

One type of financial model is total cost of ownership (TCO): how much money you will have to spend on something, such as implementing new technology. SAP has developed a TCO model that helps you understand the structure of the total cost of your ERP system.

Exploring Costs with a TCO Model

Total cost of ownership (TCO) is the sum of all costs associated with a project. If you're installing a hot tub on your patio, your TCO is not only the several hundred dollars to purchase the hot tub, but also the costs of delivering it, a plumber to help you install the pipes, a cover for the tub, water to fill it, chemicals to clean it, and so on. If you add these all up, you may be surprised to see that the purchase price may not be your biggest cost.

Your mySAP ERP license is just one part of your TCO. If you're smart, you will make the effort to understand all the other costs up-front. Your CFO will want to know, guaranteed.

Determining IT costs is nothing new. In 1987, Gartner (an industry analyst) pioneered the practice of determining IT costs in a structured way. At the time, the approach was focused on the end user and broke down the costs per individual user and the cost of the necessary IT equipment. Over the years, Gartner extended its analysis and methods. Today, Gartner provides a comprehensive IT cost analysis that takes into account not just the user's IT equipment, but also all the training, hardware, and software involved. Many other folks have jumped on the TCO bandwagon, which is why today there is a plethora of models for TCO analysis.

SAP has come up with its own TCO framework that includes a TCO model that takes the specifics and complexity of ERP software into account. Here we walk you through the gist of that model to help you make sense of the TCO puzzle.

Exploring the SAP TCO Framework

The SAP TCO Framework process involves three steps:

1. Using a questionnaire, customers collect all the relevant information about their company from key stakeholders, such as the company structure, the existing IT landscape, and the practices that are used to implement and maintain that landscape and any associated costs.

2. SAP transfers the collected data (anonymously) to a great big database from lots of companies and analyzes it.

   As time goes on, the TCO database expands as more customers participate in this program.

3. Based on the results of its analysis, SAP suggests specific procedures that enable customers to modify their own business practices and reduce their total cost of ownership.

As SAP and its customers gain more experience in the use of these cost-reduction procedures, the TCO model gets tighter and more effective.

Figure 10-1 illustrates the various components of the SAP TCO Framework. The framework is made up of the SAP TCO Model, SAP TCO Reference Parameters, SAP TCO Database, and SAP TCO Reduction Procedures.

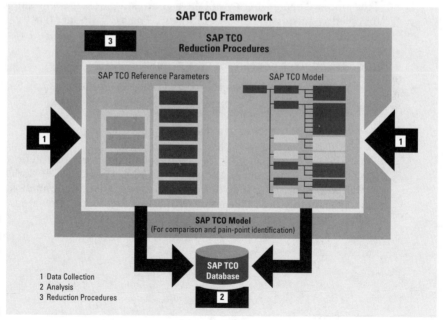

Figure 10-1:
The components of the SAP TCO Framework.

Here's how the parts of the Framework break down:

- **TCO Model** identifies the areas of cost, just as we did in our earlier hot tub example.

- **TCO Reference Parameters** define concrete parameters to measure the cost in the areas defined in the TCO model. By using these standardized parameters, you make your own TCO analysis comparable to others.

- **TCO Database** functions as the central storage area for the completed questionnaires that are the basis for the reference parameters and the collected cost data.

- **TCP Reduction Procedures** is a collection of recommendations for reducing costs in specific areas.

The SAP TCO Model: The key to understanding your costs

The heart of the TCO Framework, the thing your CFO will focus on, is the TCO Model. This is where you take a good, long look at every single cost involved in making the mySAP ERP leap. The TCO Model objectives take into account

- All SAP solution-relevant cost components

- Direct costs, as well as the costs arising from the use of an SAP solution

- A lifecycle-oriented focus

- A distinction between investment costs and ongoing costs

The SAP TCO Model identifies cost areas called *categories* and organizes them in a tree structure, as shown Figure 10-2. The SAP TCO Model has three levels, with increasing specificity as you move down the branches. The model can help you to take a holistic look at the costs associated with making the transition to mySAP ERP.

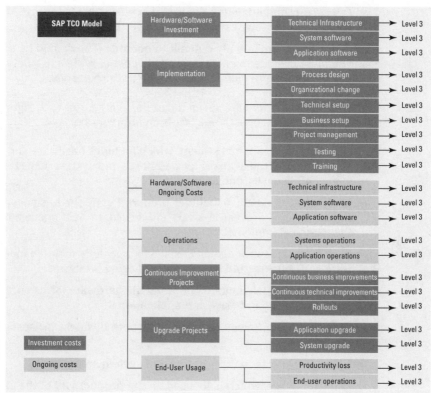

Figure 10-2:
The SAP
TCO Model.

Defining costs by category

For a TCO model, you must record cost data so that it's clearly associated with its source. Specifically, this means taking different cost types into account. The main cost type difference, which is reflected in the SAP TCO Model, is between investment costs and ongoing costs, and direct costs and indirect costs.

- ✔ *Investment costs* are one-time costs and typically fall under the headings of hardware/software investment, implementation consulting, and upgrade projects.

- ✔ *Ongoing costs,* on the other hand, typically relate to operations, maintenance, and end-user usage.

✔ *Direct costs* might include the actual licensing costs for mySAP ERP, a cost that is obviously tied directly to getting ERP in-house.

✔ *Indirect costs* are initially difficult to quantify. They could be training that you must provide to end users, or the cost of replacing a network security component to enable outsourcing to third parties.

In the TCO Model, there are seven major cost categories (see Figure 10-3). The first six are direct costs; the last is an indirect one:

✔ Hardware/software investment, which includes hardware and network infrastructure, the licenses for databases and system management software, SAP licenses, and so on.

✔ Implementation, which includes preparation on the business side of things, such as process analysis and design, project management, and the technical implementation.

✔ Hardware/software ongoing costs, which include maintenance for hardware and software and replacement of aging hardware.

✔ Operations, which include operating the hardware infrastructure, operating systems, databases, and applications.

✔ Continuous improvement projects for both business processes and technology.

✔ Upgrade projects for application and system software.

✔ End-user usage, which is focused on the productivity of the end user. Although this indirect cost is hard to measure, it can have an enormous impact on your overall cost structure.

Figure 10-3 provides another interesting perspective on your cost categories: It shows where costs can occur over a period of time.

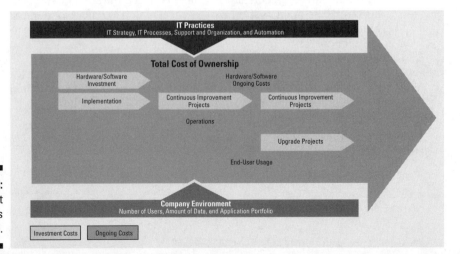

Figure 10-3:
TCO cost categories over time.

How can mySAP ERP help you reduce TCO?

So how do you spot opportunities for cost savings in your business? Here are a few examples that come right out of the mySAP ERP box.

The self-services for managers and employees, the portal-based user interface, the Microsoft Office integration, the role-based work center, and many other recent additions allow you to reduce TCO in the end-user productivity area of mySAP ERP.

On the technical side, mySAP ERP in conjunction with SAP NetWeaver gives you a lot of

flexibility in deployment. You can centralize your deployments in one or a few locations instead of having data centers and staff in every country you operate in. This reduces TCO in operations and upgrade projects.

mySAP ERP also allows you to deploy it for shared service centers (functions such as accounting shared by various departments use common services). This reduces TCO in user productivity and operations costs.

SAP has published lots of information about its TCO model, including a white paper and a paper specifically on TCO reduction, which is available in the SAP Service Marketplace at `service.sap.com` in the TCO section. (You have to register as a customer or partner to have access to the SAP Service Marketplace.)

Calculating TCO

Using the TCO Framework and all the great questionnaires SAP provides, you can work together with SAP and business consultants to gather data from your company and get comparisons by industry to begin to calculate your TCO model. This is your benchmark against which you can track actual costs. After your data is in the TCO database, you can analyze it to identify areas for TCO reduction, comparing your company with organizations of a similar size in your industry.

The two biggest costs you typically encounter are in implementation and operations.

Making a Plan with Value-Based Services

SAP offers a useful evaluation service to help you get your arms around TCO and start planning your implementation. Called SAP value-based services for SAP solutions, these services can help take the guesswork out of IT planning. Whether you are just identifying areas where cost savings can be made, developing proof of concept, estimating your TCO reductions, evaluating potential return on investment, or developing a roadmap for future deployment, SAP value-based services for SAP solutions help to reduce your risk, ensure you get the maximum return, and support your long-term business goals.

What do these services involve? Value-based services involve working with SAP, your line-of-business executives, and your IT managers to

- ✔ Define capabilities that deliver specific strategic advantage and help realize key objectives of your enterprise

- ✔ Quantify the potential cost savings and revenue enhancements achievable with SAP

- ✔ Evaluate and justify the proposed expenditure through a business case analysis

- ✔ Develop an implementation strategy to help you realize program benefits within an acceptable time frame

SAP provides company-specific value analysis. Depending on your needs, these value services can apply to a specific project that you've already defined, a broader effort for overall process improvement, or a long-term roadmap for business enhancement. Depending on your needs, these can range from a one-day workshop to identify areas of potential savings to a full-fledged project to identify return on investment (ROI). Such analyses can typically be completed within 2–12 weeks, depending on the size and complexity of your business.

Value-based services consist of three areas: business assessment, business case development, and value assessment.

Business assessment

SAP business assessment focuses on the business benefits you could get by implementing or enhancing IT projects. It enables you to quantify potential business value before the project begins, and then uses business value as the guiding principle throughout design and deployment. SAP Business and Value Assessment starts by analyzing the strengths, weaknesses, risks, and opportunities related to your business processes. It then reviews existing IT capabilities and future requirements and identifies areas where you can take action to best achieve results and prioritize activities.

Then you can create an initial plan, a project roadmap that describes project scope, approach, and milestones with a high-level analysis of costs and benefits.

Business case development

The second piece of value-based services, SAP business case development, helps you to build a value proposition for your IT investment. The analysis concentrates on IT costs, process efficiency, and strategic value impact. It can also provide a postimplementation review of the value you achieved.

SAP business case development provides the following:

- ✔ A defined program scope, including processes, regions, and product lines.
- ✔ A qualitative description and quantitative performance metrics that apply to your current situation.
- ✔ A qualitative description of your proposed situation based on industry best practices, specific recommendations for process design, or a long-term deployment roadmap.
- ✔ Quantitative estimates of implementation and deployment costs.
- ✔ A cost/benefit analysis, which can take the form of payback analysis, internal rate of return, net present value, and so on.
- ✔ Quantitative estimates of business benefits. These can include strategic value impacts such as effects on cross-selling; customer satisfaction; process improvements involving expenses, assets, and liabilities; and reductions in IT expenses resulting from a more effective IT infrastructure.

Setting quantitative goals for an IT project and then measuring the results help you to understand the business value that your IT investments provide, and also give you a framework for managing process improvement as you go along.

Figure 10-4 shows some typical areas where business cases have been used in mySAP ERP. Some of them fall into the area of revenue generation with new processes; others involve reducing costs and making your assets more efficient.

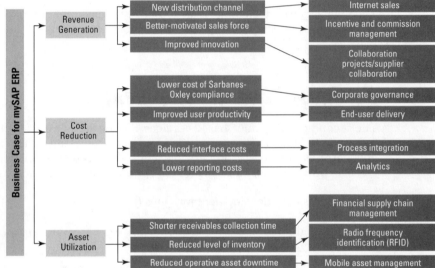

Figure 10-4: Examples of areas for business cases.

Value assessment

SAP Business and Value Assessment helps you identify the potential value of an investment in an IT project by comparing existing and proposed cost/benefit structures. This gives you a baseline for high-level return on investment calculations.

SAP Business and Value Assessment provides the following:

- ✔ Quantitative evaluation of the proposed IT investment
- ✔ Analysis of strengths, weaknesses, risks, and opportunities
- ✔ Visibility of relevant business process areas and owners
- ✔ Detailed transformation plan and roadmap
- ✔ High-level ROI analysis, including an analysis of IT costs and process efficiency

As a result, you can define gaps in your IT capabilities and process performance levels. You estimate capital expenses and identify the owners of business processes who can contribute knowledge and resources. This helps you capture the potential benefits of an IT investment and adjust costs and value drivers accordingly.

Here's a practical example. Figure 10-5 shows the results for a specific customer. Surprisingly, much of the savings came from some of the most mundane areas. The value derived from changes in the travel management and procurement procedures saved the company almost €500,000 and went a long way to justifying the cost of the implementation.

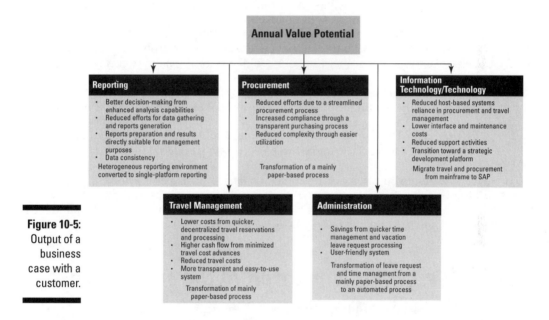

Figure 10-5: Output of a business case with a customer.

Tackling the Change Management Challenge

In the following sections, we wax a tad conceptual about implementing ERP in your organization. That's because such an implementation involves more than technology and business value calculations; it involves people.

Here we give you some advice about what attitude to use in approaching an ERP implementation, or, in fact, any strategic change in the way you do business.

ERP exposes problems to solve them

One thing you have to understand and help others in your organization to understand is that when you find a better way to do anything, you are in the business of exposing your past inadequacies. That means that you're going to tread on the feet of those who absolutely love the status quo, or who were involved in defining current processes. People become defensive or even protective of how things are done now (even if the way they are done now is painful).

If you ever had to move from one house to another, you know that digging out all that stuff in the basement that you've accumulated for years is painful. You have to go through a lot of junk, throwing some out, giving some away, and thinking that the old lamp you used to hate might just fit in perfectly in your new house. Change makes you look at all your problem stuff, so we tend to blame change, rather than our problems, for the pain we feel.

The bottom line to this piece of advice is that change is painful for everybody. Implementing solutions such as mySAP ERP, ESA, and SAP NetWeaver requires a serious shift. Try to keep folks focused and try to sympathize with their pain. Change is a process, and you're all in this together. And luckily, you have a lot of SAP support to help you get through.

The more you can involve people in change, the easier it will be. If they're involved, they feel invested. If they're outside the process, they feel like victims. Form employee advisory committees, test groups for rollouts, and focus groups to get people on board with the process.

Everybody is married to the status quo

Of course, the upside to change is that every person who ever uttered the phrase "Can't we find a better way to do this?" should be pleased that you're doing just that, right? But human nature is fickle, and these same people who thought they hated the current system could be the ones who rush forward and say "Hey, don't monkey around with what we've got — you're just making it worse."

Getting people to jump onto the bandwagon of a new system can be a long, challenging road. It's up to you to prove the value. You start by communicating the goals of your implementation right up-front. Then, you have to phase things in so there are no big surprises. Don't tackle everything up-front. Define an incremental plan and follow it. Test a process in one location, not ten. Learn from that smaller implementation, and then try it at another location.

The fact that you can use SAP components built on best practices should make things easier. After all, best practices for an industry encapsulate logical ways of doing business that support productivity and efficiency, so your people should be able to see benefits early on.

Change is hard, but the rewards can be worth it

Here's a shocker: 95 percent of the questions you have to ask yourself in implementing ERP are business questions, not technology questions. To understand why this is so, you have to consider your key tasks in this process. You have to do the following:

✔ Understand your own business and industry

✔ Define your processes and the services that support them

✔ Find ways to change your employees' behavior to make use of the self-service and collaborative tools and friendlier interfaces to technology that you are providing

The good news is that in working through these questions, you find out a lot about your business at the same time that you're making improvements to it. Always remember that technology should serve your business strategies and processes, and not the other way around.

A last few words to the wise

Finally, here are a few specific tips on how to approach your mySAP ERP implementation to get everybody on board right from the outset:

✔ **Have a clear idea of your goals and specific ways to measure them.** As we have said throughout this chapter, proving the business benefits of the implementation of an ERP solution is key. Anticipate, track, and measure your goals all along the way.

✔ **Get an executive sponsor.** Many projects have gone awry due to lack of senior-management sponsorship. Naturally, any project runs better when you know that management supports it; an ERP project is no exception.

✔ **Hold a dialogue between IT and the business people.** Keeping an open dialogue between IT and the business users is essential. Many organizations create a new role in their organization that sits between IT and the business departments, acting as neutral advisors and mediators in projects. This person keeps track of user requirements (which, of course, tend to change) as well as the compromises IT makes (which also tend to change).

✔ **Keep the implementation team on board to exploit their knowledge.** ERP does not stop after it is installed. New services and composite applications allow you to extend and grow the benefits of your ERP implementation over time. To ensure some sort of consistency, keep at least some of the team members working on continuous improvement.

Chapter 11

Building an ERP Roadmap

*I*f you've read bits and pieces of this book, you've probably picked up quite a bit about the features of mySAP ERP, SAP NetWeaver, and the whole service-enabled approach to your enterprise. But what will the experience of implementing mySAP ERP in your organization be like?

To give you a peek into the ERP implementation experience, this chapter covers some specific SAP programs and features that help you through the process after you've made the decision to go with mySAP ERP. Your account executive at SAP can guide you to more detail about these programs and tell you how to tap into them.

Zeroing in on Business Goals

Over the years, SAP has talked with a lot — and we mean a *lot* — of businesses. In doing so, it has gained tons of insight into how various industries do what they do. SAP has documented best practices and worked with partners to define useful services and tools. All this wisdom is available for you in the business process platform they have built.

As we've said many times in this book, the key to an effective, innovative enterprise isn't technology: It's an understanding of your business processes. To make Web services a reality in your corporate backyard, you need to bring technology and business together in a business process platform (see Figure 11-1). That platform consists of SAP NetWeaver's underlying technology, a repository of out-of-the-box services, SAP composite applications, and customized services and composite applications. Putting all this in place in a way that matches your corporate landscape is what an implementation is all about.

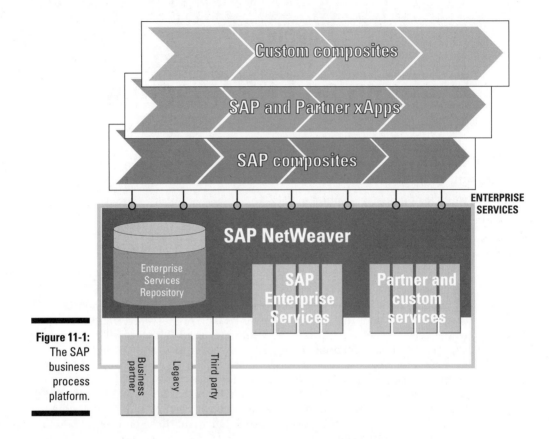

Figure 11-1:
The SAP
business
process
platform.

Understanding Your Industry

Over the years, SAP has found that a discussion of mySAP ERP should never
start with a discussion about specific tools that come out of the mySAP ERP
box, or a bullet list of features in SAP NetWeaver. Discussions should start
with your business objectives and an understanding of your enterprise's
vision.

From years of listening to businesses talk about what they do, SAP has developed more than 25 SAP industry solution maps (see Figure 11-2). These maps
help you focus on the core processes and functions that help your company
to compete, strengthen your relationships with partners, and become better
attuned to the markets and customers you serve.

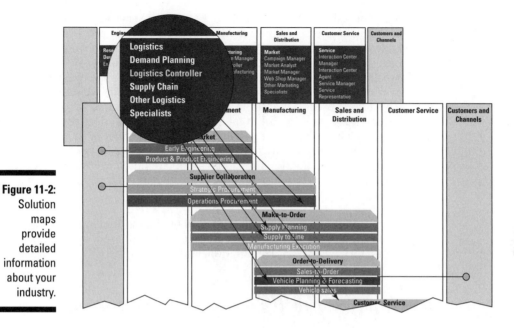

Figure 11-2:
Solution
maps
provide
detailed
information
about your
industry.

The SAP industry solution maps document and illustrate the end-to-end business processes (business scenarios) of a typical enterprise in a given industry. You can use the maps to follow the relationship of the enterprise with suppliers and partners, and customers and channels (the so-called *extended enterprise*). The scenarios shown in these maps are linked to the business processes within mySAP ERP; this gives you a head start in making the jump to SAP solutions and the world of services.

You can see all the industry solution maps by visiting www.sap.com/ solutionmaps. SAP also offers a tool called the Solution Composer that you can use to create new maps or modify existing maps. The Solution Composer helps you to visualize and plan your own company-specific IT solution. It's available at www.sap.com/solutions/businessmaps/composer.

Finding a Roadmap

Putting Web services at the heart of your IT strategy allows you to pay attention when opportunity knocks, while at the same time making the best use of your current assets. For those companies that succeed, the paybacks can be significant. Enterprise Services Architecture enables this flexibility.

But before you can get the full benefit of Enterprise Services Architecture, you have to make the decision to adapt. Adapting existing processes and the underlying technology that supports them can be complex, costly, and slow. Moreover, managers tend to dread fully revamping an existing system without some assurance that the new tools will be better than the old. What systems should you retain? What should you throw out the window? How do you weave together the old and the new? Enterprise Services Architecture is the blueprint for an architecture that enables innovation and standardization in a single environment, allowing IT management to deliver at the speed and efficiency the business requires. But how do you reconcile custom-specific applications with the functionality of packaged applications? And how do you make decisions without disrupting your carefully and methodically assembled system?

Because making the switch into a service-enabled environment means lots of change, SAP developed the ESA Adoption Program, a step-by-step approach that's useful for any SAP implementation, including mySAP ERP.

Reviewing the ESA Adoption Program

Because we love lists, we start by giving you one for ESA. Here are the four phases of the ESA Adoption Program:

- **Discovery:** Here's where you align IT and business. This is the stage where you make sure the company vision, values, challenges, opportunities, and priorities are clear to every stakeholder. In this phase, you perform TCO analyses (see Chapter 10 for more about these analyses).

- **Evaluation:** This is where you build a roadmap. You identify focus areas, outline business processes, define the services you need, and identify where you can streamline, automate, and extend processes. In general, this is where you study your IT landscape to identify any gaps or overlap. SAP supplies a tool to help with this: SAP Solution Manager.

- **Implementation:** Now it's time to lay out timelines for various processes and match them to applications and your technology infrastructure. SAP Solution Manager gives you access to the tools, content, and methodology you need to implement and make the best use of your SAP solutions so both the technology and functionality do what you want them to.

- **Operation:** This important phase is where you implement ongoing monitoring of the system and look for ways to lower costs and measure benefit and continually improve the way your systems are designed and the way they deliver solutions for your business.

SAP turned the journey to an ESA-based enterprise into a series of logical steps. The methodology is designed to streamline and simplify an otherwise complex journey and to create an evolutionary path that helps you avoid great big potholes along the way. The toolkit SAP has developed reduces adoption to a series of relatively easy, sequential activities. The goal is to help you lower costs and shorten the time you need to get to the land of ESA.

Why have an adoption program?

The Enterprise Services Architecture Adoption Program was created to help SAP, partners, and customers position, adopt, and implement Enterprise Services Architecture and the SAP NetWeaver open integration and application platform that supports it. The program uses a structured portfolio of services and associated tools that support four areas of making the move to ESA: discovery, evaluation, implementation, and operation (see Figure 11-3).

The roadmap to get to ESA consists of

 ✔ Business scenario solution mapping

 ✔ IT process technology mapping

 ✔ Drill-down and identification of potential enterprise services

	Discovery	Evaluation	Implementation	Operation
	Grasp the Vision	**Build Your Own Roadmap**	**Go Live**	**Become a Showcase**
Core Services	ESA-SAP NetWeaver Value Session ESA Opportunity Workshop TCO Discovery	SAP NetWeaver Roadmap ESA Roadmap	Plan services Build services Run services	ESA/SAP NetWeaver reference Governance guidelines ESA/SAP NetWeaver Community
Key Tools	1500 reference books DVD sales kit SAP NetWeaver Knowledge base	Competitive positioning 12 case studies ROI/TCO calculator Partner catalog Solution Map	SAP best practices CSN services	Customer Appreciation Program (CAP) Elite Customer Program
Community		**Visit ESA Today at SDN @ SDN.SAP.COM**		

Figure 11-3: An overview of the ESA Adoption Program.

Unique customers, unique needs

The adoption program is designed to accommodate the many different needs, budgets, resources, and objectives of the great, big corporate universe. Just like fingerprints, no two implementations are alike; still, using the adoption program's tools works as an effective guide whether you sell toys or investment counseling.

The fact is, as companies begin to make decisions about enhancing business processes and strategies, they utilize Enterprise Services Architecture in many different ways. Some customers rethink their entire IT strategy and want a comprehensive Enterprise Services Architecture for the entire business. Others have more immediate needs and adopt ESA just for current projects or for a specific part of their business where they need a ton of flexibility. The Enterprise Services Architecture Adoption Program anticipates all of these approaches.

ESA Adoption: A four-phase approach

As we mention in the section "Why have an adoption program?" earlier in this chapter, the adoption program is a series of logical steps (see Figure 11-4): discovery, evaluation, implementation, and operation. Each step is supported by a compact portfolio of field-tested "enablers," a dozen or so support services that include a variety of tools, templates, samples, and workshops. Like a ten-page Chinese restaurant menu, the program's flexibility allows you to select one enabler from column A and one from column B as you need them.

	Discovery	Evaluation	Implementation	Operation
User Productivity		Operating an enterprise		
		Knowledge workplace		
		Remote access		
Business Information Management		Embedded reporting, query, and analysis		
		Business planning		
		Enterprise data warehousing		
Data Unification		Content consolidation		
		Master data harmonization		
		Central master data management		
		Global data synchronization		
End-to-End Process Integration		Enabling B2B processes		
		Enabling A2A processes		
		Business process modeling		
		Enabling auto-ID infrastructure		
Consolidation		UI consolidation		
		Content consolidation		
		Adaptive computing		
Custom Development		Developing, configuring, and adapting apps.		
		Platform interoperability		
		Building composite applications		
Unified Lifecycle Management		SAP NetWeaver operations		
		Software logistics		
		Change management		
Application Governance		Unified user management, authentication, and access control		
		Message and data security		
		Service-based IT security		
Business Event Management		Business event resolution		
SOA		Enterprise service enabling		
		Service orchestration		

Figure 11-4: The roadmap to get your enterprise ESA-ready.

During the discovery phase, the emphasis is on education and understanding. Participants get together and explore the value and cost of various implementation alternatives. Tools used during this step include Opportunity Workshops. These are interactive sessions designed to identify how Enterprise Services Architecture might enhance a customer's business processes. Typically, this is where an organization's IT and business leaders sit down together (ordering out for pizza is optional, but definitely encouraged) to brainstorm the ways and areas in which a service-oriented architecture could foster innovation and lower costs.

During the second phase, evaluation, SAP works with customers to design a company-specific roadmap. Workshop activities focus on identifying the scope of ESA, the business processes that it might enhance, and the corresponding IT projects that are likely to make a company more competitive and more responsive.

The implementation phase of the adoption program is where you get down to putting Enterprise Services Architecture to work. Because SAP offers some 200 different support services to help you with planning, building, and running Enterprise Services Architecture, a key objective during this phase is to help you choose specific support tools to give you the best results.

Finally, during the operation phase, SAP provides a number of helpful tidbits to help you govern your applications and maintain a consistent strategy over time. There's a close focus on ROI during this stage, with SAP providing tools that help measure results and quantify benefits derived from Enterprise Services Architecture and from SAP NetWeaver as the underlying technology platform.

Unifying users

One really neat thing about the adoption program is the way it supports collaboration among the many people who are responsible for positioning, designing, and implementing Enterprise Services Architecture. On the customer side, business and IT leaders, IT architects, and project managers are all involved at different stages, depending on a project's scope and timetable. Similarly, SAP team members such as professionals from the SAP Consulting organization (including its business consulting and technology consulting groups) and marketing people come to call. With such diverse perspectives keeping a lookout, the adoption program serves as a valuable tool for outlining responsibilities, determining priorities, and keeping track of timelines.

For more information about the Enterprise Services Architecture Adoption Program, visit the SAP Developer Network (SDN) at www.sdn.sap.com and click the Enterprise Services Architecture (ESA) Today link.

A roadmap case study

Network Appliance, Inc. (NetApp) is a world leader in unified storage solutions, a data-intensive enterprise. Since its inception in 1992, NetApp has provided technology, product, and partner firsts that continue to drive the evolution of storage. Its storage solutions include specialized hardware, software, and services, providing seamless storage management for open network environments.

NetApp has approximately 3,200 employees across 32 global offices and revenues of $1.6 billion (FY2005). Network Appliance folks have cited the following benefits of the ESA Adoption exercise. According to this customer, the ESA Adoption program

- ✓ Indicates where a company's IT infrastructure needs to be to remain competitive

- ✓ Illustrates the potential lowering of IT TCO by lowering integration costs

- ✓ Highlights SAP Consulting expertise in Enterprise Services Architecture

- ✓ Forces companies to answer business-driving questions that can be supported by IT

- ✓ Enables companies to envision how they can leverage their existing IT investments

- ✓ Helps to document and simplify a seemingly daunting task via the roadmap

- ✓ Matches business processes with IT solutions (partners technology with business)

Getting the Most Out of SAP Solution Manager

SAP Solution Manager is a central toolset for open, end-to-end application management. All the information about your SAP and non-SAP systems is at your fingertips. SAP Solution Manager (see Figure 11-5) comes free with mySAP ERP and your annual maintenance fee.

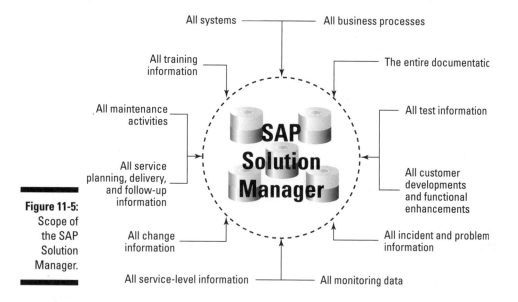

Figure 11-5:
Scope of
the SAP
Solution
Manager.

Who needs SAP Solution Manager?

This one is pretty straightforward: If you implement or upgrade to mySAP ERP, you have to use SAP Solution Manager to manage your implementation. That's OK: It will become immediately invaluable to you as you set things up now and far into the future.

SAP Solution Manager provides a large bundle of features that accelerate your mySAP ERP implementation. After your system is up and running, it requires maintenance and upgrades. SAP Solution Manager helps you maintain and monitor your systems, following SAP's best practices for application support. When you need a service from SAP's support organization, SAP Solution Manager provides direct access. These can be accessed directly and centrally via SAP Solution Manager. During the entire lifecycle of your implementation, SAP Solution Manager helps reduce your TCO and keep it low.

SAP Solution Manager doesn't just sit around documenting things. It also offers you advice about which processes you might need, which pieces you just might want to customize, areas of your business that might benefit from outsourcing, and logical upgrade paths for the future. With features such as roadmaps, testing tools, and system management tools, SAP Solution Manager is useful during your implementation period and beyond.

Getting the lowdown on what's in SAP Solution Manager

So what exactly comes with SAP Solution Manager? Is it animal, vegetable, or mineral?

SAP Solution Manager provides tools and content that

✔ Speed your implementation

✔ Help you to run an efficient operation

✔ Provide great access to all support services

In a nutshell, the following sections describe the features and functions that SAP Solution Manager provides.

Faster implementation

Implementation time is a challenge to the best of us. It requires coordination of resources and budgets, communication with a whole host of people, and documentation every step of the way. Here's how SAP Solution Manager helps:

✔ **Implementation and upgrade roadmaps:** These roadmaps provide you with valuable information that you should keep in mind during the different phases of your installation or upgrade project.

✔ **Automated system landscape information:** SAP Solution Manager is your central portal for managing your system landscape. After initial setup, every support package installation and upgrade release automatically updates your system information.

✔ **Business process repository:** Any know-how that you gain during your implementation projects is documented in your own business process repository within SAP Solution Manager. So what if your implementation team members move on to another job or retire? The knowledge of your internal business scenarios and processes stays in one place. When operating your system, you can reuse this documented business process know-how to simplify those inevitable troubleshooting episodes.

You can use SAP's standard business process repository as a template when building your own repository. SAP provides more than 260 business process configuration variants covering more than 90 percent of all business processes that mySAP ERP supports.

✔ **Project documentation:** SAP Solution Manager keeps track of any business processes that you set up and any configuration you create. It retains all knowledge of your internal process flows and implementation details inside your enterprise system centrally in your business process repository. As a result, this part of the SAP Solution Manager provides a useful process-related documentation for your entire system. In fact, many people find that SAP Solution Manager helps them gain more insight into their own businesses as they use it to analyze and track their implementation.

✔ **Global rollout:** This piece of the toolset helps you to standardize processes across your organization and its various locations by providing methodologies and preselected, relevant functionality. You can more easily implement standardized settings at local sites because you can prepare sets of customized activities related to a particular business process. Furthermore, you can create Business Configuration Sets for your subsidiaries and avoid going through the drudgery of reentering configuration settings for every local system.

✔ **Synchronization of custom settings:** With SAP Solution Manager, you can keep things consistent as you customize your distributed SAP IT environment. It enables you to administer customization with less risk, less error-prone replication of custom settings, and simpler consistency checks. SAP Solution Manager saves you from the drudgery of manual synchronization by automatically distributing custom settings to various systems and by centrally managing all requests to synchronize settings.

✔ **Testing:** SAP Solution Manager makes test preparation and execution much easier. It provides a single point of access to the complete system landscape and centrally stores testing material so you can manage cross-component tests. The detailed information you get on test coverage and the quantities of open and solved bugs lets you track testing and monitor test results very efficiently.

Efficient operation

After things are up and running, we won't kid you: You will have ongoing support and maintenance issues to deal with. Here's how SAP Solution Manager helps:

✔ **IT and application support:** The service desk included in SAP Solution Manager gives you a jump-start on problem resolution. It helps you manage those inevitable incidents more efficiently and helps you keep support costs under control. Centralized handling of support messages makes your support organization much more efficient.

✔ **Solution monitoring:** SAP Solution Manager performs centralized, real-time monitoring of systems, business processes, and interfaces, easing the burden of your administration effort. It can even monitor intersystem dependencies, where one system counts on another to perform its function. SAP Solution Manager doesn't sit around waiting for trouble to occur: Proactive monitoring helps you avoid critical situations, whereas automatic notifications help you to respond to issues with lightning speed. Besides the service desk, the solution-monitoring feature ensures that mySAP ERP is operating as it should.

✔ **Service-level management and reporting:** SAP Solution Manager allows you to easily define service levels and take advantage of automated reporting. Service reporting covers all systems in the solution landscape and gives you one, handy consolidated report containing the information you need to make those all-important IT decisions.

✔ **Maintenance planning and change request management:** To ensure that you can make improvements to your business applications as you head into tomorrow, SAP Solution Manager allows solid maintenance planning and simplifies the process of implementing changes in running systems. The change management process can be very customer-specific; you can centrally launch and monitor all steps within this process, such as request, approval, implementation, testing, release, and transport of a change.

The very best access to all support services

SAP Solution Manager offers easy access to all support services that SAP has set up for mySAP ERP, such as consolidated EarlyWatch alerts for your whole solution and GoingLive services. GoingLive supports you during the implementation phase, while EarlyWatch supports you during ongoing live production. These services involve support such as information, tools, workshops, and system performance checks. SAP Solution Manager also makes recommendations for services, such as SAP Safeguarding, which helps you manage technical risk; SAP Solution Management Optimization, which helps you get the most from your SAP solutions; and SAP Empowering, which helps you manage your solutions.

Chapter 12

Following ERP into the Future

More than 20 years ago, enterprise resource planning software started to play a significant role in helping IT executives to cut costs and increase efficiency. These earlier solutions included standard financial, human capital management (HCM) or human resources, and basic operational (order entry, materials management) features. These early off-the-shelf ERP applications enabled IT organizations to reduce application backlogs and implement standard business processes.

Today, however, companies are faced with a very different world. They have less time to get it right and more pressure to do so. Today, innovation occurs with stunning speed, even as the window of opportunity for capitalizing on innovation seems to get smaller every day.

In 2004, SAP launched its next-generation ERP solution, mySAP ERP 2004, which was followed a year later by mySAP ERP 2005. mySAP ERP is an evolution from the traditional ERP solution. It not only allows companies to become more efficient, but it also allows companies to react faster to business change.

But mySAP ERP was just the first step toward a whole new direction for ERP. So where are mySAP ERP and ESA headed in the future? In this chapter, we look into our (informed) crystal ball.

The SAP Roadmap for ESA and ERP

As we discuss throughout this book, Enterprise Services Architecture (ESA) is SAP's open architecture where technology is turned into business processes using enterprise services. This is all done using Web services as building blocks to automate enterprise-wide business scenarios. ESA is central to the future direction of mySAP ERP.

The ESA Roadmap, recently published by SAP, helps you to benefit from a modern service-oriented architecture that allows high flexibility while keeping down the cost of change.

In a nutshell, here's where the road ahead leads: Future development will further integrate SAP NetWeaver technology with the applications, specifically mySAP ERP, leading to the creation of the Business Process Platform (BPP). Applications will be based on ESA and provide enterprise services.

Specifically, the current roadmap for current and future versions of mySAP ERP is as follows:

- ✔ **2005:** SAP delivered an inventory of enterprise services, including the first service-enabled scenarios focused on collaboration, end-user needs, and business process flexibility. Customers buying mySAP ERP 2005 can make use of the SAP ESA Adoption Program, take the first steps in their own ESA Roadmap to make the transition to ESA, build business process composition skills, design their own enterprise services, and get experience with service-oriented architecture.

- ✔ **2006:** SAP will provide an extended ESA inventory with hundreds of ERP enterprise services, which are implemented and delivered on top of mySAP ERP 2004 and mySAP ERP 2005. You'll also be able to execute major blocks of the ESA Roadmap by extending the ESA Inventory with your own enterprise services. Additional content (new roles and analytics functionality) may also be made available during the year.

- ✔ **2007:** Here's where you'll be able to more fully benefit from ESA and reach new levels of differentiating yourself by composing custom processes, as well as using new composite applications.

These future developments are geared to bring more flexibility and reduce the cost of ownership for mySAP ERP. Plans are underway to make technical implementation and maintenance much easier, organizing the process of planning things like how many servers are needed, and setting the stage for easier upgrading down the road. In addition, these future releases offer some really cool tools such as Adobe for Printing and more guided procedures to help users make their own way through business processes.

Future mySAP ERP releases will provide more functions for specific industries. Up until now, the industry solutions were shipped in various ways. Some were shipped with mySAP ERP; others were add-ons that were shipped up to six months later. Starting with mySAP ERP 2005, almost all the industry solutions are shipped together with the ERP software. You can activate the appropriate industry solution using new technology called the *switch framework*. The switch framework essentially allows you to switch on the industry functionality you want instantly.

Table 12-1 outlines SAP's guiding principles for future developments in mySAP ERP.

Table 12-1   **Guiding Development Principles for mySAP ERP**

Guiding Principle	Business Benefit Objective	SAP Development Focus	Examples of New Capabilities
Increase efficiency	Bring all the relevant applications, information, and services to the chosen device of an individual to allow him to complete his daily tasks faster. Ensure rapid adoption for even casual users and promote increased collaboration. This can apply to an employee or business partner such as a supplier or customer.	Using a portal as entry to system, support for multiple devices (PCs, PDAs, mobile phones), standardization of user interfaces across all solutions, creation of roles and content, and integration of standards to support.	Preconfigured user business roles (generic and specific) with focused business process content. Guided procedures to assist occasional users through complex tasks. Latest and unified user-interface technology. Use of Adobe forms for information-gathering.
Creating value-adding capabilities	Ensure that capability to fulfill current and future business requirements is available in a standard ERP system. This is not limited to standard human capital management (HCM), financials, and operational capability, but also corporate services such as real estate and travel management capability.	Continuous focus on key areas of HCM, financials, operations, and corporate services. Exploration of new composite solutions. Incorporation of industry standards, and legal and regulatory requirements. Extension of business processes outside traditional organizational limits.	New financial, general ledger, and financial supply chain management. RFID technologies. E-learning and e-recruiting. Easier business consolidation and express planning. Occupational health improvements.

(continued)

Table 12-1 (continued)

Guiding Principle	Business Benefit Objective	SAP Development Focus	Examples of New Capabilities
Analytics for transparency and compliance	Organizations, employees, customers, and partners need relevant information and need to understand the activities across the entire business network to make informed decisions. Additionally, organizations need to be compliant with an ever-growing number of regulatory laws.	Creation of central reporting tools, adoption of business process monitoring, creation of predefined content with roles, embedding of analytics into all business processes, and creation of integrated planning framework.	Strategic enterprise management. Predefined analytical dashboards. Business content for roles. Tools to support regulatory compliance. Service-level management.
Increasing software solution flexibility	Ensure IT organizations have the agility and flexibility to enable, modify, and deploy processes to support the fast-changing business requirements in a timely manner. Give organizations the ability to easily integrate heterogeneous system landscapes using Web standards.	Service-enabling of specific functionality, development of a services platform. Development of an open framework for composite solutions. Easier integration of systems, both technically and using master data management.	Service-enabling of functionality (financials, invoicing, billing, HCM, enterprise learning, and talent management). Creation of composites for dispute and collections management.
Improving the TCO	Reduce the total cost ownership over the lifecycle of the solution, from implementation through operation and continuous improvements. Ensure that existing investments in IT infrastructure are leveraged.	Compatibility from one release to the next is assured, simplified system implementation, operations and upgrades with Solution Manager, flexible deployment options for outsourcing and shared services, and consolidation of applications.	Simplification of system landscape — reduced number of instances needed for solution. Consolidation of industry solutions. Preconfigured solutions. Best practices for mySAP ERP. Flexible deployment options (financials, travel accounting, travel administration, HCM, payroll, time and attendance, benefits administration, and enterprise learning).

Embracing SAP NetWeaver

For the next three years, mySAP ERP will continue to build on SAP NetWeaver, working toward the creation of the BPP. But before we head off into tomorrow, we'll try to figure out where we're going by looking backward for a moment.

The traditional footprint of SAP R/3 (up to release SAP R/3 4.6c) was a stand-alone system, where employees mostly acted as the integrators in business processes, running around gathering what they needed to get their work done with different systems, as shown in Figure 12-1.

With the introduction of SAP R/3 Enterprise, the technology layer of SAP R/3 made use of much of the SAP NetWeaver Application Server (SAP NetWeaver AS) for the first time (see Figure 12-2). This made the system a bit more efficient.

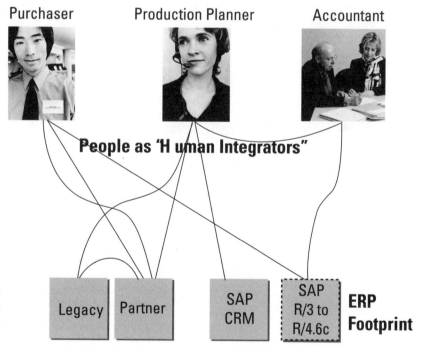

Figure 12-1:
Hard-wired
enterprise
systems.

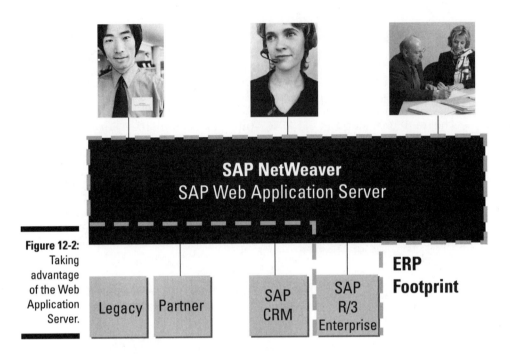

Figure 12-2:
Taking
advantage
of the Web
Application
Server.

The SAP NetWeaver AS formed the new technology foundation for all SAP applications, which didn't just use the SAP NetWeaver AS, but were actually built on it. Also, mySAP ERP from 2004 forward makes extensive use of other SAP NetWeaver components, such as the SAP NetWeaver Portal and the SAP Business Information Warehouse (SAP BW), to offer role-based access and integrated analytics.

See Chapter 4 for more about analytics and Chapter 3 for more about role-based access.

In future releases of mySAP ERP, the further integration of SAP NetWeaver is as sure as ants at a picnic. Analytics will play a bigger role to ensure that all the information in a company is available to everybody who needs it. Tighter integration with portals will offer a much better user experience as role-based information is actively pushed to the user (see Figure 12-3).

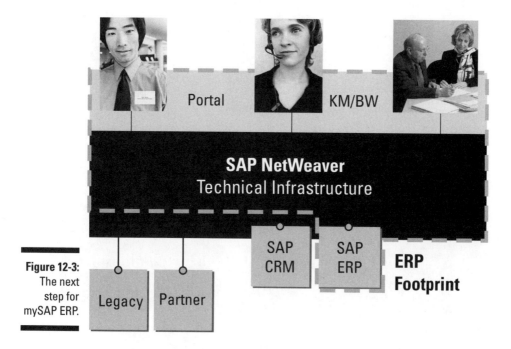

Figure 12-3:
The next
step for
mySAP ERP.

mySAP ERP 2004 was also one of the first solutions within SAP to make use of composites, where you can quickly build and maintain flexible applications on top of your existing infrastructure. Composites will be a major development focus of future mySAP ERP releases. Already in mySAP ERP, processes such as Create Product, Change Product, or New Employee Hire act as composite processes. In mySAP ERP 2005, more composites were introduced, such as Guided Procedures in self-service applications. All of these use SAP NetWeaver as the underlying technology.

Additionally, partners can make use of the infrastructure to create and develop their own composites, and organizations can leverage both SAP and partner composites to create their own individual applications (see Figure 12-4).

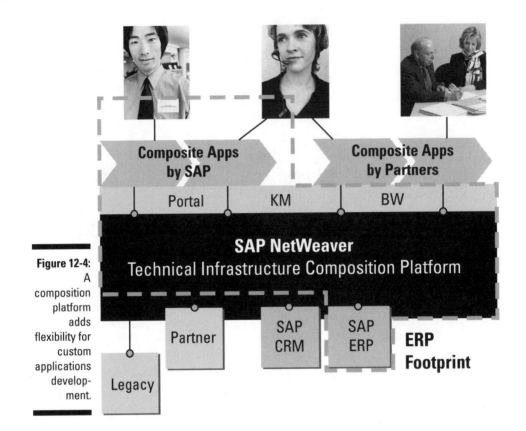

Figure 12-4:
A
composition
platform
adds
flexibility for
custom
applications
develop-
ment.

Future development of mySAP ERP will further embrace Web services as a foundation of Enterprise Services Architecture. A repository to contain and describe services (see Figure 12-5) is being further developed, and plans were announced in 2005 to introduce the first batch of several hundred services. Services including basic functionality (for example, currency conversion), UI services (such as sales order status), and complex services (such as Create Purchase Order and Generate a List of Absent Employees) will be included.

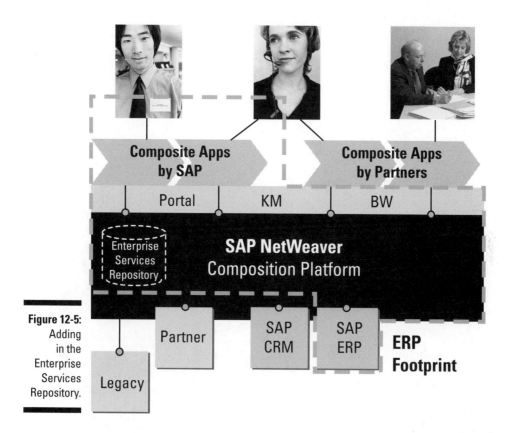

Figure 12-5:
Adding
in the
Enterprise
Services
Repository.

Finally, with the repository complete, SAP NetWeaver will become a platform for orchestrating business processes (see Figure 12-6). Functionality will be moved from some applications and centralized within the platform. This functionality can then be used by a variety of different applications. For example, the functionality for a call center could be moved to the platform, where it can be used by ERP applications for an employee call center. However, a CRM application can also use the functionality as the basis for a custom interaction center.

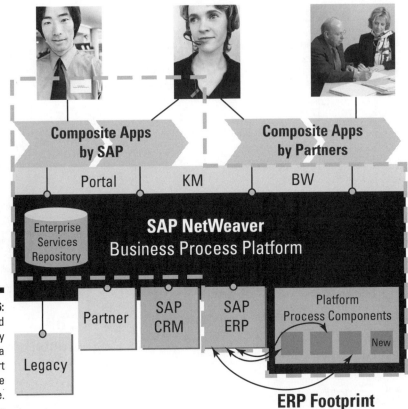

Figure 12-6:
Shared
functionality
becomes a
bigger part
of the
picture.

Using this approach, mySAP ERP, along with other applications, will use
common elements within the platform. This means a lot less complexity
and more flexible systems because the new composite applications can be
built around the services offered by the platform, whether from SAP or from
partners.

Enterprise Services Architecture adopted by mySAP ERP

mySAP ERP is one of the major players in keeping the promise of SAP's
Enterprise Services Architecture Roadmap. As SAP NetWeaver is the technical foundation of ESA, SAP invested heavily in the integration of various SAP
NetWeaver features that are fundamental to enabling the service-oriented
approach, including

✔ Transparent service definition in the SAP NetWeaver Infrastructure (SAP NetWeaver XI)

✔ Flexible processes definition via guided procedures integrating Adobe Forms

✔ Fast and user-friendly master data search via embedded search functionality

✔ Enhanced flexibility via Web Dynpro–based user interfaces

✔ Increased efficiency by leveraging Enterprise Portal features

✔ Better insight via embedded analytics and integrated analytical applications

But what will happen from a business point of view? Following the ESA Roadmap, mySAP ERP 2005 allows

✔ Increased efficiency, higher automation, and greater productivity. These will all save time and money by reducing errors and reducing the number of steps in a process.

✔ Higher flexibility that allows easier integration. This will allow you to build end-to-end business processes reusing existing assets.

✔ Faster innovation by using new processes that benefit from collaboration inside and outside of your company.

How will all this come about? By further implementing ESA, improvements to the platform, and changes in mySAP ERP.

Composites grow in importance

Future development of mySAP ERP will rely heavily on the use of composite applications. Composites use the handy building blocks of services to create flexible applications that you can quickly create and modify. These applications will not only improve the collaboration within your enterprise, but also offer you a clear shot at higher efficiency. You get these efficiencies by using the blueprint character of the composites from SAP on top of mySAP ERP. You can easily adopt the processes and create nifty-looking and functional user interfaces with the modeling capabilities and the visual toolset that you find in the Composite Application Framework. For streamlined processes, SAP will offer wizard-like guided procedures that are especially helpful for more straightforward processes.

Using dashboards

Analytics — those charts, graphs, reports, and so on that tell you how your business is doing — have become feature-rich in mySAP ERP. Dashboards give users a graphical integration of all their analytics, and visual tools in SAP

NetWeaver enable you to quickly create new or adapt existing dashboards by using new services. This functionality will improve in the future with the increasing number of enterprise services that SAP will deliver with the next mySAP ERP versions.

SAP will deliver more services that push important events to the people — regardless of the environment they are in. New dashboards will not only provide the relevant information at a glance but also will offer options to act on those events. Integrating Microsoft Office documents and other unstructured data, as well as being able to search and retrieve relevant information across applications, will also allow better decision-making.

Services and scenarios grow

A common shared Enterprise Services Repository that includes mySAP ERP enterprise services integrated with the other services in your enterprise is at the root of many improvements in years to come. With the existing tools of SAP NetWeaver, open standards, and tighter tool integration in the near future, IT gets more flexible.

In the next versions of mySAP ERP, you'll see more integration scenarios and composite applications that make intelligent use of services based on SAP NetWeaver. Enhancing processes with these robust engines while increasing the flexibility in a step-by-step approach will also lead to faster innovation. You keep control of your projects and get a faster return on investment.

How mySAP ERP Will Change Going Forward

In the preceding sections, we talk about how the changes in the Business Process Platform and following the vision of the ESA Roadmap will have an impact on your business. Now it's time to take a peek, specifically, at how the features of mySAP ERP will change going forward. We have structured the changes along the mySAP ERP solution map that you can find on the Cheat Sheet at the front of this book.

People get even more productive

As with mySAP ERP 2005, future versions will provide intuitive access for every employee to all the information, applications, and services they need to do their work. Intuitive design and online access to broader, more accurate information will be another boon to employees.

SAP will continue the new user-centric approach focused on the productivity of people in developing future versions of mySAP ERP. All this underlines the evolution of mySAP ERP as a next-generation ERP solution.

Think about it: In SAP R/3, the focus was on data and process consistency. This is still true in mySAP ERP; however, in the future, SAP will continue to add flexibility, speed, and convenience for the user.

Giving people more analytical applications

mySAP ERP 2005 delivers more than 100 predefined analytical applications (such as blocked order lists, recruiting analytics, and manufacturing order lists) that utilize a rich and highly interactive user interface to deliver information. Future mySAP ERP releases will include more analytical applications that address many business issues as well as specific requirements for different industries.

The future direction of SAP Analytics for ERP will be clearly centered around two main areas:

- ✔ Enabling business people with analytics in their day-to-day work by providing embedded decision support right in the process
- ✔ Enabling the analytics architecture to make use of enterprise services in order to provide flexibility and adaptability

Enterprise Services Architecture will be the future foundation for SAP Analytics for ERP, allowing you to seamlessly connect real-time and replicated data, operative and strategic data, and SAP and third-party data.

Analytics is and will be an integral part of the mySAP ERP solution and one of its functional building blocks. The development focus will be on providing whole scenarios across business processes with analytics that cross over any divisions of data or applications. This will include measuring the performance of scenarios or processes by using Business Activity Monitoring. To see the current availability of analytics in mySAP ERP, see Figure 12-7.

mySAP ERP *Analytics*				
End-User Service Delivery	**Strategic Enterprise Management**	**Financial Analytics**	**Operations Analytics**	**Workforce Analytics**
Manager Self-Service	Legal and Management Consolidation	Financial and Management Reporting	Procurement Analytics	Strategic Alignment
Employee Self-Service	Balanced Scorecard	Financial Planning, Budgeting and Forecasting	Inventory and Warehouse Management Analytics	Reporting and Benchmarking
Interaction Center	Risk Management	Profitability Management	Manufacturing Analytics	
Roles	Management Cockpit	Product and Service Cost Management	Transportation Analytics	
Delivery Channels	Strategic Planning	Overhead Cost Management and ABC/M	Sales Analytics	
	Value-Based Management	Payment Behavior Analytics	Customer Service Analytics	
	Financial Statement Planning	Working Capital and Cash Flow Management	Program and Project Management Analytics	
	Investment Planning		Quality Management Analytics	
	Stakeholder Relationship Management		Enterprise Asset Management Analytics	

Figure 12-7: The current availability of analytics and user productivity with mySAP ERP.

mySAP ERP Financials

Financials is where ERP started, and they are still at the heart of any organization. Building on 20 years of financial management features, the future development of mySAP ERP Financials will focus on supply chain management and financial and management accounting as well as support for building shared service organizations for the financial functions within an organization. The current functionality of mySAP ERP Financials is outlined in Figure 12-8.

mySAP ERP *Financials*			
Financial Supply Chain Management	**Financial Accounting**	**Management Accounting**	**Corporate Governance**
Credit Management	General Ledger	Profit Center Accounting	Audit Information System
Electronic Bill Presentment and Payment	Accounts Receivable	Cost Center and Internal Order Accounting	Management of Internal Controls
Collections Management	Accounts Payable	Project Accounting	Business Risk Management
Dispute Management	Fixed Assets Accounting	Investment Management	Whistle Blower Complaints
In-house Cash	Bank Accounting	Product Cost Accounting	Transparency for Basel II
Cash and Liquidity Management	Cash Journal Accounting	Profitability Accounting	
Treasury and Risk Management	Inventory Accounting	Revenue and Cost Planning	
	Tax Accounting	Transfer Pricing	
	Accrual Accounting		
	Fast Close		
	Financial Statements		
	Parallel Valuation		

Figure 12-8: The current mySAP ERP Financials functionality.

Figuring out the financial supply chain challenge

Supply chain management involves coordinating the supplies you have coming into your operation so you're neither understocked nor overstocked. This concept can save a company big bucks as it keeps inventories lean. *Financial supply chain management* refers to the cash flow that runs parallel to the supply chain within or between companies. Keeping enough cash on hand to stock up on supplies, but not so much cash that it's not available to other parts of your operation, can also save you money. The financial supply chain automates and optimizes all financial processes between companies, connecting customers, suppliers, banks, and other service providers. The challenge is to seamlessly integrate your financial processes to get specific benefits, such as

- ✔ Optimizing working capital
- ✔ Significantly reducing the cost of the financial processes
- ✔ Greatly improving cash flow planning

The ability to optimize the financial supply chain is closely linked to technology and your organization. Technologically, the Enterprise Services Architecture is the basic prerequisite for communicating flexibly, efficiently, and securely with business partners both within and between companies. You also need open standards so that different standards don't slow the electronic exchange of business documents.

The acceleration and automation of the financial supply chain has to be backed up by integrated, analytic applications to help people make wise decisions about when and where your cash flows. You have to be able to access all information that is relevant to you through a completely redesigned, intuitive user interface.

With mySAP ERP 2005, SAP still provides proven solutions for electronic invoicing, automatic invoice verification, and structured complaints processing, but SAP has now added solutions for protecting against customer default risks as well as currency risks and interest rate risks. These integrated parts of mySAP ERP Financials allow more precise and up-to-date planning of your cash flow.

So where is this all going in the future? Because any delays in getting payments cost lots of time and incur avoidable fees, with mySAP ERP 2007, SAP will give you ways to securely and electronically handle all payment transactions based on Web services. This shift will eliminate doing any piece of the process manually. A little thing called *straight-through processing* (STP) provides the magic here. Here's an example of STP: After payment orders are submitted to a bank, the order status can be monitored online and the payment can be canceled as long as the bank hasn't yet completed the transaction. This kind of access to processing information gives your company more control over payments.

You can implement STP via a shared service center or using service providers for outsourcing. The Web services provided by SAP, based on a service-oriented architecture, provide this flexibility as well as the necessary interfaces.

Financial and management accounting

With mySAP ERP Financials, companies of all sizes and from any industry can effectively and cost-efficiently meet national and international accounting requirements, such as US-GAAP and IAS compliance, multicurrency capability, and multiple language support. So where are mySAP ERP Financials today, and where are they going tomorrow?

With mySAP ERP 2004, SAP delivered a completely revised version of the general ledger that beats the classic general ledger by providing several key features:

- A standardized general ledger that meets all business requirements
- Closely linked financial and management accounting
- Real mapping of parallel accounting principles and valuations
- Delivery of industry-specific, extendable general ledger templates
- The ability to split payments in such a way that, for example, part of a payment can be allocated to a product profit center and another to a service profit center in your general ledger
- Increased transparency and, consequently, improved auditing capabilities for corporate governance
- Faster period-end closing

With mySAP ERP 2005, SAP continued to offer its current customers migration solutions that were first put to the test with mySAP ERP 2004 and are now available to all customers. The new general ledger also meets all legal, national, and international accounting principles. For example, stricter legal requirements regarding revenue recognition gave rise to extensions and improvements in this area; these new features will be delivered with mySAP ERP 2007.

In mySAP ERP 2005, user interfaces and critical operational business processes in financials and management accounting, such as all activities related to period-end closing, were reworked entirely. By mySAP ERP 2007, all current and future user groups will be provided with new user interfaces and integrated, role-specific analytic applications.

mySAP ERP Human Capital Management (mySAP ERP HCM)

More than ever, a company's people are the key differentiator for its success. Key human capital management (HCM) strategies that contribute to this business edge include things like improving workforce efficiency and productivity, delivering best-in-class HR services at the lowest possible cost, planning workforce needs and measuring strategies, finding the right talent for today and building talent for tomorrow, educating the workforce, and aligning and motivating people to achieve company goals and objectives. Together, these strategies help maximize your human capital investment.

SAP's goal is to enable execution of these strategic workforce processes through technology. Combining a whole slew of human capital processes with self-services, analytics, and flexible technology, you can consolidate your human capital processes onto one global platform, distribute them to everyone in the organization, and provide the analytical data to plan for your workforce future. The current mySAP ERP HCM functionality is outlined in Figure 12-9.

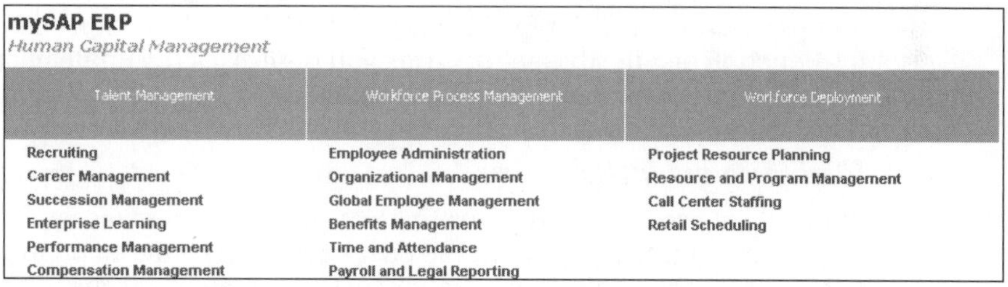

Figure 12-9: The current mySAP ERP HCM functionality.

mySAP ERP
Human Capital Management

Talent Management	Workforce Process Management	Workforce Deployment
Recruiting	Employee Administration	Project Resource Planning
Career Management	Organizational Management	Resource and Program Management
Succession Management	Global Employee Management	Call Center Staffing
Enterprise Learning	Benefits Management	Retail Scheduling
Performance Management	Time and Attendance	
Compensation Management	Payroll and Legal Reporting	

Talent Management and Workforce Processes

The human capital processes supported within mySAP ERP will continue to comprise two general groupings: talent management and workforce processes. Talent management includes processes spanning the entire "hire-to-retire" spectrum of the employee lifecycle, including sourcing, applicant tracking, career/succession management, learning, and performance management. Workforce Processes comprise the foundational employee processes like payroll and benefits, also called "deploy-to-pay."

mySAP ERP integrates and connects these pieces, creating end-to-end business processes and transforming the way your company can acquire, influence, and retain your employees. For example, connecting succession planning with development plans and performance management means you can spot high-potential employees, plan their development, and monitor their progress.

mySAP ERP will continue with the strategy of "globalization with localization." This gives you a basis for standardizing global human resource processes while at the same time providing legal compliance and best practices in each individual country.

HCM Service Delivery

If you want to be able to take full advantage of strategic human capital processes, you have to be able to make those processes available as services to everyone in the organization. As HR data and processes touch potentially every employee in the company, HCM solutions end up being used by just about everybody. Given that not all employees have browser access, you have to support multiple ways of getting at the system, for example, at a kiosk, by voice, and from mobile devices. You must also use methods like mail, telephone, and a help desk to initiate service requests.

mySAP ERP combines all these components and strategies as HCM Service Delivery, which allows organizations to implement and manage a comprehensive shared services strategy (shared services are a way to place a piece of a business process scenario in a central location to make it available to many groups). New in mySAP ERP 2005 is the employee interaction center and the introduction of a flexible set of forms and processes to supplement the existing self-services for managers and employees.

Workforce analytics

When people are involved, tools to create strategies and measure them are crucial. Workforce analytics in the past have been centered on process measurement (for example, how much it costs to create a paycheck). Workforce analytics today, integrated with ERP data, provide many more dimensions of insight: relations between human capital investment with business outcomes, workforce trends and demographics, and workforce planning. This gives you a better basis to implement strategies that you can measure and monitor over time. mySAP ERP combines workforce data with ERP data to give you an in-depth picture of how workforce factors can contribute to business planning and success.

Integration of content and services from third parties, as well as process outsourcing, plays a key role in a comprehensive HCM solution. Enterprise Services Architecture makes these strategies work, providing industry-standard methodologies to quickly integrate processes across business boundaries and to easily enable outsourcing. Providing the platform to construct composite applications and processes on top of those that SAP provides helps your organization quickly respond to new demands related to your best asset: your people.

Taken together, mySAP ERP capabilities have the sophistication and breadth to help you better manage your people investments. You can also answer questions like "Have we identified and are we developing our next wave of leaders?" and "Do we know which human capital investments have the greatest impact on business performance?"

mySAP ERP Operations

The roadmap for mySAP ERP Operations, the part of ERP that handles things like order entry, procurement, and production planning, also continues to build the focus on services and makes use of the Business Process Platform wherever it makes sense to.

In the following sections, we provide some highlights of the adoption of this ESA Roadmap in mySAP ERP Operations.

Procurement and logistics execution

Purchasing has been undergoing a quiet revolution in recent years as businesses have realized that, among other things, effective supply management is a big contributor to profitability. The current procurement and logistics functionality in mySAP EPR Operations is outlined in Figure 12-10.

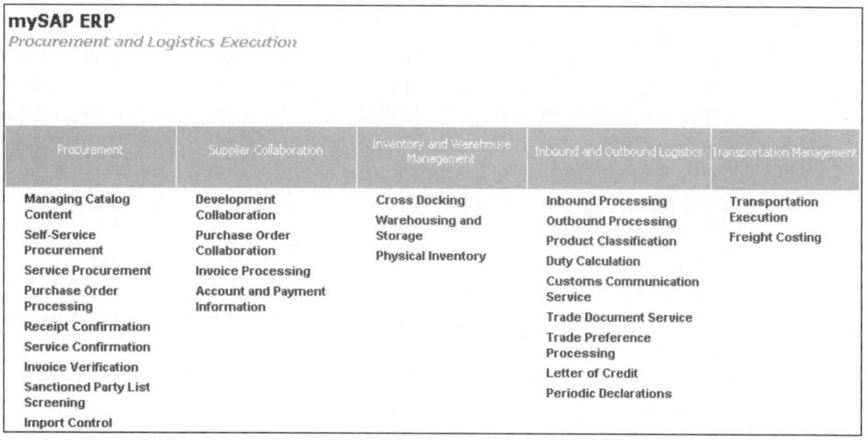

Figure 12-10: The current mySAP ERP Operations functionality in procurement and logistics.

mySAP ERP
Procurement and Logistics Execution

Procurement	Supplier Collaboration	Inventory and Warehouse Management	Inbound and Outbound Logistics	Transportation Management
Managing Catalog Content	Development Collaboration	Cross Docking	Inbound Processing	Transportation Execution
Self-Service Procurement	Purchase Order Collaboration	Warehousing and Storage	Outbound Processing	Freight Costing
Service Procurement	Invoice Processing	Physical Inventory	Product Classification	
Purchase Order Processing	Account and Payment Information		Duty Calculation	
Receipt Confirmation			Customs Communication Service	
Service Confirmation			Trade Document Service	
Invoice Verification			Trade Preference Processing	
Sanctioned Party List Screening			Letter of Credit	
Import Control			Periodic Declarations	

Future scenarios that will be delivered in mySAP ERP Operations to help to deal with the new purchasing landscape include

- ✔ **Service procurement — temporary labor:** Companies in all industries are relying on resources from third parties for their day-to-day activities and projects. This scenario supports employees from line managers or project managers to fill-in temporary staff.

- ✔ **Supplier order collaboration:** This scenario is a big motivator for employees because they get what they need to do their jobs through self-services. In the supplier order collaboration scenario, the supplier responds to the purchase order the buyer creates in mySAP ERP. They jointly agree on delivery quantities, dates, terms, and conditions (this is the collaboration bit). Supplier collaboration also includes bill creation and enterprise services, so the supplier can check on a payment's status. For the large number of small suppliers, who often don't have systems in place to exchange documents electronically, this order collaboration platform will provide a system that can save them money and effort.

- ✔ **Invoice Monitoring System (IMS):** A new invoice preprocessing feature covers various invoice exception scenarios. For example, if a customer places an order and receives the product but decides to return it, the invoice processing suddenly veers off its expected course. A Returns Exception could cover that contingency. In case of exceptions, workflow documentation is sent, including supplier notifications. Another feature speeds invoice verification by automatically matching invoices with purchase orders based on predefined variables and tolerances. You get a reduction in manual processing, comfortable and intuitive user interfaces, and a faster processing time.

Production planning and manufacturing gets more mobile

mySAP ERP lays the foundation of SAP Manufacturing. This is a comprehensive, integrated package that allows manufacturers to plan, schedule, sequence, execute, and monitor production and maintenance. The application also helps manufacturing folks to comply with health and safety standards. It gives managers and production personnel a real-time peek into manufacturing operations so they can take quick, appropriate action to keep things humming.

Over the next three years, several manufacturing features related to mobile devices will slot into place in mySAP ERP. Supply chains continue to grow leaner every day. Inevitably, however, the leaner your inventory, the more exposed your supply chain is to production issues or unexpected changes in customer demand. One result of this is that the burden of replenishing customer orders without a drop in service levels continues to shift to the factory.

Being able to tap into data about what's happening on the shop floor is therefore becoming critical. Mobile and RFID-enabled business processes are meant to close this "real-time" gap.

SAP's mobile capabilities in a manufacturing environment will come to the rescue. The main goal here is to give production personnel the ability to get away from their desktop computers, and yet still be able to monitor and detect manufacturing exceptions as and when they happen. This lets people respond proactively and resolve these exceptions before they became major headaches. Mobile asset management scenarios also make maintenance personnel more efficient, decreasing equipment downtime.

The adoption and use of RFID (radio frequency identification) in the retail and distribution environments is another shift that will start to appear on the factory floor. RFID is a way to track things with tags, sort of like a next-generation bar code. If your pooch has an implanted ID chip that the pound can use to identify her, you're already using RFID technology. In a manufacturing setting, stringent regulations are creating the need for "cradle-to-grave" audit trails that RFID tags and readers make possible. Industries such as pharmaceuticals and life sciences will increasingly see the use of RFID on the shop floor for tracking customer orders, inventory management across the production lifecycle, and quality compliance. Signals captured from RFID tags can be used to alert you to exceptions and deviations from key performance indicators as they happen.

Product development and lifecycle data management

The current product development and manufacturing functionality in mySAP ERP Operations is outlined in Figure 12-11.

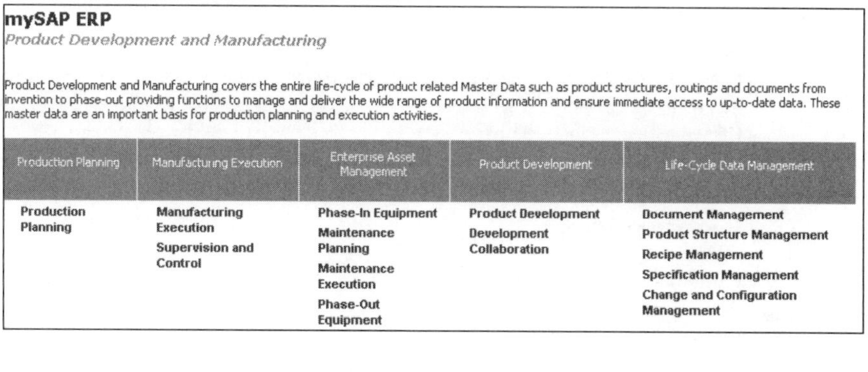

Figure 12-11: The current mySAP ERP Operations functionality in product development and manufacturing.

mySAP ERP
Product Development and Manufacturing

Product Development and Manufacturing covers the entire life-cycle of product related Master Data such as product structures, routings and documents from invention to phase-out providing functions to manage and deliver the wide range of product information and ensure immediate access to up-to-date data. These master data are an important basis for production planning and execution activities.

Production Planning	Manufacturing Execution	Enterprise Asset Management	Product Development	Life-Cycle Data Management
Production Planning	Manufacturing Execution Supervision and Control	Phase-In Equipment Maintenance Planning Maintenance Execution Phase-Out Equipment	Product Development Development Collaboration	Document Management Product Structure Management Recipe Management Specification Management Change and Configuration Management

The long-term development in managing the life of your products will be driven by SAP's product lifecycle management (PLM) strategy, leading to improvements in two major areas:

✔ **Lifecycle Data Management:** In this area, SAP will focus on enabling Enterprise Services Architecture for underlying product-related data, especially product structures. (A *product structure* is essentially all the details of what constitutes a product; it's a list of each individual element that is assembled to make the finished goods.) You'll be able to take advantage of the advanced product structure of the mySAP product lifecycle management (mySAP PLM) solution, which is known as the integrated product and process structure (IPPE). The result will be easier integration with partner and third-party applications.

✔ **Lifecycle Process Support:** In this area, SAP will focus on creating an even deeper integration of mySAP PLM with the other applications of the mySAP Business Suite. For example, they'll integrate with mySAP SRM to improve strategic sourcing, and with mySAP SCM to create a combination of product and inventory collaboration scenarios. In addition, SAP plans to improve integration into CAD solutions, engineering change management, and manufacturing and design partner collaboration. Other areas for future improvement include the management of software used in products and configuration management for software and hardware.

Sales and service

The current sales and service functionality in mySAP ERP Sales and Service is outlined in Figure 12-12.

mySAP ERP
Sales and Service

The Sales & Service area addresses the customer focusing processes like selling products and services and providing aftermarket services. It enables sales organizations to manage the sales cycle, sales and service orders and the subsequent activities.

Sales Order Management	Aftermarket Sales and Service	Professional-Service Delivery	Global Trade Services	Incentive and Commission Management
Account Processing	Phase-In Equipment	Project Planning and Scoping	Sanctioned Party List Screening	Incentive Plan Maintenance
Internet Sales	Phase-Out Equipment	Project Resource Planning	Export Control	Incentive Processing
Managing Auctions	Asset Scrapping	Quotation Processing	Product Classification	
Inquiry Processing	Product and Warranty Registration	Sales Order Processing	Duty Calculation	
Quotation Processing	Warranty Claim Processing	Project Execution	Customs Communication Service	
Sales Order Processing	Service Contract Processing	Managing Employee Time and Attendance	Trade Document Service	
Mobile Sales	Maintenance Plan Processing	Travel Expense Management	Trade Preference Processing	
Inbound Telesales	Mobile Measurement and Counter Reading	Project Accounting	Restitution Handling	
Contract Processing	Service Employee Resource Planning	Resource-Related Billing	Letter of Credit	
Billing	Service Notification Processing	Resource-Related Intercompany Billing	Periodic Declarations	
Returnable Packaging Management	Service Order Processing	Billing		
Consignment	Billing			
	Returns Processing			
	In-House Repair Processing			

Figure 12-12: The current mySAP ERP Sales and Service functionality.

Future developments in the area of sales and service will focus on the use of business objects and core capabilities provided by the Business Process Platform. For example, new features could be used for telephony integration, to manage sales opportunities and service activities, and for broader applications of Internet pricing configuration (IPC). (IPC is a Web tool used to configure products; for example, think of how you can build a virtual car on a car manufacturer's site.)

mySAP ERP Corporate Services

mySAP ERP Corporate Services is your best friend when it comes to supporting administrative processes in the areas of quality management; environment, health, and safety; project portfolio management; real-estate management; and travel management. These are the types of processes that just about every business uses to keep its doors open for business. Improving efficiency in these areas can save everybody money. An overview of current mySAP ERP Corporate Services functionality can be found in Figure 12-13.

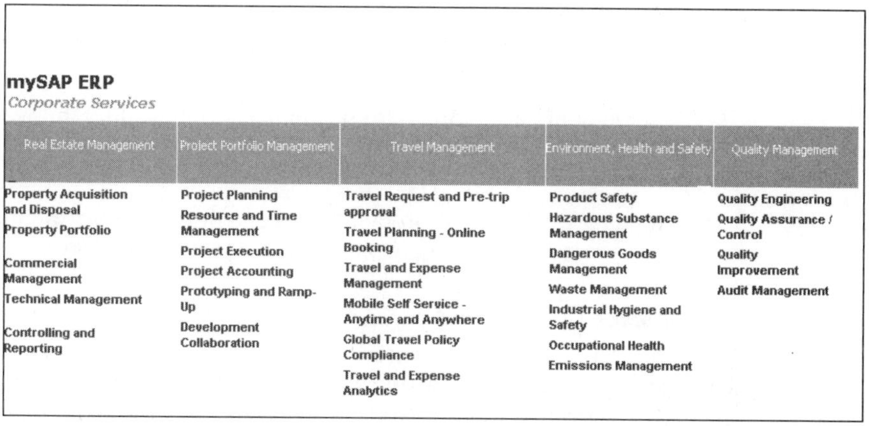

Figure 12-13: The current mySAP ERP Corporate Services functionality.

mySAP ERP
Corporate Services

Real Estate Management	Project Portfolio Management	Travel Management	Environment, Health and Safety	Quality Management
Property Acquisition and Disposal	Project Planning	Travel Request and Pre-trip approval	Product Safety	Quality Engineering
Property Portfolio	Resource and Time Management	Travel Planning - Online Booking	Hazardous Substance Management	Quality Assurance / Control
Commercial Management	Project Execution	Travel and Expense Management	Dangerous Goods Management	Quality Improvement
Technical Management	Project Accounting	Mobile Self Service - Anytime and Anywhere	Waste Management	Audit Management
Controlling and Reporting	Prototyping and Ramp-Up	Global Travel Policy Compliance	Industrial Hygiene and Safety	
	Development Collaboration	Travel and Expense Analytics	Occupational Health	
			Emissions Management	

In the following sections, we present some of the changes coming to this area of ERP.

Project Portfolio Management

Portfolio management allows you to prioritize and align projects with your business strategy. In mySAP ERP, a combination of cProjects and SAP xApp Resource and Portfolio Management (SAP xRPM) allows you to set up a comprehensive project portfolio management system:

✔ cProjects is a powerful and easy-to-use application that enables operational project management using a phase-based approach. cProjects focuses on resources and project roles, documents, and collaboration.

✔ SAP xRPM delivers the foundation for strategic portfolio management by combining financial, strategic, and operational elements of the entire portfolio.

In 2005 and future releases, SAP's goal is the transformation to a service-enabled architecture that allows a more flexible user interface, deployment options, and a lower TCO. On a strategic level, there will be support for the portfolio lifecycle as well as scoring, simulation, and review tools to help you make decisions. In addition, SAP will continue to develop analytical features for all areas of project and portfolio management.

Plans beyond 2005 include

✔ Ongoing integration between the strategic and operational layers of project and portfolio management.

✔ Continuous improvements of resource management features and financial integration, especially for service industries.

✔ Project and portfolio management will drive a successful New Product Development and Introduction (NPDI) process.

✔ Developments are in the works to manage the product innovation process more efficiently and to establish a high transparency throughout the whole development cycle.

✔ Extending the scope of project management to support the planning, execution, and reporting of Six Sigma projects.

Environment, health, and safety

As products and processes continuously change, so do the laws and rules that regulate them. Global businesses have gotten used to dealing with frequent changes in the number and complexity of environment, health, and safety regulations. These regulations have an impact on just about every area of your business, including purchasing, new product development, manufacturing, sales, distribution, service, and maintenance.

mySAP ERP provides capabilities for monitoring complex regulations, managing data and documents, tracking dangerous materials and products, carrying out waste disposal, enhancing employee and public safety, and supporting preventive healthcare.

Within the next three years, the developments in SAP Environment, Health, and Safety (SAP EH&S) will usher in SAP NetWeaver as the new technical platform, enhance the existing functionality to help you adapt to future legal requirements, and offer new processes to support customers to ensure compliance on a global scale. With the provision of the EH&S dangerous goods master data and the substance data on the ESA platform, customers can create and operate new business processes in line with essential EH&S information and ensure that they keep the compliance watchdogs happy.

In general, adapting to future legal requirements affects all areas of SAP EH&S. One of the major steps to come is the enablement of the technical and business aspects of the new European REACH. REACH stands for Registration, Evaluation, and Authorization of Chemicals. The EU will be using this new legislation to regulate the registration, evaluation, and authorization of chemical substances. Implementing REACH will involve substantial changes, in particular for companies producing or importing more than one ton of a chemicals per year. As a result, not only manufacturers but also importers and companies processing chemicals will have to rethink their processes.

Travel Management

SAP Travel Management supports all customers with a great end-to-end process for travel management. With SAP Travel Management, you can put into place a pretrip approval travel request; use a powerful online booking tool to book air, car, and rail travel and hotel reservations; and tap into a global expense management system.

In general, the SAP Travel Management system has seen a dramatic change in user-interface design. In the future, there will be additional UI elements, such as Universal Worklist Support, new entry scenarios for expenses, and further enhancements to the user interface based on customer feedback.

The trip request functionality supports, via the SAP Business Workflow tool, the complete process of pretrip approval, including requesting an advance, based on the new user-interface technology, which will be further enhanced to support Adobe Interactive Forms and SAP Internet service requests. In addition, the connection to the online booking system will be further developed, and the requirements of the public sector areas will be delivered in the form of funds management. Further enhancements are planned in the delivery of workflow templates for the trip request, which will deliver out-of-the-box standard workflow that fulfills many company requirements.

The travel planning functionality will be improved with generic standard interfaces to connect car and rail providers to SAP Travel Management based on SAP NetWeaver XI. In addition, further process improvements between the SAP Travel Management travel planning capabilities and travel agencies are in the works, including enhancements in workflow and lost-savings statistics.

In addition to the existing GDS interfaces (Sabre, Amadeus, and Galileo), there will be changes to the SAP NetWeaver XI interfaces, giving you a choice among more than 20 travel vendors for online booking.

The travel expenses functionality currently offers more than 20 country versions, and several new ones will be added, including Russia, China, Hungary, Brazil, and Australia. The credit card interface will be further enhanced to run through an SAP NetWeaver XI interface. In addition, SAP is developing full support of future credit card company data files, including hotel, air, and rental car portfolio data.

The travel expense management functionality includes a component for mobile applications called Mobile Time & Travel. The new version of Mobile Time & Travel will support a new user interface. In addition, more mobile scenarios will be supported by SAP, such as travel approval (planning, request, and expenses) by a manager via mobile devices, such as Blackberries and most PDAs. There will also be other mobile scenarios for Travel and Expense available, such as receipt entry via mobile devices or an overview of all open trips, including trip status. New Travel Planning scenarios will be delivered via mobile devices.

Analytics for SAP Travel Management will be enhanced to include reports and online graphics, such as the most-used hotels, lost savings, worldwide travel expense, and many more. You'll also be seeing templates based on Visual Composer that allow you to build company-specific dashboards. To deliver these reports, the interfaces for BW data to and from partners, such as credit card providers and booking systems, will be standardized via SAP NetWeaver XI interfaces.

Real Estate Management

SAP Real Estate Management supports customers by increasing transparency in their real estate portfolios, streamlining day-to-day business processes, and helping them make the right decisions.

Many country versions are currently supported. Future releases will provide additional country support, including more country-specific legal features for Japan, Russia, Portugal, and Spain.

Part IV
The Part of Tens

The 5th Wave   By Rich Tennant

D&G HALLOWEEN MANNEQUIN MFG

Oh, we need some integration in this process real fast!

In this part . . .

This part contains three chapters in the ever-popular top-ten list format. This is where you discover ten great ways in which mySAP ERP can make your employees more productive, ten approaches to help you innovate in a services-enabled environment, and ten resources to get you started with mySAP ERP.

Chapter 13

Top Ten Ways to Make People More Productive

*I*f you've been reading this book and paying any attention, you know by now that moving to the world of ERP provides you with lots of new functionality and technology to save money and make your business processes flexible. But that's not the end of the story. As intelligent as these technical solutions are, people still (for the time being) call the shots, so you have to make sure they use that technology productively.

mySAP ERP has many ways of bringing information to the user faster and more easily than ever before. This chapter describes ten ways that you can use mySAP ERP to make your people more productive and effective.

Using Both Generic and User-Specific Roles

One of the major facelifts in mySAP ERP is the user interface — more specifically, the way that functionality and information are presented to users based on their role in an organization.

A typical employee may have many different roles in an organization. Take for example the boss of a production plant (we'll call him Irving). Irving would probably have several roles in his organization. For example, Irving is

- ✔ An employee
- ✔ A manager
- ✔ A plant manager

Now imagine if Irving had all the information, applications, and services needed to complete these tasks actively "pushed out" to him. No longer would he have to search through complex menu structures to find the right bit of functionality; it's right there, staring him in the face (see Figure 13-1). This is the concept of role-based functionality, which you can read more about in Chapter 3.

So far, so good. But understanding one interesting aspect of role-based functionality may help save you some time. Roles can be generic in nature (in our example, the manager and employee roles are generic) or job-specific (for example, the job of the plant manager). Generic roles can be applied to as many people in an organization as you want. Just about everyone in a typical company has the role of an employee, which involves functionality such as change of address, vacation planning, or expense accounting. The manager role requires information about all the employees reporting to that manager, information about the cost centers that manager is responsible for, as well as standard manager-type functionality such as submitting new employee requisitions.

The plant manager role, on the other hand, is very specific to a particular job. In this example, the plant manager role would require access to information about yields in the plant, safety records, and various functionality needed for Irving to run the plant.

mySAP ERP contains both generic and specific roles. Employee self-services and manager self-services are examples of generic roles. Plant manager, purchasing agent, or recruitment specialist are just some of the specific roles included in mySAP ERP.

These roles are right there, out of the box, designed to be templates for companies to use as a basis to develop their own company-specific roles. They contain content and functionality based on SAP's extensive experience with thousands of businesses, but they are easy to extend and modify.

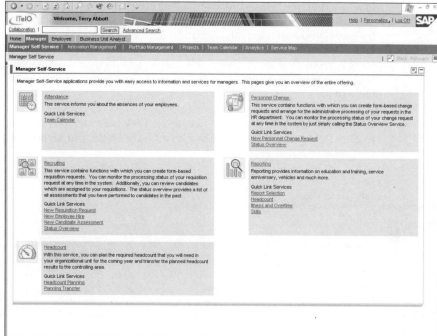

Figure 13-1:
MSS:
Generic
role-based
user
interface —
Manager
Self-
Service.

One other thing to note: Roles are not just for people internal to your organization. You can easily use the same infrastructure to assign roles to customers, partners, or suppliers. Naturally, these roles would have more limited functionality and have additional security features (for example, they would be placed outside a firewall), but they can be very useful in improving communication and enabling collaboration.

Roles play a key part in control centers and work centers, the user-friendly dashboards that push services and analytics to users where they live. See Chapter 3 for more about these very handy centers.

Work Lists

What sort of things does a role contain that might come in handy? One of the interesting pieces of content SAP has developed for roles are work lists.

Imagine that you are a customer sales representative. You receive orders and inquiries from a specific set of customers and you process them. Wouldn't it be nice if you had a list, always up to date and available in real time, that shows you all the outstanding documents you need to process? What if, with each entry on the list, there was a button or link that intelligently guesses what you want to do with an item to process it faster? That's exactly the principle of a work list.

A work list, like the one shown in Figure 13-2, provides not only access to up-to-date information about the work you have to do, but also the functionality you need to finish your work.

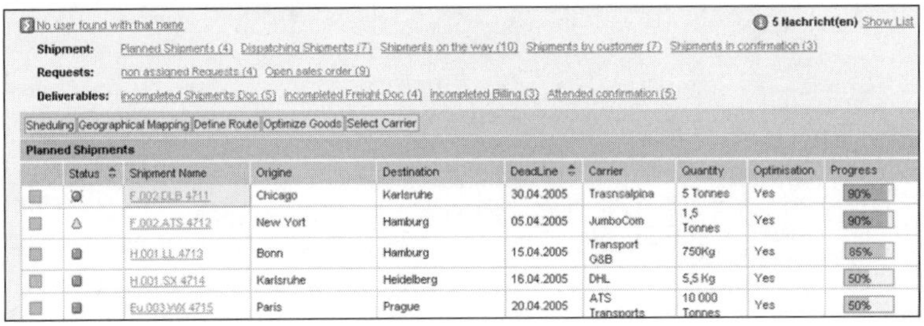

Figure 13-2:
An example
of a work
list for a
shipping
clerk.

Active Alerts

Every company has sets of goals that have to be monitored. To do this, you can define key performance indicators, or KPIs. KPIs help your organization define and measure progress toward your organizational goals.

Key performance indicators are agreed-upon, quantifiable measurements that reflect the critical success factors of your organization. Of course, companies, like people, are all different, so KPIs differ depending on the organization. KPIs can be set on

✔ An organizational level (the percentage of income that comes from new customers, for example)

✔ A departmental level (say, the number of calls that are answered within the first minute)

✔ An individual level (managers shouldn't exceed their budgets)

Active alerts are a form of trigger that alerts the user when something needs to be done. They can, for example, be in the form of little traffic lights (green, amber, and red) that appear in a control or work center. These lights are triggered when a set of criteria is met and let you know that an action is required. They make monitoring and keeping track of KPIs much easier.

The threshold for when these traffic lights change can be set on a corporate, departmental, or individual level. A manager can specify, for example, that if his monthly travel budget gets within 15 percent of his limit, the little light turns yellow, and within 5 percent, it turns red.

Some companies even offer a catalog of KPI criteria that a manager or employee can select (see Figure 13-3). This catalog is simple to manage and much more efficient than scrolling through pages of lists.

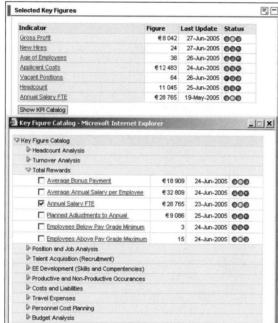

Figure 13-3:
Active alerts and a KPI catalog.

Mobile Scenarios

Mobile devices are here to stay. Mobile phones, Blackberrys, Palm Pilots, and many other devices pop up on the street, in offices, in restaurants (often annoyingly so), as well as in factories and warehouses.

Real-time information can be displayed on these devices, and you can also use them to input information or even run an entire business scenario. mySAP ERP is no stranger to mobile; it's developing many scenarios to utilize the power of these devices, especially for sales and service personnel.

Mobile sales and mobile time and travel scenarios built into mySAP ERP help salespeople on the road be more efficient by supplying them with real-time product information and customer order status.

Mobile asset management enables field technicians to access the information they need to perform functions when and where they need to, regardless of how they are connected — from a customer's office, a loading dock, or even the inside of an elevator whizzing up a skyscraper.

Voice Technology

Here's a little SAP play for your entertainment:

While our plant manager Irving pays the taxi and waits for the change, he dials 1-800-EXPENSES from his cell phone. The system recognizes him through caller ID and answers . . .

System: Hello, Irving. What expense type would you like to enter?

Irving: Taxi.

System: OK, taxi. What's the amount?

Irving: Thirty-four dollars.

System: OK, thirty-four dollars. Is this correct?

Irving: Yes.

System: OK. Do you have additional receipts?

Irving: No.

System: Thanks, Irving. Have a nice day.

Irving hangs up, gets his change, and gets out of the taxi.

Later, when Irving returns from the business trip, he receives a prepopulated interactive expense form via e-mail. He can check it for accuracy and, if everything is all right, press the Submit button to submit the form.

Sound like science fiction? It's not. Enabling "anytime, anywhere" access to your system is a key part of mySAP ERP using voice technology available today.

Voice technology gives users direct online access to systems via a phone from anywhere in the world. Various scenarios similar to the expense reporting example here are in place. For example, your sales representatives can call to get information about a customer's order before a meeting. Many utility companies offer this type of service to customers for meter reading.

This technology speeds data entry, but above all, the user acceptance is almost universal. After all, not everybody feels comfortable with a PDA, but who hasn't used a phone? Keep an eye out: This functionality is coming to a phone near you soon.

Embedded Analytics

Analytics has traditionally been done by someone outside the normal business process. For example, a manager might have had to ask accounting to run some numbers on departmental costs so she could complete her yearly budget. She'd take the spreadsheet the guy in accounting sent her, and then create a graphic and place it in a budget form. This took time and effort, and the information was never really up to date.

With mySAP ERP, the main focus is still on improving and managing business processes, but it is now enhanced through SAP's innovative approach to enterprise analytics. Embedded analytics takes the analytical functionality and makes it part of the fundamental business processes, such as the work center capacity data shown in Figure 13-4.

What is the advantage to this approach? Companies can eliminate any delay between the moment of insight and action. By presenting analytical information within the context of a business process, the end user can immediately react to the information and take the necessary steps to set things right.

You can read more about analytics in Chapter 4.

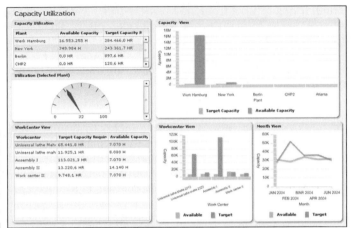

Figure 13-4:
Analytics
built in to
the business
process.

The point is that if you make good use of embedded analytics, you can make people more productive. Here's an example that illustrates how embedded analytics improves business processes and why SAP's analytics offering is unique. Say a manager receives a purchase order request. In order to make an intelligent decision, he needs to know the effect the purchase will have on his budget (budget forecast) and existing equipment (equipment monitor). Embedded analytics can actually anticipate the information he needs and push information to him as soon as he receives the request, enabling him to act right away to accept or decline the request.

RFID Technology

You probably come across hundreds of RFID tags every week without even knowing it. RFID (radio frequency identification) is a technology that allows an object or person to be identified at a distance, using radio waves. Many stores use them to replace bar codes used for inventory tracking on DVDs, CDs, and other products.

RFID is the most important and commercially promising type of "real-world awareness" technology. Without real-world awareness technologies, companies have to use a manual process to keep inventory levels up to date, resulting in delays, errors, and increased labor costs. RFID can automate operations such as inventory, shipping notifications, and purchase orders by integrating them directly into business processes.

RFID technology

- ✔ Creates "real-world awareness," increasing supply chain visibility
- ✔ Avoids duplicate data entry
- ✔ Speeds transaction times
- ✔ Reduces human error
- ✔ Prevents counterfeiting

Major companies, from retailers to airlines, are already embracing the technology. One airline has announced that, in the future, all baggage will be tagged with RFID tags. Readers will be installed on planes so that when a bag enters the plane, the computer system is instantly "aware" of where the bag is and where it will be going. No longer will it be breakfast in Bahrain, lunch in London, and luggage in Laos. (Well, we can hope.)

SAP RFID does the following:

- ✔ Supports supply chain execution, with which you can pick, pack, track, and trace inventory
- ✔ Supports enterprise asset management, which improves your ability to identify equipment, select work orders, record work, and update equipment history

SAP RFID technology can be integrated into existing IT landscapes.

As RFID is a hot topic and a relatively new area, the standards and ways RFID can be used are constantly in flux. To find out more, check out `www.sap.com/rfid`. If RFID gets you so excited that you want to become actively involved in the SAP RFID Community, `www.sap.com/community/rfid` offers discussion groups and the latest tips and presentations on how to make the most out of this technology.

Form-Based Processing

Forms are traditionally paper-based things, which seem to have been around since Gutenberg first designed the printing press. They are familiar, they always look the same, and the data is easily entered. Then the form (with duplicates) is sent off to some anonymous office in a basement somewhere, where the handwritten data is then keyed into a computer system.

Now imagine if the forms you use every day appear on your computer screen. You can fill in the form just as you did before, electronically sign it, and then send it off instantly to the system, where the data is automatically read and processed. This is form-based processing.

Using form-based processes, end users can call up a form in their portal environment, such as a request for a budget transfer or a request for a change in work time. This form is already populated with data from the application, such as the name and number of the department to which the budget is to be transferred and the name and contact details of the applicant. When you submit this form, a workflow engine finds the appropriate person to process it, routes the request to that person's inbox, and then takes that person into the related transaction so that, in some cases, the processor only has to click the Transfer button to complete the transaction.

The whole process is traceable for the end user and manager and can include approval steps and forwarding functions where they make sense.

Forms are not limited to internal work, however. Using the PDF forms, built in to mySAP ERP, many people are using such forms to communicate with customers. For example, a car insurance company can send out an electronic form to potential customers (see Figure 13-5), who can simply enter all the data required, either offline or online, and send the form back to the insurance company. After the form is returned, the information can be "sucked" out of it by the system, and a quote for the potential customer can be generated instantly.

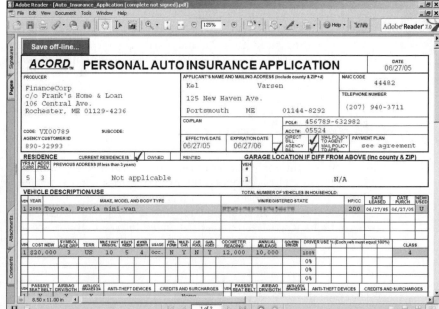

Figure 13-5: Example of an interactive car insurance form.

Guided Procedures

To reach their maximum efficiency, people need to be more focused on what they want to achieve, rather than be concerned about the ins and outs of the process itself. For example, a manager hiring a new employee doesn't want to think about the process that the HR department has to go through to hire someone; the manager just needs to get another body on board and get that person productive as soon as possible.

A guided procedure can help this poor, understaffed manager get help. This wizard-like procedure guides her through the process to the desired goal, without her having to pay much attention to the process involved. This also eliminates the chance that somebody forgets a step and makes a mistake.

Guided procedures are normally a pretty linear process. In the example of a new employee hire, the steps may be

1. Ensure that an employee has a work contract.

2. Ensure that an employee has a PC, chair, desk, and phone.

3. Ensure that an employee has an office space.

4. Ensure that an employee is signed up for training.

Wouldn't it be nice if all these steps could be presented to the manager in a simple step-by-step fashion to ensure that the new employee can be productive and efficient as possible within hours of starting? The new employee could also benefit from a guided procedure. He arrives and has a simple guided procedure to follow to provide bank account details for his paycheck deposit, to select a benefit plan, and to order business cards. This is now possible, and Figure 13-6 shows what it looks like.

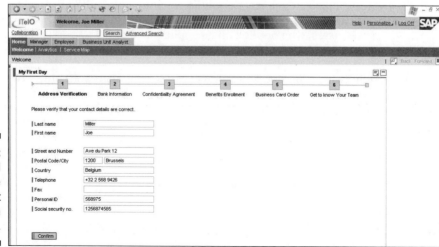

Figure 13-6:
A guided procedure for the first day of a new hire.

Easier User Interfaces

At the end of the day, the way most people interact with a system is based on what they see on their computer screens, which is known as the *user interface.*

Users find it much easier to work with a system if it has a "standard" user interface across all applications. For example, most Windows users are familiar with the Microsoft Office standards: The Save command is always on the File menu, Help is always available by pressing F1, and so on. This makes working with Microsoft Word, PowerPoint, or Excel easy because they all adhere to the same standards.

SAP is also ensuring standards for its applications. As business applications are a little different from traditional office functionality, slightly different standards have been adopted. SAP bases its user interface on flexible templates (called *patterns*) repeated throughout the applications. Regardless of whether you are using a customer relationship manager function or a supply chain management application, the layout and elements on the screen are familiar and comfortable.

Patterns are sets of elements grouped together. For example, the navigation and search tools are always on the left side of the screen, and error messages are always displayed in a content area on the right. The tables displaying information always look the same, and can be sorted in the same manner, regardless of the business content they contain.

This consistency ensures that all users, even users who only occasionally access the SAP system, can find their way around with minimal effort, don't require expensive training, and can be productive sooner.

But having an SAP standard does not touch all users in an organization. Some people may just use standard office functionality and only need to use an SAP system for an occasional vacation request or time tracking. For these non-power users, why not link office applications and SAP applications? This is the concept behind Mendocino.

Mendocino is a joint development of SAP and Microsoft. These two giants are jointly developing this new product that will help companies gain a competitive advantage by changing the way information workers access, analyze, and use enterprise data to make better business decisions. Mendocino will link SAP process functionality directly to Microsoft Office applications so that users can access SAP's business processes and decision support tools directly via Office applications, such as Microsoft Outlook. Examples of Mendocino functionality include

- ✔ **Time management:** Using the Outlook calendar as a front end for SAP time reporting
- ✔ **Budget monitoring:** Receiving reports in the Outlook inbox and working offline
- ✔ **Leave management:** Adding leave requests as Outlook calendar items integrated with SAP approval guidelines
- ✔ **Team management:** Getting up-to-date information about employees as Outlook contacts
- ✔ **Report distribution:** Distributing mySAP ERP transactional reports via Outlook

The preview release of Mendocino is planned for late 2005; the final product should be available in mid-2006.

Mendocino development will be focused on extending current SAP scenarios and adding new self-service scenarios. These scenarios enable new capabilities, such as integrating business smart tags to all Office products and bringing additional business processes to the information worker's desktop environment (see Figure 13-7). Mendocino will also make tools available to customers and third-party providers to enable them to build their own scenarios.

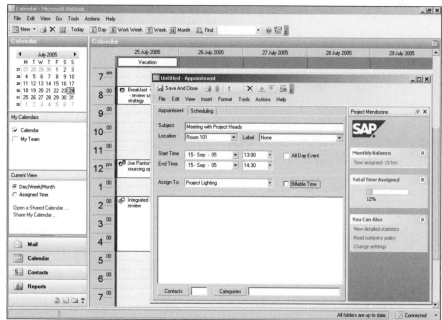

Figure 13-7: The new Mendocino interface.

Chapter 14

Top Ten Ways to Enable Innovation

In This Chapter

▶ Creating a framework for identifying how a company should innovate

▶ Service-enabling applications to support the innovation process

▶ Sharing knowledge

A big benefit of mySAP ERP is the support you need to make your organization more innovative. But how does this work?

Innovation is something difficult to measure: For each company, it means something different. Try as it might, SAP can't supply an innovation button you can just click to innovate. Instead, SAP provides tools and services to support the innovation that each company needs for long-term survival.

Creating the Framework for Innovation

Most companies think that innovation is a dandy thing, but they need a framework for that innovation. A company has to set guidelines for which areas of the company should be innovating at any point in time. This, of course, differs from company to company. A toy company may look to new products or production as the primary area of innovation, whereas a bank might focus on new ways to offer financial services to its customers.

But no matter what your industry, any framework for innovation has to involve defining strategies, identifying key performance indicators, setting plans, developing budgets, and making sure everything operates according to these plans. When changes occur, this framework has to accommodate flexibility.

To set this framework for innovation, you need some sort of strategic management. The toy company management may set developing four new products or reducing the cost of production by 10 percent as a strategic goal. From there, managers can brainstorm about ways to reach these goals.

An ideal tool for setting these goals is SAP Strategic Enterprise Management (SAP SEM). Based on a data warehouse, SAP SEM enables your company to set a strategic path to reach its goals and to monitor and track your progress.

Setting such a framework is not a guarantee of success and doesn't foster innovation in and of itself, but it does help to focus people in the areas they should be concentrating on.

Composing Service-Based Applications Strategically

As we discuss throughout this book, if you break down the functionality of applications to services, that functionality can be used more easily and deployed faster and more flexibly than ever before. It is like using Lego bricks to create a application: The pieces can easily be broken down and rebuilt as needed.

Now you can't run around enabling everything immediately; companies need to think very strategically about which areas to service-enable. The idea is to first identify areas where you want to innovate and need maximum flexibility; this is probably where you can really differentiate yourself to your customers. Then you create a careful roadmap to work out how to identify and create the services you need, not forgetting that services can come from within the organization or through partners.

Offering Services to Others

Who remembers the first man on the moon? Everyone. But who remembers the second, besides his wife? Second place, by definition, never has the distinction of first place. The same is true in the race to offer services to others. By being the first to identify a market niche and take control of it by offering services to that market, you can set the pace of innovation.

Consider this example: The number of insurance policies one insurance company was issuing and maintaining was rising exponentially. The company's systems were at a breaking point. A new, flexible system was developed, based on services. The system was modular and scalable, so scalable that the company was able to offer its system as services to other insurance companies. Everyone was happy: The other insurance companies could concentrate on their core business of calculating and hiking up premiums, and the administration and issuing of contracts were cheaply outsourced. The company created a strategic advantage by being the first on the market with such an offering.

Companies who outsource functions are the pioneers of using services. Many trucking companies offer services to their clients to track deliveries or packages, and were among the first to think strategically about how to offer those services. For example, UPS, DHL, and FedEx all offer tracking functionality. Although this service was groundbreaking when it was first introduced, now it's a must for any carrier. This type of trendsetting pops up in all sorts of industries.

Using Services from Others

To enhance and offer innovation to customers, many companies build in services from other companies to beef up their existing applications (whether they are service-enabled or not).

Services from third parties can be quickly integrated into standard business processes using mySAP ERP, which has some real benefits. For example, an Internet shop can offer a link to the tracking service offered by a trucking company, which displays the precise location of the package ordered by the customer. Everyone is happy. The shop has outsourced its logistics cheaply. Without having to build the application itself, the shipping company can automatically answer customer queries about the delivery without resorting to expensive call centers, and customers know exactly where their packages are.

Have an active dialogue with your suppliers, banking partners, and strategic business partners to see what type of services they might offer, or let them know the types of services you need to make your offering in the market more attractive than anyone else's.

Using Model-Driven Development Tools

When you develop a new process within an organization, the IT department is normally involved in implementing that process. This takes time and is always a source of friction between the business managers and the IT department.

Today, with a new wave of model-driven tools and with functionality supplied as services, the processes can be modified and even created by employees themselves. SAP NetWeaver Visual Composer (see Figure 14-1) is such a tool. It allows users to easily "compose" a new application by connecting the dots. All an employee needs to know is which service supplies the functionality she needs. With some basic knowledge, she can model the business process.

Ideas for innovation can be implemented far faster than ever before, and IT folks are freed to do more strategic work.

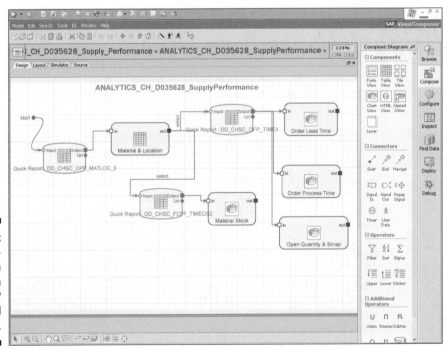

Figure 14-1:
A model-driven approach with SAP Visual Composer.

Connecting Analytics to the World

SAP Analytics for ERP gives you new insights into your corporate data. The idea is to combine data from different systems to identify trends that can help you innovate. These systems can be internal, for example, combining purchasing, HR, and sales to see whether the salesperson with the latest equipment really does sell more. But these views really come into their own when you combine them with external data.

External information provides real context to internal information. For example, if your company is growing at 8 percent, you may be tempted to sit back and spend your bonus. However, if you link the information to a stock database and see that most of your competitors are growing at 18 percent, you may want to keep that bonus in the bank.

Many commercially available external databases contain myriad information. You can link these databases to company-specific data to provide contextual data that can give people ideas about how to innovate.

For example, a pesticide producer implemented analytics from mySAP ERP and gained real-time information about sales to customers. The producer decided to do some geographical analysis: It used a geographic mapping system to link customers to map coordinates, and then the company analyzed sales over time.

Lo and behold: The producer identified a common pattern of sales, which followed the path of insect swarms. The little bugs typically started in the south and, as the weather got hotter, moved north. The company decided it could calculate the path of the swarm; when an outbreak was about to occur, the company warned people in the path of the swarm that the insects were coming and preemptively offered them a solution. This innovative way to use existing sales figures and link them with external information boosted sales and brought the producer customer loyalty by providing real value. The company's predictions have improved with time, and now the model uses weather information as well as historic data to make best guesses about insect movement patterns even more accurate.

Working with Composite Processes

In your organization, your goal may be to offer your services in an innovative way to ensure maximum value for your customers. For example, a credit card company may offer a loyalty system, baggage insurance, and a purchase-protection scheme.

Often, innovation is stifled when a process is disrupted or blocked. Imagine if a customer calls your credit card company and has to be transferred to different departments for each of the different services that your company offers. Each handoff from one department to another means that your customer is kept waiting, which causes him frustration and creates inefficiencies in the entire organization.

So after a new innovative process has been developed, using different parts of different systems, how do you deploy it to the people who need it? Furthermore, how do you make it easy enough to ensure that they *do* use it, especially when there are bottlenecks in an organization?

Luckily, a composite process can solve all that. When a new customer creates an account, the customer is guided by the representative to other services. This process adds value to the customer and to the company itself.

A composite process reuses parts of other business processes from different systems and is typically implemented by guided procedures. Composite processes additionally allow you to flexibly manage and deploy the new innovative processes — say, a new banking offer from the credit card company that can simply be added to the financial services offering process.

Utilizing Composite Applications

Composite applications help you identify and color in "white spaces" in your organization. Functionality that you couldn't previously add cost-effectively because the content was hosted by disparate systems can now be offered to your users. Composite applications tap into disparate information sources and processes and bring them together on an enterprise level with a common interface.

An example of this is risk management. Many different types of risk can be found in an organization: risk associated with financials, with product launches, or in the area of human resources. A composite application may bring all these areas together to make sure you have an organizational overview of risk for your entire business.

Composite applications can also be used to manage an entire chain of processes to ensure that innovation does not get lost. For example, when introducing a new product, you could bring the processes of idea management, portfolio management, and product definition together with a common interface to manage this entire chain. In this way, you can make sure that the appropriate ideas become commercialized to offer more innovative products to your customers.

Collaborating and Sharing Knowledge

Innovation normally comes from ideas from a number of people. Particular frameworks often foster innovation; brainstorming meetings are a good example. However, a good brainstorming session is not always possible, especially if the parties are scattered around the globe.

mySAP ERP offers a number of ways to foster collaboration between different departments or organizations. A framework for structured project planning, execution, and shared knowledge fosters innovation.

The collaboration tools in mySAP ERP include cProjects, which work in tandem with cRooms and cFolders. cRooms are real-time virtual meeting rooms, and cFolders offer a way to easily share documents around the world. Of course, unstructured information is also important to make decisions, and mySAP ERP also includes a search tool that can process massive quantities of data to bring users real-time information.

Deploying Hardware Efficiently

For many organizations, the decision about how to deploy hardware (servers, networks, and so on) has always been a challenge. Especially for innovative firms that are growing, the flexibility of these underlying systems needs to be well planned and executed.

Luckily, mySAP ERP has been designed to support just about any size of business, with options to scale the area that is growing fastest without upsetting the rest of your system landscape. This scalability has been proven by thousands of SAP customers, from smaller organizations to huge multinationals.

Thus, for example, with new innovative offers on your Web site, the traffic may increase exponentially. With flexible underlying technology, you can deploy and scale the systems you need to make sure customers always get the response times they expect.

Chapter 15

Top Ten ERP Resources

The world of ERP is a big one, and the step into it is a mighty leap. Although the potential rewards are big, you don't want to make that leap alone. Luckily, lots of resources are available — both in human and online form — to help.

Some of these resources are specific to your ERP solution. We've included several from SAP that can help you with mySAP ERP. Others are more generic. Pick and choose the ones you need, and good luck with your ERP future!

Your SAP Account Rep

If you're looking at mySAP ERP as your ERP solution, your account representative is your new best friend. He can pull together a team of people to advise you about the best way to get started. Detailed up-front analysis of your business and needs, as well as ongoing support to maintain and tweak your system, is available.

If you don't have an account representative, visit `www.sap.com/contactsap/directory` and contact the SAP office nearest you.

ESA Adoption Help

If you're ready to make the leap to adopting ESA, the ESA Adoption Program can help. This is a formalized, step-by-step approach to help you move into a service-oriented environment with a focus on maintaining your existing systems as much as possible. The program includes four key steps to support a customer's transition to ESA, including

- Grasping the vision through ESA opportunity workshops and total cost of ownership (TCO) discovery sessions
- Building a tailored roadmap based on individual customer needs
- Implementing the offering and going live
- Harnessing the value of ESA while effectively managing change

At each step, SAP provides customers with a portfolio of field-tested support services that provide a variety of tools, templates, samples, and workshops customized for your organization. These services include an ESA and SAP NetWeaver vision value session, a TCO discovery session, an ESA-enabling roadmap workshop, and an ESA operations session on governance and security to support your new IT environment.

User Groups

SAP users are an active bunch. User groups all over the world share advice and information about their SAP and ERP experiences.

Here are a few links to get you started:

- In the United States, connect with Americas SAP Users Group (ASUG) (www.asug.com). ASUG holds a huge annual conference every year, as well as smaller regional events and specialized events via Webcasts.
- Die Deutschsprachige SAP-Anwendergruppe (DSAG) is the German-speaking SAP User Group. This active bunch can be found at www.dsag.de/.
- A busy user group in England is at Warwick University (www2.warwick.ac.uk/services/finance/sap/usergroups/).
- In Australia, hook up with the SAP Australian User Group (SAUG) at www.saug.com.au/.

Go to www.sapgenie.com/usergroups (note that this is not an official SAP site) for a list of groups, or contact your SAP account representative to find out about the group nearest you.

SAPGenie.com also offers lists of user forums and publications, as well as resources for developers such as utilities and for clients such as information on outsourcing.

ERP Events

The SAP SAPPHIRE conference (see Figure 15-1) is the preeminent SAP event, held at various locations throughout the world every year in the spring. Go to www.sapsapphire.com for the latest information and to register to attend. The conference provides presentations on all aspects of SAP solutions, including new innovations in the latest releases of products such as mySAP ERP (which is updated annually) and future directions for SAP. You can also meet with SAP partners who might be able to help you with your specific challenges.

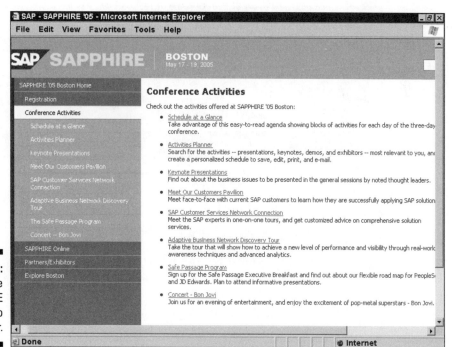

Figure 15-1: Go to the SAPPHIRE Web site to register.

SAP TechEd is a useful conference with workshops, presentations, and networking opportunities for the more technically minded. You'll find topics of interest for developers, consultants, business people, and partners. Go to `www.sapteched.com` for more information about the next session. Topics that were presented at the 2005 TechEd in Vienna, Austria, include

- ✔ SAP NetWeaver and Enterprises Services Architecture
- ✔ User productivity
- ✔ Business Process Integration
- ✔ Custom development
- ✔ System and platform consolidation

There are also many conferences out there geared toward more specific industry needs, such as HR Summit, Public Sector Summit, SAP Financials, Banking Summit, Information Security Decisions, Data Center Decisions, and SAP NetWeaver Conference. You can find a list of these with links at `www.sapgenie.com` or `http://searchsap.techtarget.com/events/` (see Figure 15-2).

Figure 15-2: Look for events at TechTarget.

SAP Insider (discover more about the parent publication in the section "Publications," later in this chapter) produces several SAP-type events. Go to www.sapinsideronline.com to explore them all.

Web Sites

SAP's Web site (www.sap.com) is a great place to start finding out about SAP-specific offerings.

CIO Magazine maintains a Web site that includes an Enterprise Resource Planning section (www.cio.com/research/erp). Here you can find useful articles about the basics of ERP, as well as case studies and research reports. There are also sections on CRM, SCM, and e-business.

IT Toolbox (www.erp.ittoolbox.com) maintains an ERP Information and Tools site. This site offers useful FAQs, discussion groups, and blogs related to the IT side of the ERP equation.

ERPFan Club and User Forum (www.erpfans.com) is a collection of ERP information, chat rooms, news, and links. You can also search for books on ERP and even ERP-related job postings.

If you're in the manufacturing industry, try going to www.managementsupport.com/erp.htm. Here you'll find the ERP Guide, a huge PowerPoint presentation on all aspects of ERP. You can even take slides from the presentation and build your own presentation to show to your management folks.

If you want to compare ERP software, go to www.erp-software-comparison.com. You can define your role, define your business needs, get a shortlist of software, and run a comparison.

Publications

Business 2.0 (www.business2.com) offers a print publication that helps you keep up with the latest in technology for your business. The site frequently has articles on ERP-related topics.

SAP Insider, produced by Wellesley Information Services, is sponsored by SAP and offers a quarterly publication on SAP activities. Visit SAP Insider at `www.sapinsideronline.com`.

SAP Info, published by SAP (see Figure 15-3), is a monthly magazine you can get in print or subscribe to online. E-mail `press@sap.com` for information about subscribing, or ask your account representative.

SAP NetWeaver For Dummies, by Dan Woods and Jeffrey Word, published by Wiley, is a great introduction to SAP NetWeaver's extensive capabilities.

Enterprise Services Architecture, by Dan Woods, published by O'Reilly, (2003) is a basic overview of the Enterprise Services Architecture approach to your IT systems.

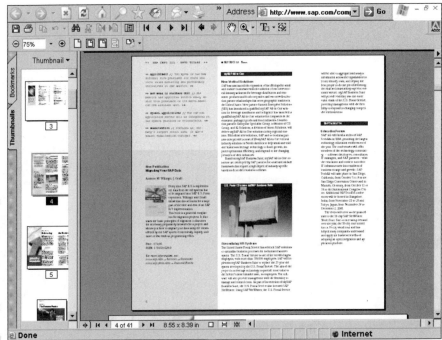

Figure 15-3:
You can read *SAP Info* articles online in Adobe Acrobat format.

SAP Partners and the Ramp-Up Program

SAP has built strategic partnerships with many businesses to provide best practices and consulting. Go to www.sap.com/partners to find out more about SAP's ecosystem of partners.

The SAP Ramp-Up program involves you in new programs and products from SAP. You are the first to get the next big thing from SAP with extra support from its project management team; in turn, you help by providing feedback to bring the solution to market.

Here are some of the benefits of being part of the Ramp-Up program:

- ✔ **Project scoping:** Project scoping compares the solution scope with your expectations. If any concerns arise, SAP conducts a feasibility check to determine to what extent it can meet your requirements.

- ✔ **Project coaching:** After an implementation project begins, SAP Ramp-Up provides an expedited channel for support to resolve issues quickly. For more complex issues, the SAP Ramp-Up back office ensures that product development and product management become directly involved. Each project is assigned to a dedicated expert in the SAP Ramp-Up back office.

- ✔ **Knowledge transfer:** SAP Ramp-Up staffs implementation projects with highly skilled consultants and organizes communities that enable team members to capture and share knowledge with you.

SAP Developer Network

If you're a developer working in the ERP world, go to the Web site for the SAP Developer Network at http://sdn.sap.com (see Figure 15-4) to register and discover more about mySAP ERP, ESA, and SAP NetWeaver.

At this site, you can get information about working with any of SAP's products, read case studies, tap into e-learning and other training options, and access links to documentation and books.

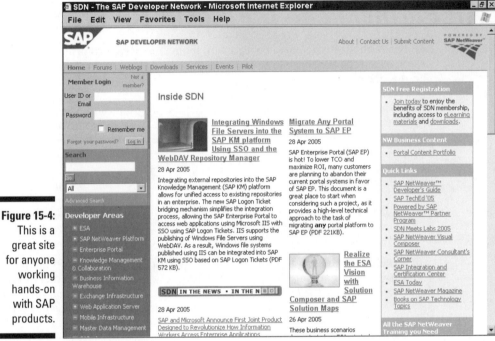

Figure 15-4:
This is a great site for anyone working hands-on with SAP products.

Solution Manager

SAP Solution Manager is a free product that comes with SAP NetWeaver, so if you're using mySAP ERP, it's already available to you. This is a very useful central platform for dealing with the implementation and operation of an SAP system. With SAP Solution Manager, you can get step-by-step guidance on how to set up your system landscape, plan upgrades, and manage testing activities as you plan to go live. It even includes a roadmap for upgrades.

In mySAP ERP 2005 and later editions, you have to use SAP Solution Manager to perform an upgrade, so you might as well get to know about this handy tool. You can read more about SAP Solution Manager in Chapter 11.

Industry Solutions

SAP provides more than 25 industry-specific ERP solutions. SAP has produced industry-specific solution maps that help you implement mySAP ERP in your specific business. SAP preconfigures your system with best practices for your industry. Ask your SAP account representative about industry solutions for your business or visit www.sap.com/industries/ or www.sap.com/solutions/smb for small to midsize business solutions (see Figure 15-5).

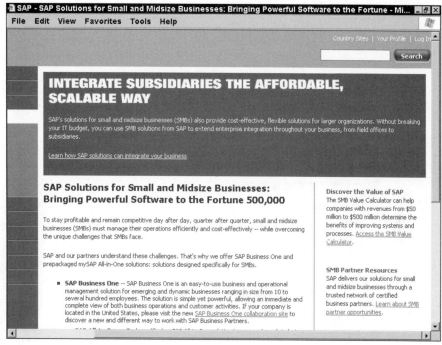

Figure 15-5:
Find out
about
smaller
solutions
here.

SAP currently offers the following industry sets:

Manufacturing industries

✔ Aerospace and defense (A&D)

✔ Automotive

✔ Chemicals

✔ Consumer products

✔ Engineering, construction, and operations (EC&O)

✔ High-tech

✔ Industrial machinery and components (IM&C)

✔ Mill products

✔ Mining

✔ Oil and gas (O&G)

✔ Life sciences

Service industries

✔ Logistics service providers

✔ Media

- Postal services
- Professional services
- Retail
- Railways
- Telecommunications
- Utilities
- Wholesale distribution

Public services

- Defense and security
- Healthcare
- Higher education and research (HE&R)
- Public sector

Financial services

- Banking
- Financial service providers
- Insurance

SAP also offers vertical (such as publishing) and microvertical (one level deeper into an industry, such as print publishing or Web publishing) help for small and midsize businesses called mySAP All-in-One solutions. These solutions, available regionally from SAP solution partners, include the following:

- More than 50 microvertical solutions each for the consumer products, retail, and service provider industries, from apparel and beverages to textiles and wholesale car parts.

- Some 30 to 45 microvertical solutions each for the automotive, engineering, construction and operations, industrial machinery and components, and mill products industries, from aircraft construction and air-conditioning systems to metal molding and packaging materials.

- Some 25 to 30 microvertical solutions each for the chemicals, high-tech and pharmaceuticals industries, from cleaning agents to optical technology and synthetics manufacturing.

- Various tailored solutions for diverse microverticals, from advertising, churches, and office furniture to public amenities, state authorities, and technical real estate management.

Glossary

application components: *See components.*

application engine: *See engine.*

application platform: The newest generation of SAP applications that are being systematically developed. They will be made available as business objects, engines, and components in order to make them reusable and extendible. This platform will be increasingly leveraged by all SAP solutions, including mySAP Business Suite.

application service: *See also Web service.* Services used by an application component, an engine, or a utility.

BPM: *See Business Process Management.*

BPO: *See Business Process Outsourcing.*

business events: Internal or external occurrences that trigger business activities or processes. For example, a changed delivery address or an additional product ordered by a customer would be a business event. An event such as an additional product ordered may trigger activities such as the recalculation of customer value and attractive pricing for future products. Business events are relevant in ESA because they allow business logic to control process flow.

business object: An identifiable business entity, such as a customer, a contract, or a product that is defined once and becomes the building block of the business. It is described by a data model, an internal process model, and one or more service interfaces.

business process: A set of logically related tasks that are performed to achieve a defined business outcome. Business processes are usually carried out within one organizational department and are typically supported by at least one solution, such as mySAP ERP or mySAP CRM. Examples of business processes include vehicle delivery and cash receipt. A business process is usually a part of a business scenario.

Business Process Management (BPM): Describes the modeling and analysis of business scenarios and business processes; orchestration, automation, and deployment of these scenarios within the enterprise; and active monitoring of the performance of these business scenarios. BPM is an integral part of ESA. Meta-models of the business process are used for composition of new services and many composite applications.

Business Process Outsourcing (BPO): Placing the responsibility for a business process with an entity outside of your business. Also called *outsourcing*.

business process platform: The combination of the SAP application platform with the composition platform (that is, SAP NetWeaver), which supports the creation, enhancement, and seamless execution of business processes and business scenarios. This platform can be leveraged by SAP internally to develop packaged composite applications, leveraged by partners to provide additional services and composite applications, and leveraged by customers to extend the solutions to address their specific and evolving business needs.

business scenario: Carries out an end-to-end business task and spans processes across multiple organizational units and applications, both inside and outside the enterprise. Business scenarios address customers' key business requirements. A business scenario is either specific to one industry (in which case it is called an *industry-specific scenario*) or it could be applicable to multiple industries (in which case it is called a *cross-industry scenario*). An example of a business scenario in the automotive industry is order-to-delivery.

CAF: *See Composite Application Framework.*

collaboration room: A shared workspace on a portal where people can meet online and exchange information about a specific task, activity, or project. Collaboration rooms are created by users.

components: Modular, reusable pieces of application software. In the future, most applications will be constructed as components and composites to comply with the requirements of ESA. Functionality offered by these components is usually accessible as a service.

composite application: An application on top of other applications or application components that makes use of data and functions that are provided as services by underlying applications or application components and combines them into a coherent business scenario. It can add its own business logic and provide specialized user interfaces to fully support the business scenario.

Composite Application Framework (CAF): A reusable basic design structure that provides a development environment in which different services can be composed and orchestrated into new composite applications. CAF is an integral part of SAP NetWeaver.

composition platform: Term used to describe SAP NetWeaver. SAP NetWeaver is the SAP platform for composition and orchestration of services in a transparent, secure, and quality-assured way. The Composite Application Framework (CAF), Business Process Management (BPM), and Enterprise Services Repository (ESR) within SAP NetWeaver allow the model-based composition and orchestration of services to enable or enhance business processes, thereby expanding this integration platform and application server into a composition platform.

control center: The user's home area. It consists of a set of pages organizing the user's activities across and beyond roles. It summarizes and combines all information the user needs for structuring, organizing, and monitoring daily work. From a control center, a user can access one to many work centers for domain-specific activities. The control center provides work-related information such as news, work triggers (messages, workflow items, and exceptions), the status of ongoing work, tasks, work scheduling, and resources from various applications.

custom composite application: *See also composite application.* A composite application that is developed exclusively for one customer, either in-house or by third-party developers.

engine (also called an *application engine*): A software component that performs a specific and well-defined search, analysis, or computation upon request with little or no human intervention. An example would be a pricing engine that calculates the price of a product based on customer- and market-specific information. To support ESA, the functionality of the engines is usually exposed as services.

enterprise resource planning (ERP): A set of software applications that are intended to integrate and streamline business processes. Traditionally, the processes that ERP concentrated on were financials (such as accounts receivable, accounts payable, and general ledger); human resources (or human capital management); and logistics (procurement, transport, and storage of goods).

enterprise service: *See also Web service.* A service used in the execution of a business process step, having a significant meaning and impact for the business of the enterprise. An enterprise service fulfills strict rules regarding version compatibility and stability defined by the enterprise service interface, and built on Web service technology.

Enterprise Service Bus: *See Enterprise Services Infrastructure.*

Enterprise Services Architecture (ESA): The blueprint of a service-oriented architecture for current and future SAP customers. It combines the reliability and extensive functionality provided by SAP's extensive enterprise applications with the flexibility of services based on open standards. Leveraging SAP NetWeaver, it allows the seamless integration of SAP, legacy, and third-party software into composite applications that can enhance and innovate key business processes. As a consequence, ESA also is the governing architecture for SAP's current and future generation of software solutions. ESA, in itself, is not a product, but rather the concept supporting various products and solutions.

Enterprise Services Infrastructure: SAP NetWeaver's service infrastructure based on ESA principles for defining, developing, identifying, invoking, and managing services. Generally referred to in the industry and by some analysts as the Enterprise Service Bus. This is a central piece of the Composition Platform.

Enterprise Services Inventory: The list of enterprise services and associated definitions published by SAP in 2005 in order to help partners and customers plan their own ESA roadmap. This inventory is updated every year. A subset of services from this inventory can be implemented at any given time, and these implemented enterprise services will be stored in the Enterprise Services Repository.

Enterprise Services Repository (ESR): The central repository in SAP NetWeaver, where enterprise services, business objects, and business processes are modeled and their metadata is stored. This repository is an integral part of SAP NetWeaver.

ESA: *See Enterprise Services Architecture.*

ESR: *See Enterprise Services Repository.*

Guided Procedure: A flexible, highly functional workflow environment that enables users without specialized software development skills to set up and execute collaborative business processes by providing reusable templates.

integration platform: A set of tools in SAP NetWeaver for the integration of data and functions from diverse applications to support the alignment of people, information, and business processes across technological and organizational boundaries. These include SAP NetWeaver Exchange Infrastructure, SAP NetWeaver Business Intelligence, SAP NetWeaver Master Data Management, and SAP NetWeaver Portal.

key performance indicator (KPI): A checkpoint for gauging company performance.

KPI: *See key performance indicator.*

Mendocino: A joint product from Microsoft and SAP that enables Microsoft Office applications to interact with applications such as mySAP ERP.

metadata: Data that provides information about the content, quality, condition, and other characteristics of other data.

model: A description of a physical, abstract, or hypothetical aspect of reality that serves to communicate, construct, and analyze that aspect. Within software, engineering models are created, on the one hand, to represent reality in a way that supports the construction of software, and, on the other hand, to act as abstract descriptions of certain aspects of software systems. Typically, models are used to generate software or to be interpreted directly at run-time. There are different types of models for different domains, including the user-interface model, business process model, run-time execution model, and data model.

modeling: The process of creating a software model. Typically, modeling is done using a so-called modeling tool, which uses graphical representations of objects and components such as data sources, relationships, interface elements, and so on to define their relationships. SAP NetWeaver provides leading-edge modeling tools with CAF and Visual Composer.

outsourcing: *See Business Process Outsourcing.*

packaged composite application: *See also composite application.* A composite application that has been productized by a vendor to sell to customers.

portal: A Web-site gateway to the Internet or a network. A group of links, content, and services that help users locate the information and services they need.

role-based: An approach to providing content and services to users based on sets of policies that support their function in the organization.

SAP NetWeaver: *See composition platform.*

SAP NetWeaver Business Intelligence (SAP NetWeaver BI): Part of SAP NetWeaver that provides the tools needed to make the right decisions, optimize processes, and measure strategic success. In SAP NetWeaver BI, data from all enterprise sources is merged effectively and can be comprehensively analyzed. Results of analyses can be graphically represented in a wide variety of formats, such as grids, graphs, and maps.

SAP NetWeaver Exchange Infrastructure: A tool used to integrate processes and enable applications to talk to one another.

SAP Web Application Server: Operates underlying programs in the SAP runtime environment, among other things functioning as a Web server to display a portal in a browser and enable enterprise services.

SAP xApps: Packaged composite applications that are sold separately from mySAP Business Suite, mySAP All-in-One, and SAP Business One, with their own release schedule. SAP xApps enable new business processes or significantly enhance existing business processes.

scenario: A sequence of business processes used to achieve key business objectives. A scenario is either specific to one industry (in which case it is called an *industry-specific scenario*) or it could be applicable to multiple industries (in which case it is called a *cross-industry scenario*).

service: *See Web service, application service, and enterprise service.*

service composition: *See also composite application.* Creation of new services by aggregating more granular services either through programming or modeling for a particular transaction context. Enterprise services are typically composed in this fashion from application or Web services. Application services are similarly composed in this fashion from compound services.

service consumer: Typically a software entity that invokes a service (usually a composite application or a portal). Can also be used to refer to the organization of the user who invokes this service.

service consumption: The invocation of a service (Web service, application service, or enterprise service) by a service consumer. This is the logical next step after service discovery.

service discovery: The process by which a service user (typically a composite application or user portal) interacts with the service repository to determine the correct service to be invoked for a specific business context.

service enablement: The isolation of a specific functionality of an enterprise application and its implementation through proprietary or open standards in order to make the functionality accessible as a service. Such service enablement is the basis for ESA-compliant applications.

service orchestration: The model-based arrangement of a set of services to enable or enhance an entire business scenario or business process, loosely coupled across multiple user contexts, systems, business partners, or enterprises.

service provider: Typically the application that supports and publishes a service. Can also be used to refer to the organization or the user who is the owner of this service.

service-oriented architecture (SOA): A software architecture that supports the design, development, identification, and consumption of standardized services across the enterprise, thereby improving the reusability of software components and creating agility in responding to change. ESA is SAP's vision for an SOA that more effectively addresses business-level challenges and is rapidly deployable.

shared services center: A way to place a piece of a business process scenario in a central location to make it available to many groups. Shared services centers can be useful for outsourcing parts of your process to an outside vendor.

SOA: *See Service-Oriented Architecture.*

Solution Manager: A central service platform made up of frameworks, tools, and services to help you implement, manage, monitor, and support SAP and non-SAP business solutions.

solution map: A map of a complex, tailored industry solution system that gives a company an overview of industry-specific business processes. Solution maps were drawn up in cooperation with industry-specific user groups, partners, and SAP development teams in an effort to define the requirements of individual sectors of industry.

Visual Composer: An SAP modeling tool that allows business users to create user interfaces through an easy-to-use graphical modeling environment.

Web service: A standards-based way of encapsulating the functions of an application that other applications can locate and access. For a consumer or provider, a Web service is a black box that may require input and delivers a result. Web services provide integration within an enterprise as well as across enterprises on top of any communication technology stack.

Web Service Description Language (WSDL): An XML language for describing Web services. WSDL enables someone to separate the description of the abstract functionality offered by a service from the concrete details of a service description, such as "how" and "where" that functionality is offered.

work center: Organizes data and activities of a specific set of tasks (for example, purchase order management and invoice management). A work center consists of a set of user interface "pages" organizing and supporting the user's activities in his work area (work set). From a control center, a user can access one to many work centers for domain-specific activities. One user may have several work centers, according to his responsibilities.

WSDL: *See Web Service Description Language.*

xApps: *See SAP xApps.*

Index

• S •

Notes